The British and How to Deal with Them

The British
And How to Deal With Them:
Doing Business With Britain's
Ethnic Communities

by

Ram Gidoomal, Deepak Mahtani
and David Porter

Middlesex University Press

First published in 2001 by Middlesex University Press

Middlesex University Press is an imprint of
MU Ventures Ltd
Bounds Green Road, London N11 2NQ.

A CIP catalogue record for this book is available from
The British Library.

ISBN 1 898253 42 0

Designed and typeset by Porterfolio.
Manufacture coordinated in the UK from authors' CRC by
Book in Hand Limited, London N6 5AH.
Cover design by HT Graphics.
Printed and bound in Great Britain

Contents

Foreword by Lord Sheppard of Didgemere

Even a casual observer will note how the civic disorder in places like Oldham and Bradford is widely reported in terms of rivalries and tensions between indigenous and ethnic communities. It is possible they will draw the conclusion that, for many major towns and cities in Britain, the diverse nature of their communities is a problem and a problem that the powers that be are struggling to manage.

Yet the discerning observer will recognise and appreciate that the multi-cultural nature of British society and the British economy represents a major asset that should be exploited. The authors, Ram Gidoomal, Deepak Mahtani and David Porter, challenge the belief that multi ethnic communities are a threat and emphasise the extraordinary opportunities presented by Britain's diversity.

In writing this book the authors start by presenting this alternative view, of communities contributing some £25 billion of disposable income to the British economy, responsible for a significant proportion of all business start-ups, and producing many of the entrepreneurs who feature in the most recent *Sunday Times* 'Rich List'. Britain's ethnic businesses offer major opportunities as trading partners for indigenous firms, and the communities are a source of the important skills, expertise and knowledge needed to compete in world markets.

But there is a downside to the analysis as well. Most indigenous British businesses are failing to develop effective links with the ethnic businesses that could be part of their supply chain, and in many cases they are not reaching the ethnic consumers in their home market. A serious lack of inter-cultural 'literacy' lies at the heart of this failure. It is a sad fact that far too many UK businesses, and business people, simply don't know how to do business with anyone who isn't 'British'. There is also evidence that, for similar reasons, the extensive array of business support services provided by Government and its Agencies frequently fail to reach those individuals and enterprises in the ethnic business communities that could benefit from them. Britain's major asset in these ethnic businesses, and the entrepreneurs in our ethnic communities, could easily be wasted.

Everyone has a part to play if this is not to be the case, including the indigenous business community, central and local government, and education. There is an agenda for action here that we would be foolish to ignore.

All this has a particular relevance for Middlesex University, which aims to be recognised as a leading modern regional university, with an international reputation committed to serving the needs of its students and its regional communities. Many of our students come from areas of North and North West London that have large ethnic populations, and our student body is among the most diverse of any university in Britain.

Many of these students will be the first from their families to enter higher education. Their diversity has enriched the academic and cultural life of the University, and is enabling us to pursue our mission in new and imaginative ways. We are working actively to support community development and regeneration in the North London region, work which involves many partnerships and collaborations with businesses, schools, colleges, voluntary organisations and community leaders. In this task we are benefiting greatly from the advice and assistance of Ram Gidoomal, who is also one of our Visiting Professors, and his colleagues.

I commend this book to you. I hope it will help you to see the 'British' business in a different light, and encourage you to take advantage of the fascinating diversity of opportunities the ethnic communities and their businesses present.

Lord Sheppard of Didgemere KCVO Kt
Chancellor Middlesex University

Foreword by Mike Fairey

We don't need to see the results of the 2001 Census to know that ethnic minorities are a vital dimension of many consumer markets. And they are an even more important part of the business sector.

Some 12% of new businesses are started by ethnic minorities, so for banks, the vocabulary to communicate with these entrepreneurs has really got to be part of the language of business today.

This book provides an invaluable insight into the cultural nuances and is an excellent source of reference. This kind of knowledge can make the difference between winning the trust and business of tomorrow's business leaders, and missing out and offending an individual and the community. The challenge for those of us who advocate opportunity for all is to turn good intentions into action.

If inspiration were ever to be the missing ingredient, this book seems to have the recipe for success.

Mike Fairey
Deputy Group Chief Executive
Lloyds TSB Group plc

Preface and Acknowledgements

There was once a UK businessman, Mr Jones, who needed to buy widgets.

But not just any old widgets. He needed a specialised overseas widget, one that had made its country of origin world-famous for widgetry. There was no other widget that would suit his particular needs. He'd designed his new product line around it.

So Mr Jones decided to cut out the middlemen and make a business trip to buy direct from the manufacturing country. It would be expensive, and it would be more difficult to achieve a profitable mark-up and an attractive selling price for his product. But it was worth it to get the product right.

He planned his trip carefully.

Before leaving Britain, he rang his destination and booked an interpreter. That wasn't cheap, but he wanted to be sure he would be able to understand everything that would be said. Then he rang the local bookshop and a government department, to order several books about the country he was going to. No point in spoiling everything because he'd missed some vital cultural nuance. Thinking it over, he decided to hire a local personal assistant when he arrived, just to make sure. More expense! The day before his flight Mr Jones decided to visit his bank, to arrange cover for all these unavoidable outgoings.

He didn't know a word of the language of the country he was going to visit, so it's not surprising that on his way to the bank he didn't recognise that several people he passed in the street were speaking it; nor that several handbills on the door of the local assembly rooms were written in it. You couldn't blame him for not knowing that the wedding being celebrated in the assembly rooms was typical of the country he was bound for, or that the participants were wearing the national costume. And he couldn't be expected, surely, to know that the young man he brushed past at the bank entrance was from a family originating in that country, held a diploma from its national college of business studies and often served as guide and cultural facilitator for executives travelling there.

The bank could have been more helpful – if Mr Jones had briefed them more fully about the purpose of his trip. But he didn't know that the bank happened to handle the overseas account of a factory a few miles away, owned by a family from that very country, residents of the UK for the past forty years. Mr Jones didn't even know the factory existed. That wasn't surprising, for its customers were almost entirely from ethnic minority communities and the factory did almost no business with the majority community.

It was a pity, though. For the factory was a widget factory. It prided itself on making widgets that were just as good as those made in the mother country. In fact it had recently received a business award for excellence in widget manufacture.

But Mr Jones had no time to find out anything of this.

Mr Jones had a plane to catch.

Part of the reason we have written this book is to provide the information that might have saved Mr Jones a lot of money, and might also have led to some very profitable business collaborations.

Every working day in the United Kingdom, people look overseas for goods, skills, services and expertise that can already be found here in abundance.

We provide an overview of the ethnic business communities of Britain, with many pages of information and useful resources, and we also give you the opportunity to hear a varied range of business people from the UK ethnic business communities speaking for themselves. These include:

- A Dutch executive of Shell
- An American IT executive
- A South Asian retailing entrepreneur
- A Japanese banker
- An African business consultant
- A Malaysian-Chinese biotechnology entrepreneur
- A Polish chef
- Several representatives of inter-cultural business services

We show you the characteristics of Britain's ethnic communities and how to build cross-cultural relationships. This book is a map of territory that is largely uncharted. It celebrates a national resource that has often gone completely ignored.[1]

But we have other reasons for writing, and not all of them make such cheerful reading. Mr Jones might well find that the widget factory on his doorstep is about to close down. All over Britain the ethnic business communities are facing problems and obstacles to growth that could easily destroy them.

There is a time-bomb ticking under the UK ethnic business economy, and time is not on our side. The ethnic unrest and violence in Bradford and other northern cities in July 2001 illustrate one major social problem which we discuss in this book. But there are other less visible problems that have massive implications for the ethnic communities and for the UK economy as a whole. One cannot easily separate them. For example, business interests in Bradford fear that the unrest has set back ethnic relations and partnership twenty years; there is already the beginnings of talk about a business exodus, the scale of which remains to be seen.

We'll show you that Britain could face a future of falling behind in world competitiveness, of failing to achieve world-class business status, of abandoning any hope of becoming a showcase to the world in culture, fashion, food, music, the arts and much more, and of seeing the end of hopes of London becoming one of the three capitals of the world (which was Mayor Ken Livingstone's vision in May 2001).

There are steps that Britain must take, if we are not to squander the potential of our ethnic business communities.

And there are fundamental changes that we must make as a nation, if Britain is to become an inclusive world player.

In this book we propose an agenda for change.

---

1. Our book is not intended to add to the literature of international cross-cultural businesses and how business practices differ across the globe, but focuses on cross-cultural issues within Britain. The two topics have much in common (you'll find the same broad general characteristics among Greek people in Liverpool as you will on the island of Kos), but we focus on the ethnic minority communities as part of British society; with unique ethnic qualities but located in the same geographical, administrative, legal and social context. So the opportunities, challenges and problems we discuss will be specifically UK ones – although from first-hand knowledge of international business, we are convinced that the underlying issues and principles involved can be applied to multi-cultural situations across the globe.

When a title page bears three names, the reader is entitled to know who is responsible for what part of the finished book.

This is a book with three authors and one writer.

Ram Gidoomal is a South Asian businessman whose family came to Britain from East Africa in one of the first waves of immigration in the 1960s. His business background is with the multinational niche marketing corporation the Inlaks Group, and with a number of public sector and charitable sector enterprises. He sits on the boards of several government-appointed think-tanks, advisory groups and regulatory bodies, and he was a candidate in the 2000 London Mayoral elections. He brings to this book global experience of dealing with business people on several continents, and of operating from offices in Geneva, London and Scotland. He also lectures and consults across the full range of ethnic minority business communities and has served on such programmes as The New Deal (Minority Ethnic Advisory Group), the African Caribbean Westminster Initiative, and The Prince's Trust.

Deepak Mahtani, also a South Asian businessman, is director of several companies, including the cross-cultural business consultancy Winning Communications Partnership Ltd which specialises in advising public and private sector companies on issues relating to ethnicity. With Ram Gidoomal he is a director of the charity South Asian Development Partnership, which in 1992 published a groundbreaking study of the UK South Asian contribution to the UK economy, *The £5 Billion Corridor*. He brings to this book awareness and understanding of cross-cultural business relationships in businesses as diverse as City banking houses and IT consortiums, and wide-ranging practical experience in seminars, conferences and academic institutions. He was born in Hong Kong and lived for fourteen years in Japan and for a further fourteen years in Switzerland, before coming to Britain in 1995. He is a member of the Community and Race Relations Advisory Panel to National Police Training.

David Porter, who is a member of the majority community, is the author of many books, including business histories and biographies. He conceived this book and has written the text, drawing heavily on the expertise and experience of Ram Gidoomal and Deepak Mahtani to shape the contents and direction of the book. We have used the resources of Winning Communications Partnership Ltd and of South Asian Development Partnership in various ways. David brings to this book the experience of living in ethnic minority communities in the north of England, writing projects with communities in Northern Ireland, and travelling and writing in post-revolution Eastern Europe where he has worked with ethnic minorities in Hungary and Romania.

We are grateful to a large number of people who have helped us, especially those who allowed us to interview them extensively for the second section of the book.

We would also like to thank Tricia Porter, who has transcribed most of the interview tapes.

RAM GIDOOMAL
DEEPAK MAHTANI
DAVID PORTER

Introduction

If I had been sent to Venezuela or Japan, I would have expected 'culture shock' and prepared myself accordingly. I was not prepared for the shocks I have had these last few months in Britain. (*An Italian manager*)

The stereotype Brit strolls along the Strand with stiff upper lip and furled umbrella, or watches the shadows lengthen across the Lords turf as the Test Match draws to a close. Of course he is male; his wife is probably making his tea. He can be found too in the twilight of the Raj on the Indian polo fields (Malcolm Muggeridge believed that the only surviving real Brits were to be found in India), forging paths through unknown lands, or teaching classics in chalk-drenched schoolrooms.

That model of Britishness is almost always set in the past. Today, some would describe the stereotype Brit as someone to be found knocking back lager in Magaluf, or being arrested outside a foreign football stadium. Or it might mean being separate from – and 'better' than – other societies, like America or Europe. Some of the old school would say that the British are noble and true (usually taken to include the monarchy, the parish church, Jane Austen and the BBC). And some use 'British' as a derogatory term, even if they are British themselves. They mean un-professional, amateurish, or (if talking employment) lazy and probably (if talking football) mindlessly loutish and doomed to lose the match into the bargain. When other countries behave in such a way, they are often said to have contracted 'the British disease'.

Those models are almost always white Anglo-Saxon. To hold to them you have to ignore the evidence of statistics and the evidence of your own eyes. Britain is multi-ethnic and a significant number of its people are from ethnic minorities. Here are three examples:

□ In Belfast, the Chinese are building a new Chinatown. 'Chinatown' is an evocative word. In Liverpool, Chinatown is well established, a place to eat in restaurants where real Chinese people eat real Chinese food and down the road you can buy the spices and sweetmeats to make the dishes yourself – and authentic woks to cook them in. In London, five minutes' walk from Trafalgar Square you can, on festival days, watch the ancient Chinese dragon dance and wander through tourist-packed streets that still feel Chinese. But the UK Chinese are not just a nostalgic memento of the exotic Orient. In Belfast, one of the largest Chinese communities in Britain is celebrating its business and social development with a gleaming new twenty-first-century edifice backed by private and government funding.

□ In ethnically troubled Bradford, the South Asians are creating new business patterns that aim to draw closer together the minority and majority business communities. In this book you'll read about QED and its founder Dr Mohammed Ali. QED is seeking to tap the huge resources of the British ethnic minority communities and release skills and entrepreneurial vision that have often remained invisible. These South Asian Britons are the most easily recognised ethnic minority: Leicester is the second-largest Indian city outside India. We look at why Asian business success has remained Britain's most invisible business asset, and how change is happening (and why some change is happening that is unwelcome, like the ethnic unrest and rioting across the north of England in summer 2001).

□ Knowledgeable visitors to Peckham in London remark that its High Street looks like a little Ghana. The UK African community isn't usually considered an identifiable group as are the South Asians and Chinese, but they contribute considerable professional skills and quali-fications to Britain. In section two you can read about the pastor of a thriving black church in Middlesex who also runs a business consult-ancy, a publishing operation and a business seminar programme. Most his clients are black British professionals and business people.

What is Britishness?

The question of how Britishness is to be defined is a topical one today, when, at the beginning of a new millennium, Britain is a place of rich ethnic diversity. In some towns and many more villages the vast majority of faces are white. Superficially, little has changed for decades. At the same time some British cities have districts that look like Asian or African towns. The shops sell unfamiliar food and other goods, and mosques and minarets dominate the skyline.

But not all ethnic communities are instantly recognisable. Some are scattered almost invisibly among the majority ethnic community; others are very visible, and live in easily identified neighbourhoods with their own focal points and institutions. But even the scattered communities have times and places when they come together. There is a Polish cemetery in Hammersmith, a Hungarian church in Barons Court; in the northern counties, in the shires and in the newly devolved regions frequent gatherings, rituals and celebrations are a reminder that there are significant numbers of ethnic communities throughout the country, not just in those areas where they can be easily seen.

Diversity

Around one in eight of all Britons has an ethnic minority background. We will be looking, albeit briefly, at the historical background: how these communities came to Britain, what their cultures look like, and what particular skills and abilities their members possess. We also, in section two, look at the basic things you need to know when doing business with the ethnic minorities – for example, matters of etiquette and social custom. No book can hope to include every UK ethnic culture in detail, but we have chosen what we hope is a representative selection, and in the interviews in section three we have invited a number of their members to speak for themselves.

In the first part of the book our aim is primarily to capture the flavour of Britain's multi-ethnic, multi-cultural heritage, and to provide some landmarks and reference points in the ethnic community business landscape to help anybody unfamiliar with the territory to begin to explore the opportunities, challenges and resources that those communities offer. We see this as much as a celebration as a reference guide, for Britain today is truly a nation of rich cultural diversity. And that's something worth celebrating.

The Other Side of the Story

But in this book we also ask important questions, and raise issues that have major implications not only for Britain's ethnic communities but also for Britain herself and her economy. Issues of whether or not one should shake hands with clients of the opposite sex, or if one's body language is accidentally sending insulting messages to clients, are not the only issues in doing business with Britain's ethnic minorities.

Lost chances and wasted resources ...

This book tells a story.

It's the story of **a huge pool of talent and resources** that has too often been ignored by Britain. Why do so few British businesses take advantage of the huge business resource that the ethnic communities represent? Why do so many look abroad for help in marketing to foreign countries, when whole business communities of people, originating from those countries and familiar with their cultural and business practices, live and work in the UK? Why is so much imported that is being produced by ethnic communities in the UK – and sometimes to a better quality? There's not much point in celebrating something that you then proceed to ignore.

It's the story of a **brain-drain** that has largely gone unnoticed. You won't read about it in the tabloid press, but we are not only losing a pool of skills that Britain desperately needs; we are also sending on their way many gifted and talented people whom we educated and trained in Britain. Why? We look at some of the reasons in Chapter 4 (p. 52).

It's the story of thriving business communities that include some of the wealthiest business people in Britain – yet are built on **fault-lines** that are already becoming ominously apparent. Like the rumblings of a volcano no longer dormant, there are worrying indicators in the ethnic business communities that could point to imminent business disasters that will have repercussions for the whole UK economy.

It's a story of **wasted opportunities**. For example, South Asians have business flair that has created many millionaire entrepreneurs (and access to an enviable global financial diaspora). The Chinese are a people whose mother country, it's widely believed, will inevitably be the driving force of world economics in the first half of the new millennium, and with whom early business rapport is highly desirable. Yet co-operation and profitable business collaboration between majority and minority ethnic communities is often made impossible by simple misunderstandings or blunders that could easily be avoided – or by attempts to impose 'one-size-fits-all' solutions on problems that are geographically and economically diverse.

In telling this story, we look at specific case histories. For example,

THE CASE OF THE LOST BANK ACCOUNTS ...

It was two o'clock on a Friday afternoon just before Christmas. The manager of a busy high street bank received a phone call from the managing director of a South-Asian-owned business, a client of the bank for almost ten years. It had an excellent track record and an account balance that normally ran at seven figures.

'We're unexpectedly ordering more stock than we anticipated,' said the MD. 'We need to increase our inventories for the Christmas period. Can you authorise a temporary overdraft of £60,000?'

'I need to look at the figures,' the bank manager replied. 'I'll get back to you.'

At four o'clock the MD's phone rang. The bank manager was firm. 'I've looked at the account and the figures. We aren't able to extend you an overdraft.'

Over the weekend the MD told three of his cousins and brothers, all customers with the same bank, what had happened. On Monday all four closed their accounts. As a result of that one telephone call the bank lost business worth £4 million – because a £60,000 loan had been declined.

The bank, perplexed at what seemed a massive over-reaction to a straightforward business decision, told the story to a business consultancy. 'What did we do wrong?'

It wasn't a business mistake. The bank had not understood a simple and fundamental characteristic of the South Asian business community. That mistake cost them four million pounds' worth of business – and could have easily been avoided.

In Section 1 you'll see what the mistake was and why the family reacted as they did.

The Case of the Lost Bank Accounts is typical, in at least one respect, of the stories of many failed business relationships between ethnic communities. The bank had no idea what they had done wrong. Many initiatives between communities do not produce the results hoped for, and one party or the other – sometimes both – cannot understand why.

Often the problem is cultural unfamiliarity, causing resentment and raising barriers over relatively simple matters like misunderstanding a particular gesture, not realising the significance of casual remarks or jokes, omitting some basic courtesy, or not understanding what the real meaning is of apparently straightforward commitments. In later chapters we provide resources to help counter such wasteful misunderstandings and to interpret more accurately the way that various ethnic communities do business.

But there is a wider dimension of misunderstanding that is, potentially, much more serious. A misplaced handshake or poorly-timed witticism can wreck a contract, but if local or national government is unaware the realities of multi-ethnic Britain, the viability of whole ethnic industries can be threatened. The role of educational establishments, large corporate investors, national institutions, emergency services like the police and the armed forces has sometimes rested on misunderstanding and sometimes on thinking that is out of date or simply wrong, as the Macpherson Report on structural racism in the Police Force, for example, demonstrated.

These are matters that need urgently to be considered. Before we turn to them, however, we need to look briefly at the history of multi-cultural Britain. Doing so will give us a good perspective with which to view the cultural landscape, and will also point up some of the misconceptions that are currently in circulation about the community in which we live.

Section 1
1: Get to Know the Neighbours

As we started to write this book, the white population of California was officially declared an ethnic minority. As we were finishing it, it was announced that the same shift was imminent in Leicester, UK, and that Birmingham was not far behind.

Of course, Leicester is not a typical English city. It sits centrally in the corridor that stretches from Southampton to Newcastle and in which nearly 90% of British Asians live. It has a much higher concentration of ethnic minorities than do most cities. The fact that it is approaching a demographical trigger-point is not a sign that Britain's ethnic minority communities are about to become the largest sector of the population.[1] Current population forecasts estimate that by the year 2010, the ethnic minorities will account for only 10% of the peoples of Britain. In the London borough where two of our authors live there is a high proportion of ethnic minority residents, and in some boroughs, like Newham, over half the population has an ethnic minority background; in Hampshire, where the other author lives, the figure is around 3%.

Even so, announcements like that about Leicester are dramatic indications that British society is changing. For generations, the ethnic minority communities have tended to be looked upon as immigrants, visitors who had settled here. Now, as second and third generations appear who have been born in the UK and have never visited their mother country, and as successful members of the ethnic minorities begin to make an impact on business, the arts, the professions and even politics, it's necessary to look at these communities as part and parcel of our social landscape. They're not going home: they *are* home. Their passports are not colonial versions. They don't have to stand in the 'Aliens' queue when

---

1. Ashok Viswanathan of Operation Black Vote, commenting on the Leicester report, forecasts a slowing down of ethnic minority population growth by the third generation, when the trend for large families will stop, and predicts it will be 50 years before any sizeable shift takes place. 'But the shift is inevitable and should be celebrated.' (Ananova web site, November 2000).

they go through Customs Control at Heathrow. They are British citizens.

For many of us, it means we're going to have to redefine the word 'British'.

Roots and Shoots

Business guru Charles Handy quotes an American visiting Britain:

> Why is it that over here whenever I ask the reason for anything, any institution or ceremony or set of rules, they always give me an historical answer – 'because' … whereas in my country we always want a functional answer – 'in order to'?[2]

The point is a good one, and most of this book will take the 'functional' approach. The historical background can't be left out of the picture, however, because history has shaped so much of the way in which British society is viewed today. So let us begin by looking briefly at how we arrived at modern multi-cultural Britain.

'Britishness' was in the news very early in the new millennium, when The Runnymede Trust's Commission on the Future of Multi-Ethnic Britain published its controversial report.[3] Home Office Minister Mike O'Brien acknowledged it with the words,

> The Government is profoundly committed to racial equality and the celebration of diversity. We are a multi-cultural society.

That is, of course, saying nothing new. The dawn of a new millennium is a good time to look back, and the roots of our cultural diversity can be easily seen when we look at Britain at the dawn of the last millennium. A collection of autonomous regions, she was already occupied by large ethnic populations: Celts, Angles, Picts and more.

Britain's natural resources were fabled and she stood at international crossroads. In the ravaged north, the Danes dominated what had been the cultural centre. The south was a land flowing with beef, bacon, wheat loaves, strong beer and sweet mead, butter and cheese. 'The Italians cook with oil but the English cook with butter,' it was said in envious

---

2. Charles Handy, *The Age of Unreason* (Hutchinson, 1989), p.3. (Quotation marks added for clarity.)

3. Runnymede Trust, *Report of the Commission on the Future of Multi-Ethnic Britain* (Profile Books, 2000). Chairman: Professor Bhikhu Parekh.

neighbouring countries. The wealthy owned fabulous properties, furniture and clothing. The churches were splendidly decorated and housed treasures. The banqueting halls were richly furnished. The invasions and forays that such splendours prompted added further ethnic diversity to a people already ethnically diverse. We get most of our English words for meat from France and most of our dairy words from Germany and Scandinavia. We travel on roads left behind by the mighty Roman conquerors. The days of our week are named after Scandinavian gods.

Modern Britain was shaped in the ebb and flow of ethnic diversity; just as on the continental mainland nations were rising and falling, as wave after wave of conquerors vanquished, settled and intermarried.

The Death of Myths

The notion of 'Britishness' is shrouded in myths. Here are a few.

❑ **The Myth of the Island Race** – a melting pot of cultures and ethnic groups, which evolves into a democracy that civilises and benevolently rules an empire. That is Winston Churchill's thesis in his monumental *History of the English-Speaking Peoples*. Ironically, Churchill was still Prime Minister in the mid 1950s when Britain was dismantling much of her empire – he called it 'a hideous act of self-mutilation'[4]. Immigrants from newly independent colonies, attracted by Western benefits (and invited by Western interests), came to Britain; and Churchill realised that closing the doors would jeopardise the position of ex-patriate colonial Britons.

❑ **The Myth of the Mother Country**, in which ethnic diversity blends over the centuries into an amorphous 'Britishness'. This was hard to sustain when distinct ethnic groups arrived and the beginnings of recognisable large communities of UK ethnic minorities began to be established. Now British society was seen to be composed of many different ethnic identities. The ideal of Britain as cultural blancmange died, just as many other myths were dying, just as imperialist jingoistic patriotism had lost much of its passion in the mud of the trenches and the carnage of the two World Wars. And all that was before the major immigrations of the 1960s, when Harold Macmillan found himself in

---

4. Quoted in Lord Moran, *Winston Churchill: The Struggle for Survival 1940-1965* (Constable, 1966), p. 328.

the unlucky position of having to make unpopular legislation – even though later, all sides would regard it as inevitable.[5]

❏ Plenty of myths died in the making of modern definitions of 'Britishness'. For example, **The Myth of the Benighted Pagan Black Savage** whose civilising contact with the West has been a spiritual and cultural blessing to him (a favourite justification for slavery in Britain and in America) – difficult to maintain in a Britain whose ethnic minorities have often been the most disadvantaged members of the community.

❏ **Traditional ethnic stereotype myths**, many of which survive in popular comedy; the late Benny Hill endorsed the stereotype of the squinting Chinaman with a funny voice and limited understanding, and numerous Irish stand-up comics have traded on the popular myth that all Irish are engagingly stupid. The devious grasping Jew immortalised by Charles Dickens's Fagin occasionally surfaces in modern entertainment, and neo-Nazi movements and a sharp rise in European anti-semitism have ensured that the bitter lessons of the Holocaust have not entirely won the day.

❏ **New ethnic myths** arise, too. During the Third Balkan Wars of the 1990s, many British schoolchildren were socialised into thinking that every Serb was an ethnic cleanser, just as their parents were sometimes taught as toddlers that every German had been a Nazi during the war. Similarly, attitudes to both sides in the Northern Ireland conflict have sometimes been shaped by popular prejudice and media imbalance.

If we want to construct a definition of 'Britishness' adequate for a new millennium, these myths have to go. Instead, we must take a hard look at what exactly comprises British society today.

The Runnymede Report contains a lot of sound common sense and some visionary wisdom – and also some problematic and controversial statements. One that we think particularly confusing is this:

> The term 'race' ... is unhelpful, however, to the extent that it reflects and perpetuates the belief that the human species consists

---

5. Alistair Horne, *Macmillan: 1957-1986* (Macmillan, 1989), p. 421f.

of separate races .... The words 'race' and 'racial' are not used in this report in ways that might imply the view that the human species consists of separate races. (*Overview: Terminology*)

At the least, this is language being used in a new and potentially very confusing way. At worst, it implies that 'Britishness' is that cultural blancmange into which everybody blends.

On the day the Report was published, the BBC asked one of the present authors, Ram Gidoomal (a first-generation immigrant whose family came to Britain in the late 1960s from East Africa) to comment. He responded,

> I'm very happy to celebrate ethnic diversity and the ethnic culture that is my heritage. I'm also a British citizen, which is very important to me, and I celebrate the unique flavour of British society too. But if you ask me whether I plan to become a brown Englishman, the answer's No.

Contribution on demand

Ram's family arrived in Britain in 1966 as refugees from Kenya. Many UK ethnic minority communities arrived in similar circumstances, as refugees and often in extreme poverty. For them Britain was a benevolent empire, admitting to its shores a limited number of people who had no other place to which to go.

But most of Britain's largest ethnic communities were established in the post-war years, when immigrants arrived at Britain's request rather than their own. They were invited to work in specific jobs and were at first warmly welcomed by a country still recovering from a war that had taken its toll of the labour force.

Of the UK's ethnic minority population of around 4 million[6], nearly half are of South Asian origin; and the three largest ethnic minority groups are Indians (28%), Black Caribbeans (17%) and Pakistanis (16%). None of these had significant numbers in the UK before the 1950s, so it can be said that the modern UK ethnic demography was established in the years following the war.

---

6. Approximately 6.5% of the whole population (by the year 2020 it is expected to stabilise at around 10%).

My country needs YOU!

The first to come were Jamaicans, who arrived in 1948 to answer the call of the country they had served in wartime. Over the next ten years, the numbers of Jamaicans and other 'West Indians' in Britain gradually increased. Some came because British companies recruited in their home countries. A 1956 London Transport advertising campaign brought 3,787 Barbadians to Britain over twelve years. In 1966 further campaigns were launched in Trinidad and Jamaica. Other organisations such as the British Hotels and Restaurants Association recruited skilled workers in Barbados. Many of the immigrants worked as London Underground staff, bus conductors, and hospital orderlies. It was a contribution to the British workforce that was made because the British asked for it to be made.

When it became clear that the numbers coming from Jamaica were insufficient for Britain's labour needs, substantial immigration from the Indian subcontinent followed. Before the war very few people from the subcontinent lived in Britain (even though immigration from South Asia had begun in the eighteenth century) and those who were resident tended be among the social elite. But in the 1950s, again with encouragement from Britain, rural workers from India and Pakistan began to arrive. By the end of 1958 there were around 55,000 Indians and Pakistanis in the UK and about 125,000 West Indians. Not long afterwards thousands of Asians, expelled from Uganda and East Africa, arrived.

All these came by invitation, and they came by right, for the 1948 Nationality Act entitled Britain's colonial (and ex-colonial) citizens to British citizenship and the right of residence in Britain.[7]

The present map of ethnic minority communities took shape in those years, as new arrivals looked for friendly faces in a country where the warm welcome they received from government and press was not echoed by the Trade Unions and most of the general public. The cities that today have large ethnic minority communities are those that received the largest numbers then.

Closing the door

Since then, immigration laws have progressively tightened. Many people who argue that too many foreigners are being allowed into Britain would

---

7. See Peter Fryer, *Staying Power: The History of Black People in Britain* (Pluto Press, 1984), pp. 372-3.

be surprised if they knew the real numbers involved. The 1962 Commonwealth Immigration Act, for example, did two things. First, it responded to growing suspicion and fear of recent Black and Asian immigrant communities in Britain. Most immigrants had tended to settle in visible communities, and because they had few economic assets on arrival they often chose disadvantaged areas already suffering housing and employment shortages. Consequently the indigenous population saw immigrants as a threat (sometimes overlooking the fact that the jobs the immigrants were taking were unpopular jobs, and they had been invited to Britain to do them).

But the Act also made citizens of Commonwealth member states (previously allowed into Britain, the head of their Commonwealth, to receive the same rights that they had possessed in their home country) into aliens just like any other foreigners. Later legislation followed the same pattern. Today immigration has slowed to a comparative trickle. The ethnic minority communities in Britain have roughly doubled in the past twenty years, but growth has been from within rather than without. Of the present ethnic minority population, around half has been born in Britain and most are under the age of 25. Predictions of growth in the ethnic population are not usually based on the expectation of large numbers coming from abroad.

Multi-cultural Britain is a modern phenomenon with long roots. The population of the UK contains substantial communities of people with different characteristics, different skills and cultural identities. The result is a diversity that can justly be celebrated.

The wonder is that the majority business community so rarely does celebrate it, and even more, that it so often ignores the opportunities which that diversity presents. In the chapters that follow, we ask why.

2 : Realise the Contribution of the Ethnic Communities

It was not until 1991 that the British Official Census included a question about ethnicity. Not everybody thinks that was a good idea. Ward Connerly, the Chairman of the American Civil Rights Institute, warned in the *Daily Telegraph* that including the same question in the 2001 Census could backfire badly:

> The signs of renewed racial conflict are troubling, from what I read about the British census. According to where you live, there are boxes for Welsh, Irish and Scottish – but not for English ... There is no room for racial distinctions and racial separatism by government in a policy of blind justice.[1]

Connerly pointed to a number of historical examples of government exploitation of census data (not least in Hitler's Germany). And census data can indeed be abused. But the inclusion of ethnicity in the 1991 Census enabled a leap forward in social and population studies. For the first time it was possible to see how the ethnic communities are distributed in Britain, and to identify how they contribute to the national economy and to national life. It has been a revelation, for very few people before 1991 realised that communities that had come to Britain by invitation, to do specific and usually manual jobs, had become a major and sometimes irreplaceable element in the business life of Britain. Here are just a few of the ways in which ethnic communities are contributing to modern Britain.

❑ They have between them an estimated £25 billion disposable income.

❑ They contribute more to the system than they take from it (many ethnic communities have their own support systems and therefore make fewer demands on existing services, such as social security and benefits).

---

1. Ward Connerly, 'If Justice is Blind, the Colour of Your Skin is of No Importance', *Daily Telegraph*, 26 April 2001.

❏ They provide natural links to the ethnic diaspora (world-wide dispersed communities), opening up global markets and outlets. And by making Britain a richly multicultural country they attract inward investment.

> The UK's multiculturalism is a growing factor in attracting overseas companies ... Some 275 different languages are spoken in London, meaning that staff can be found to cover virtually any niche market. Agencies such as the London First Centre and the Invest in Britain Bureau are actively promoting the country's multiculturalism as a selling point for incoming investors. 'London's multiculturalism is a powerful force in attracting inward investment from all over the world,' said Stephen O'Brien, London First Centre's chief executive.[2]

They contribute to and enrich the arts and media; for example, in his pioneering 1986 study of Black British writers, Prabhu Guptara pointed out that,

> Britain's Book Marketing Council chose among its twenty Best Young British Novelists in 1983 the following five writers: Buchi Emecheta, Kazuo Ishiguro, Shiva Naipaul, Salman Rushdie and Clive Sinclair.[3]

More recently the millennium celebrations gave Londoners a new awareness of the cultural resources of the ethnic communities (half of whom live in the capital). The East London Mela, the Chinese Dragon Year 2000, the Hindu Council's Millennium party and the Commonwealth Arts and Cultural Foundations festivities, were just some of the celebrations that were not only organised by and attended by large numbers of the ethnic communities, but also, from the amount of city-wide participation, were clearly becoming part of the UK scene.

And there are many other contributions, sometimes made by whole

2. 'London speaks your language' (Invest in the UK, News, May 1999, www.invest-in-the-uk.com/news9905.html), p.1.

3. Prabhu Guptara, *Black British Literature: an Annotated Bibliography* (Dangaroo Press, 1986), p.16.

communities, sometimes by pioneering individuals who open up new worlds of opportunity for their ethnic brothers and sisters. Here are a few examples.

In *politics*, Navnit Dholakia, who arrived in Britain as a seventeen-year-old in 1956, became a life peer in 1997 and president of the Liberal Democrats in 2000. It is the first time anyone of Indian origin has held such a position.[4] In *academia*, American scholars in British universities bring a transatlantic perspective to their teaching and by their presence contribute their skills and cultural context to the British lecture room. In *agriculture*, Dutch farmers in East Anglia bring their special expertise in dealing with the problems of low-lying land and the ever-present encroachment of the sea. In *convenience food*, the ubiquitous McDonalds is having to defend its patch against new gleaming sushi palaces with food serenely gliding by on stainless steel conveyor belts. In *cuisine*, the contribution is enormous. The list is very long, and it's impossible to make a comprehensive tally.

But with such an impressive list to their credit of contributions to British life, why is it that in almost every area, the UK's ethnic communities are represented to an extent far below their numerical presence in Britain, and the majority of ethnic business communities remain outside the mainstream business life of the UK? And why do we so often look outside our borders when we don't need to?

The Skills Inflow

Over the period in which we were writing this book it was reported that Britain is bringing in from abroad:

- An American to sort out the London Underground

- A Swede to run English football

- Indians to work in IT

- Australians, New Zealanders and South Africans to teach in our schools

- Continental Europeans to work for Railtrack.

---

4. Jon Stock, 'Don't Worry, Have Curry!: Navnit Dholakia strives to make Britain a melting pot of cultures' (*The Week*, 21 Jan 2001), pp.48-49.

Socially aware periodicals like the street magazine *The Big Issue* have featured this trend too.

> New [police] officers could come from countries like Norway, Sweden and Holland in an attempt to halt a growing recruitment in the force, said a top police figure [Neil Taggart, chair of the West Yorkshire police authority] last week ...Figures released last month revealed several forces were failing to meet targets for ethnic minority recruitment, as outlined in the Macpherson report following the murder of Stephen Lawrence. Taggart said the police should copy the health service, which frequently recruits overseas doctors and nurses.[5]

Five Ways to Realise Ethnic Capital

But why go out and look?

With the wealth of talent entering Britain country as immigrants and refugees – not to mention the economic and labour resource that the ethnic communities already established in the UK represent – it's astonishing that so rich a resource has been so rarely tapped. Why is it that so many immigrants to Britain – business executives, professionals, academics and highly-skilled workers in their home countries – end up in unskilled jobs, in their own communities, while we look overseas for those same skills that are already here? How can the situation be turned round?

There are at least five things that business and government need to do as a matter of urgency.

Know your client! (especially his or her ethnic, cultural and business background)

> Better cultural understanding might have reduced the shock factor in BMW's decision to sell Rover's Longbridge car plant, according to Farid Elashmawi, president of US consultancy Global Success. He [said in a conference speech] that understanding the cultural diversity of the workforce and external partners was vital in the global marketplace. Cultural differences in communications may have been behind the apparent

---

5. Nadine Ghouri and Max Daly, 'Why the Great British Bobby Could Soon be a Dutchman or a Swede' *The Big Issue*, 14-20 August 2000, p. 5.

misunderstanding between the government and BMW over the company's plans ... 'Managing cultural diversity is the new competitive edge for firms going global and local companies hiring multicultural workforces,' Elashmawi said.[6]

Of all the ways in which we encounter our fellow human beings, doing business is one of those most influenced by how we perceive the other person.

In the pub, standing in a bus queue or making small talk at a cocktail party, we can chat about some profound issues, show each other photos of our families, and part on the warmest terms – and next day remember very little of what the other person looked and sounded like, if indeed we remember them at all.

Business discussions are different. They involve assessing the other person. Are they going to buy? Will they agree to the new policy? Will they be willing to sell? Has our sales pitch been well received? What is the significance of that remark, that gesture? Am I committing myself too soon? Is now the psychological moment to close the sale, to make the offer, to announce the bad news, to reveal the sales upturn?

We don't often make those assessments on the basis of verbal statements and responses. We're watching facial expressions, body language, whether the smile on the face is matched by smiling eyes; we listen carefully to the inflections of the voice, and read volumes into a gesture that may or may not be significant. In the unfamiliar cultural world of ethnic minority business these are often acutely sensitive, ambiguous areas of encounter. A mistake can bring about disaster – and correctly understanding what is going on can make negotiations run extremely well. In more relaxed meetings, with less hanging upon the consequences these things probably wouldn't matter. In business dealings, they usually do.

That's why we have provided in Section 3 an overview of Britain's ethnic community, with some facts about each people group and some guidance on the characteristics of their business style. You'll discover, for example, that Japanese and Chinese business people strive for an ideal of harmony, whereas American and majority British ethnic communities

---

6. Eila Rana, 'Cultural Awareness Could Have Softened the Blow at Rover', *People Management*, 13 April 2000.

tend to adopt a confrontational approach. You'll see how some communities, like the South Asian, are highly entrepreneurial, while others are more orientated towards the professions. And you'll discover that some unexpected factors are strong influences on how many ethnic communities do business – such as religion, and the extended family. We also provide a book list (p. 251) for those wanting more than an overview of a particular ethnic community.

To illustrate the value of being aware of the cultural and religious background of those you want to do business with, here is another case history.

THE CASE OF THE ACCOUNTANT KEPT WAITING

The accountant knocked at the door of the office. It was six o'clock. When the meeting had been requested, he hadn't asked for an earlier appointment. The Pakistani family that ran the small London publishing house certainly weren't clock-watchers. Saturday meetings were common; once he'd even been summoned on a Sunday to discuss a late VAT claim.

It seemed that nobody was going to answer the door, so he pushed it open. He went into the deserted reception area and rang the bell on the desk. Still no sign of life. He sat down, reached for one of the glossy magazines on the table, and began to read.

He'd worked his way halfway through the pile and the clock had almost reached seven, before there was the sound of voices in the corridor and an apologetic Director came in. 'It was good of you to wait.'

But why had the accountant waited, in the face of such a lack of the usual courtesies? Accountants' time costs money and there had been no sign that anybody was in the building at all. Nobody had even offered him a cup of tea. Wouldn't it have been simpler to have written the meeting off and gone home for his disrupted evening meal?

He'd stayed because he was himself a South Asian and was familiar with Islamic culture. He'd worked out very quickly why there was nobody to meet him. The Fast of Ramadan was ending and today was the Fast-Breaking, a day of special prayers and festivities, focused on the end of the fast at sunset. The family had miscalculated the time their fast would end; they had still been praying and so it was quite impossible for them to attend to him, still less offer him food or drink. So the accountant waited, where non-Asian accountants might well have given up – and perhaps lost a client.

Know your client! That applies as much to his cultural background and spiritual identity as his business profile.

Mind your language!

Ethnicity is an area fraught with traps for the unwary, and nowhere more so than in the way we talk – as many business people have learned at some cost, when a contract inexplicably failed at the last moment, or a previously cordial dinner-table discussion with prospective partners suddenly lapsed into a frozen, embarrassing silence. Two of the authors[7] of this book are directors of a cross-cultural business consultancy that largely exists to prevent such disasters or to carry out post-mortems on them. The cause is almost always offence accidentally given by cultural misunderstanding. Often words are heard quite differently to how the speaker intended to speak them (a notorious example is humour, which is one of the most dangerous ways of attempting to cross cultural divides).

Language has power. It can define roles and social levels, identify the dominant members and the 'inferior' members of a group, and decide who are the outsiders and who the inner ring. It can bring people together and drive them apart; it can make people feel generous and place them under obligation.

All very useful, if that's what you intended. But it can be catastrophic if you don't realise it's happening, or how critical a factor language can be in business.

❑ Japanese and Chinese executives use language to flatter those they want to persuade. They apologise profusely for the generous gifts they give. When praised themselves, they disparage their own achievements or possessions.

❑ Americans often draw attention to themselves in a very un-British way because they want to establish themselves as desirable business partners.

❑ Arabs and Indians seem to be enthusiastically agreeing to a contract or business plan, but are actually only saying that they have taken it on board as something to consider seriously.

---

7. Ram Gidoomal and Deepak Mahtani: the consultancy is Winning Communications Partnership Ltd.

❑ Australians negotiating with British executives will freely use language that Brits consider swearing – 'bloody' is an even milder word in Australia than it is in Britain. They are also likely to use very casual language that seems highly insulting to the 'pommie bastard' with whom they are hoping to close a deal. But they are often quite surprised if told that they are using language that is not normally used in formal business dealings in Britain.

If both parties know what is going on, the conventions of language can be useful business tools.

The Japanese middle-rank executive who has just been wined and dined at great expense by an advertising company pitching for a contract is not stupid. She doesn't really believe that she is so important that being given even so expensive a meal is practically an insult – but she likes being told so. An Indian trader in a Midlands fabric warehouse will not send an invoice immediately after his client has said 'Yes' to a large purchase. But he is very happy with the signal that has been sent out: his offer is obviously going to get serious consideration.

But if one party in a conversation is unaware of the way his or her words are being received, the consequences can be disastrous. And that is why we told (p. 11) the Story of the Bank that said 'No'. Here's why the clients closed their accounts.

THE CASE OF THE LOST BANK ACCOUNTS – A POST-MORTEM

The loss of several million pounds' worth of business as a result of turning down a relatively small temporary overdraft was only partly a banking error. Certainly the account was secure collateral – the overdraft would have actually increased flow through the account over Christmas. After ten years, the manager should have known that the businessman was an excellent risk. A track record had been established that should have been ample reason for authorising the overdraft. So there had been an error of banking judgement.

But that was not why the family pulled its business out of the bank.

The problem was a relational problem, and it was most of all a language problem. The bank manager should have thought about how his words might be received.

Words caused the problem and words were the vehicle of downfall. In South Asian circles, word of mouth is a powerful force. The strength of ethnic minority relationships is stronger than that of the white mainstream relationships. It can work for you or against you. Networking happens overnight. If somebody is satisfied with you, it works in your favour; his brother or sister will call you – 'Can we bank with you? Can we buy from you? Can we hire your services?' If it goes against you, the word also spreads, like wildfire.

The family's reaction was not an act of revenge or pique. According to their way of doing business they had no choice but to act as they did. For the bank manager, in refusing the loan, was actually (though he didn't know it) casting serious doubt on the honour of the customer, his business and moral standing, and his intention, as well as his capability, to repay. And because he didn't realise the seriousness of what he was saying he made no attempt to soften the force of what were to him everyday words. To the businessman, however, it was a grave insult to his family's honour. 'Look what the bank has done! It is a matter of shame: shame upon our family, shame upon our community! Let's shift our accounts.'

Don't stereotype!

In this book we attempt to steer a neutral path along the linguistic road. Whenever we can, we use terms preferred by the ethnic communities, rather than ones coined (from whatever motive) by members of the majority community. Like most writers on these topics we prefer 'black' to 'coloured' for obvious reasons (two of the authors are brown, one is pink; all three are coloured), and we avoid words that carry a value judgement, such as 'half-caste' (we strongly prefer 'mixed race'). We don't share the Runnymede objections to words like 'race' and 'minority' – we use them as straightforward factual descriptions. 'British' is a statement of government and geographic location, not a forced identity-label. Even so, linguistic policy is always a matter of choosing between unsatisfactory alternatives. We are aware that the words 'ethnic minority' are disliked by many in those communities[8], but the alternatives are often just as unsatisfactory. Canada has christened its immigrants 'newcomers', for example, but this could be understood negatively and in any case more than half the ethnic minority UK population was born in Britain.

All this matters because of the role of language in ethnic debate.

---

8. That was, for example, a finding of the February 2000 Consultation of the Race Equality Unit's Race Equality Support Programmes (cf p.8 of the Consultation Report, published May 2000).

Discriminatory language usually betrays underlying attitudes, just as someone talking about leadership exclusively in terms of 'he' almost certainly believes that leadership is essentially male.

Language reinforces and strengthens stereotypes. Using the word 'coloured' usually implies 'non-white', and to a greater or lesser degree marginalises 'coloured' people.

The media and entertainment industries are full of stereotypes carried in powerful words. The tabloids favour the vocabulary of marginalisation. Stage comedy exploits visible differences, strong accents and unusual ways of speaking. Words enter the common language bringing values with them. 'Black' is a metaphor for evil that has gradually shifted to focus on those whose skin is dark. 'Yellow' occurs in various contexts, often facetious, to mean 'Chinese'. The typical 'Red' (Russian) in action drama and pulp fiction is bound to be a global villain or warmonger. And you'll still find characters in light fiction who describe a particularly brave, comradely and moral person as 'the whitest man I know'. You don't have to be wedded to political correctness to appreciate the need to take care over language.

'Vive la différence'

There's a great deal of lazy language used about ethnicity. Take that old worn-out phrase 'They all look the same to me' – patronising, of course, but also unperceptive. Consider the Chinese. We all know the cartoon-strip round-faced, narrow-eyed, beaming, pencil-moustached Chinese face. It's a parody of the Mongoloid features, shared in various forms by a majority of Chinese. But there are over 50 ethnic Chinese groups, including Indo-European, Malayo-Polynesian and many more. Each is different from the Mongoloid facial type.

The same is true of the Indian peoples – not surprisingly, for both China and India occupy very large areas of the earth's surface and account for large sectors of the world population. It's insulting to say they all look the same. (It's also a bad basis for business, because it breaks a fundamental business maxim – 'Know your client'.)

Take religion. For many Westerners, Confucianism is the only spiritual framework of the Chinese. But there are millions of Muslims and Buddhists in China, and many minor religions. Around 60% of the Chinese population – over 50 million – is Communist, but it should be remembered that Marxism has been described as the last great world religion. 'Confucius he say …' is not as typical a Chinese saying as many have assumed.

Such stereotyped attitudes can play havoc when doing business with Britain's ethnic minorities. For example,

❑ The common mistake of ignoring 'invisible' ethnic communities – such as highly integrated, light-skinned communities like the Dutch – can seriously weaken a strategy of 'targeting the ethnic minorities'.

❑ Sometimes wilfully holding on to mistakes alienates prospective business partners. An example is the choice of English spelling one uses for Chinese names. Generations raised on 'Peking' and 'Mao Tse-Tung' dislike having to learn the newfangled 'Beijing' and 'Mao Zedong'. The former is the Wade-Giles system of transliteration, devised by two Westerners, and the latter is Pinyin, a Chinese government initiative. Wade and Giles created spellings that bore little relation to the way the Chinese pronounce names. A business person from the majority community using the old forms just because they 'sound right' will annoy an up-to-date Chinese businessman.

Think about the ethnic minority cultures with which you most often come into contact. How far are your opinions about them gained from real observation, and how far from attitudes – and probably prejudices – you have picked up from the media?

In the public sector, the publication of the Macpherson Report in 2000 has led to UK police forces, organisations and businesses across the board being urged (and sometimes ordered) to review their attitude and practice in race relations.

It's a matter of civil rights, of course. But it's also sound business sense. Time spent analysing potential business partners, staff, clients and customers is time well invested. Some firms spend very large sums doing just that!

Don't re-invent the business wheel!

The majority business community often has no idea what resources exist. Existing networks work well enough, and there seems to be little advantage in exploring new ones. Why spend time and money finding new suppliers, when the old ones are still there? It's a two-way problem, as the two following case studies show.

THE CASE OF THE INVISIBLE SUPPLIER

A large London-based UK South Asian manufacturer, producing video and CDs, had been trying for a very long time to sell a video duplicating service to the BBC. The company had been sending samples and quotations to the Corporation for more than six years. The owner was intensely frustrated. He had built up a large customer among the ethnic minority markets, but breaking into the wider mainstream market seemed impossible. He went to a cross-cultural business consultancy for advice.

The consultants arranged a meeting between him and a BBC executive and helped him prepare a presentation, as a result of which the BBC agreed to give his service a trial. A few weeks later the BBC came back to him. 'Your product is cheaper than anyone else, your delivery was quicker than anyone else, and your price is extremely competitive. Where have you been all this time?'

To which, of course, the answer was, 'We've always been here.'

Because of the difficulty of breaking into the mainstream and getting the type of exposure that creates market interest, many companies never succeed in making the transition from the minority to the majority marketplace. Yet their product or service is more than good enough to stand up in the wider marketplace. The majority market, however, has not realised that there might be excellent and competitive products and services in places they never investigated before.

Sometimes the problem is the other way round, and the ethnic minority business enterprise is unfamiliar with mainstream procedures and methodology. It's extremely difficult for many ethnic businesses to grasp how Great Britain plc actually works. What is a Board? How does employer equity operate? How do you draw up a P & L when applying to a bank for a development loan? What's a development loan anyway?

Ignorance of such things doesn't mean that such people are bad at business, nor that they are stupid. In most cases, it's simply confusingly different to the way they do business in their own communities.

THE CASE OF THE GLOVES THAT NEEDED A HAND

A South Asian manufacturer of hospital disposable gloves was trying to break into the NHS market. After failing to make any inroads for a long time he approached a consultancy for help. As it happened, the consultants had business interests in Geneva where they had very wide experience of bidding for World Health Organisation tenders for medicine and pharmaceuticals. They were able to bring to his situation a good knowledge of the tendering process in the medical profession.

For them the tender system was second nature. But their client was a South Asian, and South Asians do not usually do business by tender. So they know almost nothing about the system, whether the tender being invited is for the NHS, the Department of Education or anybody else. Consequently in dealing with the majority business community, the South Asian entrepreneurial skills and bartering flair that have been used to create some of the strongest businesses in the UK – let alone in the minority ethnic communities – can be effectively blocked.

In this case all that was necessary was to teach the glove manufacturer how to cost a tender, how to present it, and how the tendering process works.

Discover hidden resources!

> Some 75% of all the refugees who come here are professionally qualified and yet they're cleaning toilets, if they get a job at all. It's a crazy waste of talent.[9]
>
> Nick Hardwick *(Chief Executive, Refugee Council)*

It's not enough just to recognise that a vast pool of skills and resources lies untapped in Britain's ethnic communities. We are looking in this chapter at why it happens. Many of those reasons are discussed by the people interviewed in Section 2 of this book, a significant number of whom made the same points repeatedly.

Here's one.

Often a person who is highly qualified, skilled or otherwise extremely employable in his or her country arrives in Britain, unable to speak English and unfamiliar with the accepted ways of looking for work. In his or her home country such a person would be very familiar with the mechanics of job application, and would have little difficulty in finding appropriate employment. In Britain, however, there is no choice but to settle where people speak their language and there is some kind of work available – even if that work is far less skilled than that for which they are qualified.

---

9. Said in a discussion at the Royal Society of Arts recorded in *RSA Journal* (Vol. CXLV No. 5481, July 1997), p. 53.

The need to survive, to eat, to provide for relatives who may still be in the home country, traps such people in a vicious circle. Communities of skilled and professional people are occupied in low-paid, unskilled and manual jobs. Those jobs are often physically and mentally burdensome, and the lack of surplus money means that looking for work more in keeping with their qualifications is impossible. They are stuck in a poverty trap and the door cannot be easily unlocked from the inside.

Exploiting the skills pool

Opening that door from the outside – by initiatives from the majority community – is much more than a charitable gesture, though it does help to bring about desirable social change. It can also be an extremely profitable business strategy.

Any business can start working with local ethnic communities. It doesn't need specialised experience in ethnic issues: just some applied lateral thinking.

For example, suppose you are exporting to Vietnam. Maybe you are sending a business delegation there, or, like Mr Jones with whom we began this book, you plan to visit potential clients and partners. You'll need help; it's a different culture, they do business differently there and their mother tongue is not English. That's why in countries like Vietnam thriving business service industries exist: translators, cultural advisors, local representatives, tour arrangers and many more, all anxious to sell you their skills for a good price. They make a good living because there are considerable advantages to the business person coming from a foreign country. The most obvious benefit is avoiding language problems, but there is also the advantage that a great deal of potential embarrassment is prevented that might have been caused by cultural unfamiliarity. An added bonus is that money will be saved: the Vietnamese, like most Asians, are very good at getting things done. They know, more than anybody, how their own business culture works.

But why pay overseas prices and hire at a distance? There is a growing number of Vietnamese people in Britain. Many of them are qualified and skilled; all are fluent in the Vietnamese languages and are completely familiar with Vietnamese culture and social norms. So why not employ a UK Vietnamese speaker (or an entire team) to translate, give cultural training and local advice – even go to Vietnam with you as a guide?

British Telecom, when fighting for a share of the global market, were negotiating to sign a contract in India. Did they draw on the South Asian community in Britain for help? Did they get a multi-cultural team together to work on the project? Yet over 100 languages are spoken in London almost natively, and you get a better curry there than you get in India.

We have heard of a temple building project in Nairobi that was in trouble. Did they think of London for help? In Neasden, several ethnic communities working together built an authentic Hindu temple. Did anybody think of offering that expertise in the global marketplace? And not just London expertise: the ethnic communities across Britain possess large resources of talent and skills.

Government initiatives

Recent government initiatives have begun to recognise that resources are arriving in Britain and promptly disappearing into an employment limbo.

In August 2000 the Immigration Minister, Barbara Roche, announced a scheme to assess the eligibility of candidates for immigration on the basis of their business track record and their experience, rather than the traditional criteria of how much money they had or what relatives they had in Britain already. The 'Investors' scheme specifically targeted young entrepreneurs in science, technology and e-commerce. Unlike previous immigration schemes for business applicants this one did not require a large bank balance or a wealthy UK sponsor.

> It is important that our immigration policy encourages people with innovative business proposals and valuable skills to bring these to the UK. Many such people, whose presence here would result in significant economic benefit to the nation, are not catered for under the existing rules.

The scheme turned entrepreneurs' applications for entry to the UK into something like a business start-up proposal with appropriate documentation and CVs. It was part of the Labour government's programme to establish Britain as an Internet world capital. DTI Competitiveness Minister Alan Johnson explained,

> We want to attract talented entrepreneurs in e-business and other new technology fields to set up business here. They will create jobs and exploit knowledge in a way that is vital to our national competitiveness. We are committed to ensuring that by

2002 the UK will be the best place in the world to conduct e-commerce.[10]

Despite the murmuring voices pointing out that Britain's over-burdened telephone infrastructure alone[11] would make such a dream difficult to achieve, it represented a new way of looking at immigration (though Britain was not the first to propose such plans: Germany already had a fast-track immigration in place, where skilled immigrants had their applications speeded up.) By mid-2001 the results of these and similar government initiatives were beginning to be seen.

> At least two-thirds of software professionals entering Britain are from India, thanks to amendments to work permit rules last year to invite more information technology (IT)-trained foreigners.
>
> The amendments have opened the floodgates for Indian IT professionals, and with Britain facing a massive skills shortage in IT, they are pouring in.
>
> Government figures show that 18,257 foreign IT professionals came to Britain last year. Of this, 11,474 were from India – three times the number in 1999. This year the numbers are rising faster, according to official estimates.[12]

Break Moulds – Be Bold!

Underlying the issues we have explored in this chapter is the question of how we should view our society.

We are convinced that **a radical paradigm shift of perspective on the ethnic communities is needed in almost every aspect of British business life.** For too long the business community of Britain has been viewed as a 90% majority community and a 10% 'fringe' of outsiders, who are largely

---

10. Linda Harrison, 'Britain Wants Foreign Dotcom Smarty Pants', *The Register* (www.theregister.co.uk), 4 August 2000.

11. For most of 2000, the Internet Service Providing industry struggled to achieve unmetered '24/7' access to the Internet for their customers. There was a string of well-publicised failures, all due to systems unable to meet unexpected demand.

12. Sanjay Suri, 'Indian IT Professionals Pouring into Britain', *Asian Voice*, 5 May 2001.

marginalised by ethnicity (though the same could just as well be said of those who are physically and mentally disabled, those who are women, and members of several other significant minorities). The received wisdom is generally that responsible governmental, corporate and community concern dictates that there should always be a representation of these minorities within the mainstream; that good government means getting the numbers right.

It sounds good and it sounds caring. And it has led to many problems.

It has often led to *tokenism* – the attitude that if you have one or two members of the ethnic minorities on your workforce you have somehow bestowed a social good and are now off the hook. It needs little thought to recognise that this is on one hand highly patronising; and on the other hand, if what we have suggested about the resources that the ethnic communities represent is correct, it is also short-sighted in the extreme.

And it has often led to *positive discrimination* – recruiting people not on the basis of their skill or their ability, but on the grounds of their ethnicity or the colour of their skin. The result is many members of the ethnic communities who have been treated as numbers without reference to their real skills or even their personalities, working with colleagues from the majority community who feel they have little cause to respect them. Much recruitment in these situations is done purely to satisfy the requirements of anti-discriminatory legislation.

The problem with the view we have just described is that it is a 'them and us' view. It regards minorities as people to be brought into the mainstream by learning mainstream ways, and indeed by becoming mainstream themselves – 'brown English' people, whose difference from the mainstream has been successfully overcome.

But it is those differences that create the rich resource and the rich diversity which we have been discussing in this chapter. Far from 'overcoming' difference, difference should be celebrated. All the ethnic communities are part of Britain and they are part of whatever 'Britishness' is. They represent a huge diversity of skills and aptitudes, and they bring with them business assets far beyond a willingness to commit to long hours and dedicated work. They are above all globally minded and usually unfettered by the burden of having done things one way for a long time – and if ever two attributes were vital to Britain's success in the new millennium, those two are. Cause for celebration indeed!

Diversity – a Hopeless Dream?

Diversity is much talked about today. Often the discussion takes the form of a dream that is dreamed, of multi-ethnic Britain; a culturally and ethnically diverse but harmonious country, to which everybody contributes their skills and abilities and from which everybody draws all that they need and a good part of what they want. Is that just a pious hope – or is it achievable? And if it is achievable, why has it not yet happened? What is standing in its way, and how can the dream be made practical?

Dr Mohammed Ali, whom we interviewed in Bradford, believes that it is far from a dream. It is a necessity.

> If you are in business in a place like Bradford where every second child leaving school is of Asian background, and you're looking for a workforce, obviously you have a vested interest. And as the proportion of Asians in the city's population and their disposable income increases, you have an increasing customer base there too. For good business reasons, businesses are beginning to recognise that they can't afford to ignore this very important sector.

Business is at the heart of multi-ethnic Britain's future. Community growth and development are largely based on employment. Prosperity needs jobs, and if communities are to change they need the support and sometimes the regeneration that only business can provide. But business stands to gain immensely too. We believe that it is time to cash in the deposit of talent and skill that is in Britain's ethnic communities and do business together for mutual benefit and profit.

If that sounds idealistic, at least we're in respectable company. In 1997 Prime Minister Tony Blair told the Labour Party,

> We cannot be a beacon to the world unless the talents of all the people shine through. Not one black High Court judge; not one black chief constable or permanent secretary! Not one black army officer above the rank of colonel. Not one Asian, either. Not a record of pride for the British Parliament that there are so few black and Asian MPs ....

> Now make the good that is in the heart of each of us serve the good of all of us. Give to our country the gift of energy, our ideas, our hopes, our talents. Use them to build a country each of

whose people will say that 'I care about Britain because I know that Britain cares about me.'

Conference rhetoric, maybe. But the Prime Minister's commitment has been borne out by several pieces of legislation that have gone some way towards achieving that vision. At the start of Labour's second term, Chancellor Gordon Brown uttered further stirring words: 'The new Britain of enterprise for all cannot be built on inadequate investment, low skills, boardroom complacence, workplace resistance to change ...'

We applaud this bold statement, especially the phrase 'enterprise *for all*'. We are watching and waiting to see how this will be delivered to include all: not least the ethnic communities and those otherwise disadvantaged. It is significant that the day after the Chancellor's speech, a report on institutional racism in the National Health Service was published by the King's Fund.[13] It told of 'concrete ceilings', side-lining, harassment and bullying, and a catalogue of other discrimination against ethnic minorities.

So exactly how does one bring about this vision of a Britain that is good for everybody; which is, in a favourite phrase of Tony Blair's, 'simply the best place in the world to do business'? How does one bring it about, in the intensely practical world of the office, the factory, the shop floor and the like?

We now go on to explore ways in which our society and mainstream business community tend to exclude the ethnic communities rather than include them and benefit from their contribution. We will look at how the paradigm shift in thinking that is necessary if as a society we are to begin to value diversity and draw strength, energy and prosperity from it, might be made to happen.

A good starting point, and itself a shift of perspective, is to begin by looking at how the ethnic communities look at the majority community, and the way in which encounters actually take place across communities.

---

13. See John Carvel, 'Racism is Rife in NHS', Guardian Unlimited Special Reports, 19 June 2001.

3: Look at Things from Both Sides

Doing business has often been compared to playing a game, as two gurus of cross-cultural business acknowledge in the title of an important book: *Mastering the Infinite Game*, by Charles Hampden-Turner and Fons Trompenaars (Capstone, 1997). It's a good metaphor that has a lot to say about the way business works. There are many similarities between business and games of strategy, chance and luck.

Expert wargamers know that one of the simplest and most effective ways of creating a winning strategy is simply to get out of your chair, walk round the table, and look at the situation from your opponent's side. Immediately everything looks different. The mountain ridge that was an obstacle before is now revealed as an ideal defensive position. The township that seemed to be sheltering your opponent's forces is now clearly vulnerable to artillery fire. Suddenly you can see how your own defence looks from the other side, and your opponent's strategy, difficult to analyse before, can now seem obvious. Everything is different when you look at it the other way round, and new opportunities are easy to see. You realise that it is a mistake to formulate strategy when you have only your own perspective on the situation.

Business as a game isn't the only metaphor for business. You find many others: the rhetoric of sales directors urging their sales force to go out and sell, sell, sell (*business as a crusading quest for clients*); cold-calling enquirers flattering potential customers (*business as courtship*); a ruthless Board of Directors pushing though a hostile takeover (*business as war*); a tycoon adding a national newspaper to his holdings or grabbing a huge slice of Internet profit (*business as empire-building*) – and many more. Business has been the theme of Oscar-winning films, blockbuster novels and prime-time TV dramas, and few epic tragedies have quite the satisfaction of those that feature a self-made man or woman crashing ignominiously.

Yet behind all the metaphors, business is always a discourse between two parties who each have something the other wants – as customer, vendor, partner, or colleague. Whether the relationship is aggressive or mild-mannered, whether the sums involved are spectacular or small change, every business encounter is a two-way exchange. And in those encounters, looking at things from the other party's point of view can transform one's understanding of the situation entirely.

Challenge Outdated Perceptions

In 1999 and 2000 the British Council published two reports entitled *Through Other Eyes*, in which young people from 28 countries were canvassed for their opinion of the United Kingdom. The results were illuminating. The general opinion was that UK products and services are good, but our image as creators and innovators is weak. Only half those surveyed regarded the UK as a centre of artistic creativity and innovation: we were seen to be living off our past. British society was seen as divided by class and unwelcoming to foreigners. Though there were many approving comments – 'If you go for further education in Britain, you get quality education' was a Nigerian comment, and from Italy: 'I particularly liked the spirit, the liveliness, the people and their open-mindedness' – the negative comments were very different to the way that Britain tends to see herself: we are widely regarded as tradition-bound, backward-looking, stuffy and anything but dynamic.

The British Council undertook the research,

> To challenge and change outdated perceptions and to project an image of the UK as a creative and innovative society with much to offer the world's young peoples.[1]

– clearly recognising the value taking note of other points of view.

See Ourselves as Others See Us

> 'O would some pow'r the giftie gie us,
> To see ourselves as others see us …'

So wrote a distinguished member of the Scottish ethnic minority, Robert Burns. The couplet has become a proverb. It's also a prayer that could usefully be echoed by many members of the majority business community.

The British Council research focused on global perceptions of Britain.

---

1. Information, and text of the reports, is taken from the Council's web site at http://www.britishcouncil.org/work/survey/index.htm, from which both publications can currently be downloaded.

In this book, however, we are looking at ethnic communities within Britain itself. So how do we achieve that paradigm shift in perception, to see ourselves as others see us when we are in business discourse with them?

In the interviews in Part 2 of this book, some members of the UK ethnic communities speak for themselves about how they perceive the majority community, and it's not always comfortable listening.

That kind of listening is important, of course, but it is only one of several ways in which we communicate. Business people in any culture communicate at three levels, only one of which uses words. We communicate on the level of social and cultural identity; what we are as individuals and communities speaks volumes. But we communicate, too, as corporate entities, as businesses and companies, and that identity too speaks volumes.

Changing the way we listen demands a change in listening at every level.

Understand backgrounds of change

Many British ethnic minority communities originate from mother countries that in the past few years have seen enormous change.

Some have witnessed violent political change with disastrous results for the economy and for business.

❑ Some are in a state of flux, with no clear way forward and with difficult circumstances to deal with on a day-to-day basis.

❑ Some are facing soaring inflation, loss of markets, and financial insecurity so great that investment in any form is risky.

❑ Some are on the downward side of a curve that had seemed to promise vast rewards: the collapse of several of the tiger economies of the early 1990s has had severe and wide-ranging repercussions.

Consider the folk back home

UK ethnic minority businesses are often profoundly affected by such changes in their mother country.

For example, UK South Asians do business as part of the global South Asian diaspora, often using members of their extended families and other contacts to open up trading links and secure off-shore funding. It's not unusual for a member of the family, living thousands of miles away from the location of the family business, to have a controlling influence on company policy. Changes that affect the situation of members of that diaspora may affect the UK business that depends upon them.

THE CASE OF THE BANK WITH AN INVESTMENT IN THEOLOGY

Sometimes major parts of a business are conducted outside the UK, or use UK agencies that are not part of the mainstream economic system. This was the thinking behind the creation of the Islamic Development Bank (IDB), based in Jeddah, which aims to create local markets in its 53 member countries, operating according to *sharia* practice. This raises large issues of interpretation of the Qur'an (Islamic banks have set up theological Boards to scrutinise new financial systems); and the collapse of the Bank of Credit and Commerce International (BCCI) in the 1990s is still fresh enough in business memories to make many Islamic investors cautious, even though the Arab-owned BCCI was not an Islamic institution. But these are much simpler problems to deal with than those of trying to do business in Western business cultures that operate largely by credit and insurance – both of which the Qur'an forbids. Many UK Islamic businesses use banks that are based outside Britain, in their home country or region, and the IDB will give them the same facility locally.

That almost goes without saying: inevitably ethnic communities will take many business and cultural reference points from their home countries. But the implications can be missed by the UK majority business sector.

Now wash your hands ...

All too easily, majority businesses can approach the ethnic minority marketplace purely in the spirit of educators and social benefactors. From their point of view, the ethnic minority sectors are by and large communities handicapped by disadvantage (language, resources, facilities of many kinds), and frustrated by the inability to break into the mainstream market. Some of the most altruistic majority businesses consider that the benefits initially will be all on the ethnic communities' side, but that once those communities have been shown how to do things right, everybody will benefit.

But what do the majority business communities look like from the ethnic minority viewpoint?

Often help in surmounting obstacles will be enthusiastically received, especially if that help is provided through ethnic minority-led agencies such as Mohammed Ali's QED project in Bradford (see p.88). Many have struggled for years to master the basic procedures of doing business in the West, and the help of a sensitive and focused agency is for them the light at the end of a very long tunnel. An example is the hospital gloves company we mention on p. 31.

But help that comes from the majority community is often perceived as given with hands that are not entirely clean. In terms of the home-country economic backdrop, and in the destabilising and damaging change that many of those countries have undergone, the West is seen, rightly or wrongly, to have played a major part.

Sometimes the grievance goes back a long way, as in the violence against British farmers and the taking of British-owned land in Zimbabwe, without compensation and with the approval of the Mugabe government; their argument is that the British originally exploited the people and took the land unlawfully. Sometimes it is more recent: the Serbians and Iraqis blame the West for their weakened economy, and argue that the people are suffering unjustly for the actions of their leaders. Popular resentment has often been exploited by national leaders to create an ongoing climate of bitterness towards the West.

It's not a new phenomenon. Ordinary South African citizens said similar things during sanctions against apartheid. (Back in antiquity, the entrepreneurial community of Troy would probably have found it hard not to be cynical if Greek businessmen had offered to help them with start-up funding, after the long years of siege and battle leading to a famous Greek victory over the Trojans.)

When residents of such countries come to Britain, providing help in business start-ups, offering funding and making consultation available won't always look like disinterested generosity to the person who receives it. The hand of friendship might be taken with a great deal of mistrust.

These are matters that are important ones to keep in mind, as business possibilities are explored and overtures made to the ethnic minority business communities. Establishing credibility and a genuine desire to help might be necessary overtures to any other actions.

Explorers in Our Own Back Yard

There are many books about doing business abroad, explaining the subtleties of international dialogue and how to behave in other people's countries. This book focuses on ethnic minorities in the UK, but it obviously has considerable overlap with the other books. Whatever our own ethnicity, in the heart of Britain we can meet communities with a very different ethnic background and sometimes see British urban landscapes quite different to anything that's conventionally called 'British'. We are explorers in our own back yard.

And yet we're not.

The ethnic minorities in the UK aren't alien cultures any more, even if they speak a language we don't know and have a culture we don't understand. They have become British communities, most of them have British citizenship, and – most important of all – they live, and have lived, in Britain. So ethnic identity has begun to blur and merge. As in a long-established marriage, each partner has started to look like the other, in both obvious and not-so-obvious ways. These UK ethnic communities are not the same as their counterparts living in their mother countries. In Section 3, for example, you'll read how British Poles are different to Poles living in Poland – and some of the consequences that follow.

For there are consequences, and they affect how we do business. The diagram below illustrates what we mean.

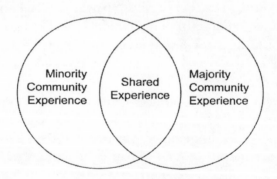

A majority business and an ethnic minority business that are in a business relationship each bring to that relationship a unique experience that the other community only experiences second-hand. But they also bring a shared experience and culture: both live in Britain, both are governed by the same government, both are exposed to the same mass media, both need an umbrella if they intend to spend much time out of doors. So though the British ethnic minorities look like the communities of their home countries, the boundaries are no longer clear-cut. There's a cultural blend taking place.

THE CASE OF THE DIRECTOR WHO LAID HIS CARDS ON THE TABLE

An example of this is our interview with Mr Horinouchi, the Japanese bank director (p. 116). When we introduced ourselves we exchanged business cards. If we had been in Japan, or in Britain meeting visitors from Japan, it's likely that there would have been a great deal of ritual behaviour and an elaborate procedure of paying respect to other people's cards – being very careful where you put them, paying compliments about the attractiveness of the card and so on. But in fact Mr Horinouchi, who has lived in England for twenty years, observed a modified version of the Japanese ritual. He placed our business cards, without comment, on the table at the side of his papers, and arranged them carefully. From time to time he looked at the cards again, and if they had been disarranged, carefully put them back into their neat arrangement. Anybody who has read one of the many books on business etiquette when visiting Japan would immediately have recognised the significance of what he was doing, but it was a diluted version, showing considerable respect to the card and its owner, but filtering the whole thing through twenty years of observing British reserve. He was doing what a British business person might have done if the British had decided to take business cards seriously.

The same thing applies to the majority business community. It too has a core of unique experience, which ethnic minorities cannot share. A visitor from China or Africa visiting a textile factory in the north of England sees a workplace and not much else. But a British visitor sees the factory in many contexts, ranging from the toil of the Industrial Revolution to the idyll of *Last of the Summer Wine*. It is full of associations and resonances that are part of the wider British culture.

Yet the majority experience, too, has been modified by exposure to ethnic diversity. Most of us eat a variety of ethnic foods. In January 2001, Tesco announced that they sell more sushi than cheese sandwiches in their stores.[2] Many of us work alongside people from ethnic minority communities, or are perhaps employed by them. The cultures of these communities have enriched British culture. The Hong-Kong-based

---

2. Channel 4 Television, *Virtual Images of Japan*, January 2001.

classical music label Naxos is Britain's largest record label. It uses artists from Eastern Europe, America, Ireland, England, Scotland, Australia and many more places. Naxos's Hungarian pianist Jenö Jandó is said to be the most-recorded pianist in the world. The music Naxos records is global too: CDs by little-known Scandinavian composers like Klami and Sallinen, Americans like Piston and Barber, and Irishmen like Corcoran and Field can all be found alongside Beethoven and Mozart in record shops and even in major branches of W. H. Smith and Boots the Chemist.

In this and many other ways, Britain – as it always has done – absorbs and draws upon the cultures of those who come to live here, and is changed, in various ways, by the process. Anybody from the UK majority population who is in their forties today first learned about the Vietnamese as a people locked in a terrible war on the other side of the world. Their children are quite likely to go to school with Vietnamese children.

Identify Difficult Terrain

There are many implications of the issues we have just been talking about. We have chosen just two, one from the minority community perspective and one from the majority community perspective.

Generational conflict

At several points in this book we mention the generational problems experienced by most ethnic communities, most notably by those that are now two or three generations old. The first generation arrives as immigrants and by sheer hard work and the need to survive in a new country establishes entrepreneurial businesses that flourish. Most of those communities regard securing a successful future for their children as their first priority and – often very sacrificially – work extremely hard to do so. The next generation is therefore highly educated, motivated and very unlikely to want to work in the family chip shop, restaurant or corner shop. The problems multiply when the founder retires or dies and hands the business on, usually to his sons in equal shares without much consideration as to whether they are all up to the task of running (and hopefully modernising) the company. In *The UK Maharajahs*,[3] two of our authors discuss this issue and describe some of the ways in which

---

3. Ram Gidoomal with David Porter, *The UK Maharajahs* (Nicholas Brealey, 1997), p.195 ff.

accountants and lawyers are beginning to recognise it and provide solutions.

Another aspect of the generational problem is the identity crisis that many young members of ethnic minority communities experience. They are members of their ethnic community – and yet they are not. They are British – and yet they are not. The cultural blend we describe above has left them in an ethnic limbo.

The consequences can be disastrous. Some sociologists have argued that it's a key factor in the rise of crime and social unrest in urban Britain (although we would question whether one factor can be isolated and blamed in what is a very complex combination of possible causes). There have been well-publicised personal tragedies, almost certainly aggravated by the generational problem.

The consequences can also be creative and exciting. Out of the confusion of identity has often come a new voice and a new identity. In the Asian communities, for example, 'British Asian' is a technical term and the existence of a new British-Asian music has been recognised even in academia.[4] Musician Bally Sagoo explains:

> I'm taking the best of both worlds and putting them together for the songs and bringing everyone together through the music. Most people probably wouldn't have ever recognised a Raj Kapoor song before and probably couldn't even relate to it. Whereas, all of a sudden, if it's sounding different, a bit of both, they might get into it ... People are listening to it, not just our kids, I'm talking about Western kids as well.[5]

Signs and messages

There are problems for the majority community, too, as cultures blend. One is the fact that competence in a language does not always mean total mastery of it. This is nowhere seen so clearly as in the use of *idiom* – the use of words and phrases unique to a language that make no sense at all if translated word for word into another language. One of our authors had

---

4. Sanjay Sharma, John Hutnuk and Ashwani Sharma (eds), *Dis-Orienting Rhythms: the Politics of the New Asian Dance Music* (Zed Books, 1996).

5. Ibid, p. 92.

this dramatically proved when one of his books[6] was translated into Hungarian. A Hungarian friend told him that the translator had faithfully translated the idioms literally, so that phrases like 'it rained cats and dogs' read exactly the same in the Hungarian text. Unfortunately, the Hungarians have no such idiom, and must have found much of the book incomprehensible.

A great deal of the language people use most freely is impossible to translate, for it draws on cultural context. An American negotiating with Russians who asks for a 'ball-park figure' will usually be met with blank looks; for what does 'ball-park' mean in a country that doesn't play baseball? Even in the UK, most of us probably only understand the term by making an educated guess or because we have watched a large number of American films.

A typical example of misunderstanding at its worst is the Swede who was negotiating with a Japanese executive who happened to be a woman. As agreement was reached he shook her hand enthusiastically and said, 'Great! Now we can go to bed together!' A Swedish woman executive would have understood that he was not suggesting anything improper: the Japanese executive was so insulted that she immediately broke off the contract and left the negotiations.

So care is necessary when talking with people whose first language isn't English, even though they speak English well and are Westernised in many ways. They may not be hearing what you are trying to say. Your choice of words might mean nothing to them; important points may be completely misunderstood. The fact that most of your listeners will be too polite to ask you to rephrase what you say doesn't make things any easier!

A related problem is *humour*. Laughter is often said to bring people together, and so it does in many ways. But it can also be the cause of much resentment. In Section 3 of this book we tell you which people groups consider humour appropriate for business meetings, but even if you are doing business with such a group, the humour might still go awry.

There are two prime traps. The first is the danger of being taken literally. Much British humour works by exaggeration, deliberate mis-statement and provocative implications – all liable to misfire badly if the words are taken at face value. The second is the danger of embarrassment.

---

6. László Tökés with David Porter, *With God, for the People* (Hodder and Stoughton, 1990), the story of the 1989 Romanian revolution.

Jokes that rely on caricaturing or stereotyping minorities are rarely well received by members of those minorities, but it's amazing how many British business people will regale their contacts in the ethnic minorities with jokes at their expense, as if daring their listeners to be bad sports.

Much better to restrict yourself to laughing about your own foibles, or the quirks and silliness that all humanity is prone to, rather than targeting a specific group.

A third area that needs care is *the dynamic of the meeting*. A successful business meeting between majority community Britishers produces a gradual relaxation of tension. Affability develops, body language becomes less tense, and people begin to use first names instead of surnames. Casual forms of address are used instead of formal etiquette. Conversation strays from the agenda to other, more personal topics such as when people plan to take their summer holidays.

In the majority community that would usually mean that the meeting was going exceptionally well. There are quite a few ethnic minority communities, however, for whom that would be the point at which the opportunities for things to go horribly wrong dramatically increased. The majority community members present might never know why the meeting broke up and the promising leads were never followed up, although the Muslims who were at the meeting might pin it down to the moment when one of their opposite numbers sat back in his chair, crossed his legs – and pointed his feet at the Muslim delegates. Indeed, it can be that the cause is lost by the way you say goodbye: when in the increasing cordiality that apparent agreement engenders, casual gestures and enthusiastic farewells unravel the carefully built-up relationship of the entire meeting. Thoughtful preparation for multi-cultural business meetings will, hopefully, prevent the well meant but unwanted handshake or informal goodbye that can spell failure when everything so far has indicated success.

What's in a name?

Understanding local customs and culture is an increasingly important matter for global markets, where not paying attention is a very costly matter indeed. The same is true when doing business with ethnic minorities in one's own country.

Names and symbols that are harmless in the home country can be disastrous when seen through another culture's eyes. In America, Nike was forced to scrap 40,000 pairs of sports shoes because they incorporated a design of a flame that had an uncanny resemblance to the Arabic script form of the name of Allah. Another shoe company, Clarks, entered the market with a pair of sandals called Vishnu and a pair of boots named Krishna. Hindu groups were not amused and Clarks had to apologise and withdraw the products.

Even brand names can cause problems. Vauxhall Nova realised that marketing in Spain was going to be difficult when it was pointed out that *nova* means in Spanish 'No Go' – hardly a good start for a launch into a new market, even for the most successful marketing expert! And computer manufacturer Commodore, in the early days of home computing, had to modify their sales pitch in France when they realised that the brand name of their most successful product, the Pet computer, sounded exactly like the French word for breaking wind.

Transforming Principles

In this chapter we have been talking about one kind of paradigm shift in thinking. We chose it because it encapsulates several priorities in cross-cultural business relations. These are,

❑ We need to be aware that there are more ways of communicating than communicating with spoken words.

❑ We need to develop a holistic view of the British people, recognising diversity as a quality, not as a problem.

❑ We need to avoid an 'us and them' mentality, and to cultivate an 'all of us' mentality.

Those three principles alone would, if widely practised, transform British business!

In the next chapter, we will look more closely at what stands in the way of transformation. The priorities and principles we've discussed so far aren't luxuries to be implemented if time allows. Time doesn't allow us *not* to implement them. Failure to make a radical shift in our thinking, to change the way we look at the ethnic communities, the majority community and the relationship between the two, will expose and aggravate the fault-lines that already exist among the ethnic business communities, fault-lines that will sooner or later impact upon us all.

So we now go on to look more closely at those fault-lines, before concluding this section with an agenda for change.

4. Recognise the Cost of Failure

Imagine a Britain with no ethnic minority communities. There never has been a Britain like that, of course – but imagine it. What would it be like?

Many service industries would be severely understaffed. Post-war immigrants arrived, invited by the Government of the day, to rescue Britain from a shortage of workers in key industries such as public transport. Those industries are still dominated by Asians and Afro-Caribbeans.

The economy would slow down, at least as regards new businesses. In 1996 Barclays Bank commissioned a review[1] that sampled 400 representative small businesses with turnovers of under £1 million, and found that ethnic minorities formed (at that time) around 5% of the population but were responsible for around 9% of new business start-ups – representing 7% of the total UK small business stock. (Which makes another finding of the report disturbing: that there is a slight downward trend in the number of Asian start-ups, traditionally a strong growth sector. The fault-line made visible?)

Many vital professions would be decimated. Medical and health services are an example. Dentistry would lose almost half its surgeons in training (48.3% of all applicants in 1994-1997 were from the ethnic minorities). Hospitals would have smaller staffs and many departments would certainly have to close. Waiting lists, of course, would increase.

Retailing would be crippled. Almost three quarters of all independent retail outlets are owned by members of the ethnic minorities. By their innovations in opening hours, stocking ethnic goods, and high presence in the community, they have changed the way the British shop. One recent example is the opening in 2000 of a drive-thru pharmacy by an Asian couple in Birmingham. Only the second of its kind in Europe, it is open 365 days a year until 8 pm except for Saturdays when it closes at 7 pm.

The arts, media and entertainment would be much the poorer. The contribution to British art and entertainment is considerable, whether

---

1. Critical Research, for Barclays Bank, *Cultural Change and the Small Firm* (Barclays Bank, February 1997).

measured by explicitly ethnic products like TV's *Goodness Gracious Me* or by the presence in the UK arts scene of large ethnic communities (some of which, like India and Hungary in cinema, have long and important cultural histories of their own).

Life in modern Britain would be duller and less interesting. Britain today is a colourful mix of cultures and people; if it were theoretically possible to extract and discard the ethnic minority communities from that mix, the result would be a great loss to national identity. One example is the ethnic diversity we would lose in our shopping: of UK retailers surveyed by Ethnic Exhibitions in December 2000, 76% had seen a significant recent rise in demand for ethnic goods and 61% had allocated extra floor space to ethnic products such as furniture, art and soft furnishings.[2] Similarly, the Argentinian CEO of the Safeway group (Carlos Criado-Perez, ex-Wal-Mart) has pioneered 'concept' shopping, a revolutionary approach to the presentation of goods in supermarkets.

There would be a fall in charitable giving. The relationship of the ethnic minorities to established UK charities is only slowly developing. However, (a) charities like Oxfam and Cancer Research Campaign have benefited substantially from fundraising in the ethnic communities, and (b) successful entrepreneurs in those communities are frequently highly motivated to philanthropy, and even where this remains within the ethnic community it reduces the burden on other charities. The estimated disposable income of the ethnic communities is £13.4 billion.[3]

Britain would lose her best chance of being a major player in the world economy. The loss of a huge IT potential, global networks, opportunities for outsourcing and off-shore services, and much more, would simply condemn Britain to being a second-league player.

Six Fault-Lines

We have talked a great deal so far about the strengths of the ethnic communities and how important it is to bring those strengths into the diversity of multi-cultural, multi-skilled Britain. We've looked at some of the barriers that need to be removed and at some of the potential minefields that must be negotiated, and we have begun to explore some of

---

2. 'Ethnic Products Boom', *Asian Voice*, 16 December 2000, p. 15.

3. Nicola Hill, 'Asian Appeal', *Guardian*, 12 July 2000 – an article drawing in part on Deepak Mahtani's experiences of working with Asian charities.

the implications for dialogue, relationships and handling business encounters which we will be looking at much more extensively in part 3.

But social change doesn't happen by default. If an inclusive and diverse society is to be achieved, policies must be pro-active. Bringing ethnic communities into the totality of British business requires an active welcome, not a casual nod of greeting. In this chapter we begin by looking at the consequences of merely accepting the status quo.

The General Election of 2001 was a painful reminder of some of the fault-lines that are opening up. In 1997 two of our authors warned of the significance of the Bradford riots of that period, pointing out the likelihood of future problems if appropriate solutions were not found, and quoting the example of a local councillor who was quite unaware of the serious social problems in the ethnic communities in the northern cities.[4] In the 2001 electoral campaign, ethnic violence flared as we predicted, leading to an armed police presence at the Oldham count – at which the British National Party achieved the largest vote in its history. The BNP vote in the General Election as a whole was significantly high, and the party's web site, www.bnp.org.uk, announced the BNP's intention to campaign for 'peaceful separation' by 'population exchange', and a boycott of Asian businesses: not one penny, it urged should be given to Asian business ... In June 2001 the *Independent*'s North of England Correspondent resorted to almost apocalyptic language in predicting likely developments: illustrated by a statistical map labelled 'The North-West Powder Keg', his article was headed, 'Whites at the top of the valley, Asians at the bottom. Is Nelson another town ready to blow?'[5]

The fault-lines are widening. Not all of them will lead to violence, but they will all weaken the ethnic minority business communities if action is not taken.

Limits to growth

In general, ethnic minority businesses tend to recruit within their own community. This 'co-ethnic' labour is usually drawn from areas that have suffered low employment, so there is an immediate short-term benefit as unemployment is reduced. Because so many ethnic minority businesses

---

4. Ram Gidoomal with David Porter, *The UK Maharajahs: Inside the South Asian Success Story* (Nicholas Brealey, 1997), pp. 183-4.

5. Ian Herbert in the *Independent*, 30 June 2001, Home News section p. 10.

are located in the inner cities, they have an important role in creating urban regeneration, achieving social and economic change and stimulating economic development.

This is obviously good news for Britain, and indeed the benefits were discussed in *The UK Maharajahs* in 1997.[6] But to leave matters as they are, hoping that ethnic minority businesses will continue to be a useful stimulant to the urban economy, may turn out to be short sighted. Many commentators argue that relying on co-ethnicity restricts markets and narrows the business context. For co-ethnicity does not only extend to recruitment; many ethnic businesses depend on co-ethnic markets.

But those markets themselves are under threat. Members of the ethnic communities can buy even their own ethnic foods cheaper in many supermarkets, and the small corner shops that served the ethnic communities have often been driven out of business by large retail chains. Those chains have invaded niche markets, extended opening hours and dropped prices as a temporary loss leader, all to gain overwhelming market share. With the loss of what was a highly competitive cutting edge (not many years ago, the only shops that stayed open late were run by entrepreneurs in the ethnic communities), ethnic minority retailers are increasingly being forced to look for added value and extra services over and above the goods they used to stock. But expanding in this way demands financial and entrepreneurial resources to which not all existing businesses have access, especially now that the days are largely gone when the whole family was prepared to work in the shop for as many hours as necessary. The second generation is often highly educated and has work commitments of its own.

In 1999 the Cities Project was launched by the Economic and Social Research Council to examine these issues. Headed by Professor Monder Ram of Leicester Business School and Dr Bahilar Sanghera of the University of Central England Business School, the project was set up to research the concerns over relying on co-ethnic consumers for survival: 'It is argued that growth is only likely to be achieved by lessening reliance on co-ethnic trading patterns and moving into wider markets. In short, "break-out" is critical to ethnic minority firms' continued development.'

---

6. Ibid, passim.

The proposed research[7] was directed at three 'hitherto neglected questions'. (a) How are second-generation entrepreneurs tackling the business and social processes involved in attempting to 'break out' of existing markets? (b) What are the internal management and labour market processes that flow from such a re-orientation of company direction? (c) To what extent will family, community and business networks that ethnic minority entrepreneurs are reputed to rely upon have to be re-configured?

These questions, particularly the last, are crucial. If nothing is done to help ethnic minority business to break out into the mainstream, the long-term consequence is likely to be a weakening of the ethnic economies and eventually a weakening of the UK economy as a whole.

What seems to be a self-sufficient infrastructure playing a part in alleviating inner-city problems is actually a fault-line that threatens serious problems.

Poor support for invention and innovation

Our interview with Dr Kim Tan (p. 138) shows that UK-grown innovation is vulnerable to the lure of overseas funding. Sometimes it is not even a lure but a necessity. Dr Tan was able to secure the funding he needed, but many entrepreneurs in the ethnic communities have not been so lucky.

It is a particularly relevant issue in the ethnic minorities as more people start up businesses in those communities than in most communities. While in some parts of south London the ethnic minority population is only 5%, over 10% of business start-ups come from these groups. If entrepreneurs and innovators feel that there is inadequate fertile soil to grow their business in the UK, they will begin to look for other countries to exploit their entrepreneurship.

An example of the loss of home-grown skills capital is the clockwork radio invented by Trevor Baylis, a Londoner who designed the radio to help communication in Africa. After being turned down by backers in Britain, Baylis was approached by two South African businessmen who, with funding from the Liberty Life Group, set up a manufacturing plant

---

7. ESRC, *'Cities' Project: Facilitating 'Break-Out': Ethnic Minority Business Development in an Inner-City Context* (document published on the Glasgow University web site, http://www.gla.ac.uk, 16 October 1999).

in Cape Town. From those beginnings Baygen Power Industries, which is registered in Britain, has become global, with distribution operations in New York, Cirencester UK, Mauritius and Cape Town. It's an inspiring story of a project that has immense humanitarian benefits and reflects very well on British inventiveness. But the bulk of the return on investment, and the jobs created by manufacturing the radio, have been lost to Britain.

The BayGen Radio story is sadly not unique. Some UK innovators are already sourcing capital from international finance centres such as Dubai and Singapore. Paresh Kotecha, for example, went to Singapore to find backing for a major refurbishing project for his international Aston Hotel chain. British banks lost £25 million of business.

If we do not take urgent steps to ensure that the ethnic communities can access schemes to support their innovative and entrepreneurial activities, we are investing money and skills in the prosperity of other countries.

Ethnic capital flight

Since 1999 the London Skills Forecasting Unit has been monitoring the contribution of the ethnic communities to the capital's economy, particularly in regard to ethnic minority employers. Although London is by no means the entire UK ethnic community landscape, as the economic centre of Britain and the home of around half its ethnic minority communities it is a useful test-bed. In February 2001 the Unit reported:

> To a great extent London's future depends on the success of ethnic minorities as they have a younger age profile than the white population ... Ethnic minority employers are firmly rooted in their local community and Borough. The [LSFU 1999] report suggests that they tend to have a local (or conversely international) market. They tend to recruit locally from within their own ethnic group. They are more likely than the White businesses to be involved in 'supporting' the local community in employment or by finance, and they are less likely to move out of London. They match the London average in terms of innovation and productivity.[8]

8. London Skills Forecasting Unit, *Ethnic Capital: Shaping London's Local Economies* (LSFU, 2001), p.6.

This is in line with what we have already observed about the strengths of the ethnic communities. But the Report goes on:

> Ethnic minority businesses may, however, be more fragile than White businesses in certain respects. They say they are uncertain about the future. The survey suggests that they create more jobs through setting up new businesses than they do by expanding existing ones. They spend about one quarter the amount of money on training as White employers. Many of these factors can be explained by their small size and by particular difficulties, such as raising finance. Ethnic minority employers are just as competitive as White employers, but they face more barriers which public agencies can help them overcome.[9]

The skills pool in London's ethnic communities is immense and often highly qualified. According to the LSFU survey, over 30% of the sample had skills of at least NVQ level 4 (the National Learning Target is 28%). In some groups such as 'Other Asian', the figure rose as high as 40% (a figure admittedly balanced by very low levels of qualification in, for example, the Bangladeshi community). The report consistently finds significant sectors of the ethnic communities out-performing the national average.

Some of these qualifications and skills are highly desirable. The computer and IT skills of the Chinese, South Asian and Black people surpass those of the White community. Britain will be short by 620,000 IT professionals by 2003, and is actively fast-tracking IT-trained immigrants (see p. 35).[10] Yet large numbers of qualified and skilled professionals are lost to the UK job market because language problems and unfamiliarity with British job-application procedures bar them from appropriate employment in sectors that are crying out for recruits. Instead they end up in restaurants and small businesses, doing manual or unskilled work, because there they can work with people who speak their language.

Some potential IT recruits bypass the UK altogether and go to America.

---

9. Ibid.

10. Ireland, too, has problems: in May 2001 the Irish economy needed to attract up to 200,000 more foreign workers to 'plug the skills shortage' (*People Management*, 31 May 2001, p. 10).

The UK's introduction of five-year work permits has yielded an average of only 1,600 extra workers since March. To help prevent the drift of Indian IT professionals across the Atlantic, European governments have approached intermediaries such as StepStone, a recruitment web site, to help them publicise their vacancies.[11]

Skills exit is another fault-line that, left unrepaired, will create lasting damage to Britain's economy. The phrase 'ethnic capital' has a double meaning. In one sense it rightly refers to London as the capital of ethnic Britain, for half of the members of Britain's ethnic communities live there. But London is also capital of a different kind, a deposit of skills and resources of which the ethnic community's contribution is a major element.

If we do not create initiatives to enable the ethnic communities to build strong business links with the majority community, so that they can take their place in a diverse and multicultural Britain, UK business will be living off its capital and its prosperity will decline.

Vulnerability of community self-help resources

The fourth fault-line, like others, might seem a positive advantage but is in fact a serious weakness.

The local ethnic communities fulfil an important role as community service providers for their people. A largely invisible system exists that functions as job centre, marriage centre, drop-in and welfare centre, counselling service and much more. It operates by word of mouth among people who know each other and are aware of community developments (Uncle Joshi is opening a new shop and needs packers, a cousin is arriving from Poland and needs somewhere to stay, little Noori is falling behind in school work and her parents are worried she might have an emotional problem). It also works through local leaders of faith communities, through members of the ethnic communities who have positions of responsibility, and through individuals whose opinions are given special weight, such as the elderly and the heads of respected families.

Of course the pub, the PTA, the vicar and others fulfil similar roles in

---

11. Jon Lamb, 'Recruiters Turn to India For IT Expertise ...', *People Management*, 24 August 2000, p. 12.

the majority community, but there they are the icing on a cake that has not always been equally shared with the minority communities. The support given by the ethnic communities to their members is often the only support, or by far the easiest support, they can obtain. Without it, the costs to the state of community welfare would dramatically rise. An example is the various community projects organised by Muslims in Bradford that are described in Section 2 (p. 88ff). The value of such hidden resources is recognised by community development projects throughout Britain.

These are strengths – but they are also weaknesses. They are fault-lines in the bedrock of ethnic minority society. Such community services run on small and diminishing resources and often face the threat of social breakdown, especially in the inner cities where ethnic tensions can become heated, such as Oldham in 2001 as we mentioned at the beginning of this chapter.

If the ethnic communities are not helped to strengthen their own support systems, and are not brought as soon as possible into the full remit of the mainstream support systems, the results could be catastrophic, and will certainly be expensive. Government must work with existing support systems to ensure their survival – funding and other help should be given to community projects, faith projects, ethnic radio and TV and newspapers.

Economic degeneration

A fifth fault-line is the fact that most economic regeneration in ethnic communities is created by the community itself, rather than as a result of government intervention.

Again, this looks very good at first sight. But local systems rarely have the luxury of addressing problems on a long-term basis. Mosques and corner shops can't often afford to make five-year plans, and local systems are often not in control of all aspects of a local situation. The short-term solutions are often highly effective, but that very success can mask a deteriorating overall trend. By the time the problem is realised, it may be too late to take cost-effective action.

Local ethnic community development must be brought into the overall local plan, and the benefits of economic regeneration must be made available to ethnic communities. Local and national government should take special care not to fall into the common misconception that

the ethnic communities are doing very well on their own. Usually, they aren't. The costs of rebuilding a derelict local economy are much higher than those of investing in regenerating a declining one.

Culture exit

The loss of skilled people – either by allowing them to be submerged, unused, in their ethnic communities, or by an escalating brain drain in which talented people, often educated and trained in Britain, take their skills abroad – is a serious matter. But the problem relates to much more than the loss of skills, disastrous though that is. Much more is being lost.

People leaving the UK business employment take with them not only their skills, but also their culture.

❑ **They take with them their fluency in their language**. This is a hidden but significant loss. If Britain intends to become a major global player, people who can speak foreign languages are a valuable capital. The UK ethnic communities contain large populations of people whose mother tongue is a key language in the new international business world – for example the South Asian languages, the languages of the Far East and the languages of Eastern Europe. Hungarian, for example, is a very marketable language, and many UK companies invest heavily in having their staff trained in it. But there are significant numbers of highly educated, business-orientated Hungarians living in Britain who could be employed either full time or on a consultancy basis who would not need to be taught the language.

❑ **They take with them their dreams and ambitions**. Some of those who leave for jobs abroad are among the most highly motivated people in Britain. Their motivation is so high that they leave close-knit communities and even more closely knit families to pursue their dreams. As Dr Tan told us in his interview (p. 149), Britain seems to have a gift for educating and training talented youngsters and then waving them goodbye.

THE CASE OF THE TEAM THAT DREAMED TELEPHONES

Sam Pitroda, head of telecommunication giant WorldTel, is a man who had a dream: an Indian who had amassed a fortune in the USA from telecommunications, he dreamed of putting a telephone in every Indian village by the year 2000. He returned to India, got the backing of the Gandhi government, and set up headquarters in a hotel building in Delhi. There he directed a team of brilliant young Indians, any of whom could have earned big money in America. They preferred to work for Sam. They worked long hours, slept when they could, and maintained their enthusiasm so that they completed their phase of the project ahead of the deadline, comfortably within the technical restraints, and well under budget. The result of their work can be seen in the yellow telephones that are now part of rural Indian life. **That kind of enthusiasm is not an exception. It is characteristic of many of the people in the Chinese and South Asian communities that are heading up change and growth in Silicon Valley and in IT world wide. To harness it is easy: to ignore it, and let it find another country to flourish in, is foolish.**

❑ **They wither if planted in inhospitable ground.** People in the ethnic communities, like people anywhere, find banging one's head against a brick wall to be intensely frustrating. There is a pressing need to develop a fertile environment in which ideas and energy can flourish. Our interview with Isidora Popovic, p. 162, shows how effective the work of agencies like the Prince's Trust has been in providing financial help, consultancy and practical training for young people with business ideas. But Britain still has some way to go before it can be called an entrepreneurial society. The banks are only slowly introducing the kind of help to entrepreneurs that most American banks provide as a matter of course.

Virgin boss Richard Branson, possibly Britain's best-known entrepreneur, argues that the British establishment feels threatened by entrepreneurs. 'Very few [entrepreneurs] have found favour within the establishment ... At Virgin we have tried to upset the way things are done, change the things that are done, whether that's in the financial services, the air industry, rail industry, soft drinks, telephones, across the board. And some people won't like that ...'

Recent fast-tracking policies for skilled immigrants have not yet meant that immigrants arriving in Britain can be assured of finding opportunities to develop – and contribute – their talents. **Continued, intensive exploration of how to harness the contribution of all sectors of society – for example, through organisations developing their own fast-track procedures – is needed.**

These six fault-lines – and many more that could be added to the list – spell out a profoundly gloomy message. If nothing is done the fanciful picture we sketched at the beginning of this chapter of Britain without its ethnic minority communities could be in danger of actually happening. The more likely outcome is hardly less gloomy. Britain with a declining economy, burdened by the loss of some of its most vibrant economy sectors, socially diminished by the loss of most of the rich blend of ethnic cultures that has given British society its distinctive character, and culturally impoverished by the loss of large elements of its arts, entertainment and media.

Add to that the loss of a wealth of global contacts, international business expertise, access to markets, specialised niche industries, a large part of all retail outlets, and much more – and those fault-lines start to look like major threats.

An Agenda for Action

Dealing with those fault-lines is good for business, and will certainly make Britain a stronger nation with a more competitive and healthy economy. But there are reasons taking urgent and effective action that are only incidentally concerned with self-interest. Here is Jack Straw, then Labour's Home Secretary, putting the case for altruism[12]:

> Race equality is a moral imperative. It also makes best use of the available pool of talent and allows everyone, regardless of colour or race, to achieve their full potential. So there are economic and social benefits too. Furthermore, our great nation is built on diversity, change and immigration. It is all the richer for this. Few of us can look at our lineage, including me, and not find links beyond these shores. However for some of us, particularly black and Asian ethnic minorities, it can be more difficult to achieve our potential, simply because of racial prejudice and discrimination.
>
> One of the Government's central aims is to achieve a society where there is respect for all, regardless of their race, colour or

---

12. Rt Hon Jack Straw, Home Secretary, introducing *Race Relations (Amendment Act) 2000: New Laws for a Successful Multi-Racial Britain* (HMSO, February 2001).

creed, and a society that celebrates its cultural richness and ethnic
diversity. In doing this, the Government wants the public sector
to set the pace in the drive for race equality, to lead by example.

So, whether we want to enhance the quality of life and achievement of
some of Britain's most disadvantaged minorities, or whether we want to
harness the business potential of those communities to increase business
performance at company, industry, national or international level, or
whether we want to do both – how exactly is it to be achieved?

5. Do It!

We want to end this first part of the book with an agenda for action. It is based on a formula used in seminars organised by South Asian Development Partnership.[1] Like the entire contents of the present book, the agenda can be summed up under four headings, easily remembered by the acronym 'ABCD'.

Acquire Awareness

We have seen that many British citizens, let alone members of the majority business community, are unaware of the potential of the ethnic minority communities. Awareness has to be worked for, whether in the case of individual behaviour or that of government policy. We suggest that awareness involves *understanding* and *exploring*.

Understanding

The need to understand the resources and opportunities represented by Britain's ethnic minorities has been a major theme of this book so far, and we mention it again here to emphasise that it is a first step in developing awareness. But besides recognising resources and opportunities, it's vital to recognise diversity within ethnic communities. We earlier pointed out the dangers of stereotyping and of the tendency to lump all members of a community together when in fact they have relatively little in common. **Any effective initiative, whether by one company or by local or national government, will only succeed if it is targeted at people as they are, not as they are mistakenly assumed to be.**

This must include correctly understanding the map of British ethnicity. We have discussed how to gain a new appreciation of *who* the ethnic minorities are, but we also need to understand *where* they are.

---

1. Deepak Mahtani, Robin Thomson and Steve Neumann, *The South Asian Opportunity* (South Asian Development Partnership, 1997). Material is also drawn from Nick Isbister and Tim Cole, *Diversity* (Career Innovation Research Group, 1999), produced for limited internal distribution.

New Labour swept into power in 1997 on a manifesto that placed a high priority on the ethnic communities, and the comments by Home Secretary Jack Straw quoted above are an example of several ways in which that commitment has been addressed. But much needs still to be done, as Tony Blair acknowledged when receiving his second large mandate in the 2001 General Election; and part of the task calls for radical shifts of thought in geographical perspective as in much else.

The map of UK diversity is well known. Around half of Britons of ethnic minority background live in London. The vast majority of South Asians live in the corridor that stretches from Southampton to Lancashire and into Yorkshire. It includes the two major centres of South Asian population – the West Midlands and Greater London – and 'the second largest Indian city outside India', Leicester. Sometimes referred to as the M1/M6 corridor, its ethnic community was reckoned in 1992 to contribute in excess of £5 billion to the British economy.[2]

The largest ethnic communities are also the most visible: the South Asians, Africans and West Indians. But they are not the only ethnic communities in Britain. We provide information about the others in the reference sections later.

The ethnic map of the UK is not evenly distributed. Yet many government initiatives seem to assume that it is and that a 'one-size-fits-all' solution will do. But there are large differences between the Asian community in Harrow, for example, and that in Bradford. In our interview with Dr Mohammed Ali (p. 90) you'll see some of those differences, such as its unusually high rate of new arrivals per annum. A government policy for the Asians of Bradford should be different to one for the Harrow Asians because they are two different communities. But all too often, the initiative is the same. Even neighbouring London boroughs are very different from each other in their ethnic communities, yet the Government approach has been to prescribe exactly the same procedures and help to all of them. For example, a Home Office document outlining categories of grant under its Race Equality Support Programmes[3], while acknowledging that situations varied across the country, did not explore

---

2. South Asian Development Partnership/SOLOTEC, *The £5 Billion Asian Corridor: Opportunities for TECs* (SADP/SOLOTEC, 1992), p.10.

3. Race Equality Unit, *Connecting Communities: Race Equality Support Programmes* (Home Office Communications Directorate, 2000)

the idea of targeting help to ethnic communities in different regions in ways specifically tailored to those communities' needs.

The consequence of not changing this way of looking is certain to be that the effectiveness and value of government initiatives in this area will diminish: as we said earlier, one of the main reasons for understanding diversity is to be able to target effectively. That calls not for segregation but for segmentation: marketing to specific groups of people demands targeting *markets* by targeting *communities*. That is the approach of several highly successful companies such as Saga, who sell insurance to people over 50, and another company that sells only to women. Chester A. Swenson writes:

> We have moved from a manufacturing-driven to a consumer-driven economy; the mass media itself is fragmenting; we are celebrating ethnic and social diversity, rather than pouring everyone into a homogenous mold; and the growth rate of the population is slowing with a resultant impact on the demand for goods and services.[4]

But without an understanding of the nature of our domestic ethnic diversity, targeting will be impossible.

The third type of understanding that is urgently needed is an understanding of the cultural issues and pressures faced by the UK ethnic minority communities. We give you a variety of information on these matters in the reference sections of this book, and we have already discussed the topic in this section.

Exploring

Awareness also demands that we explore our attitudes. What do we really think about the ethnic communities? What are the barriers to mutual understanding and acceptance?

The exploration has to be two-way. Ram Gidoomal, during election week 2001, heard a white woman say that her neighbour was selfish; he wouldn't recycle anything, so was a burden on the waste disposal services and an annoyance to the neighbourhood. Urged to challenge him about it, she replied: 'Oh, I couldn't do that, he's an Iraqi!'

---

4. Chester A. Swenson, *Selling to a Segmented Market: The Lifestyle Approach* (NTC Business Books, 1990), p. xv.

She was afraid that he would interpret her annoyance as racist. The channel of understanding was not open through which she could treat him like any other neighbour. As a result the problem continued, and neither side got any closer to understanding the other.

Similar problems surround the debate on asylum seekers, where it is difficult for any side to discuss quotas without being accused of racism.

Practical initiatives are needed. Ethnic minorities need help to develop citizenship skills; the majority community needs to be educated in understanding the immigrants in its midst. Building this two-way awareness takes time, but is an essential first step.

Build Bridges

Better awareness leads to better relationships. These can be strengthened by pro-active bridge-building between communities. Bridges achieve two things.

First, bridges between communities help establish common concerns and links between those communities. Shared values can be one form of bridge, for example joint action in the face of a common threat such as development or lack of adequate amenities. Another might be the need for an improved transport system. Any initiative that encourages social interaction between communities will help build bridges: often arts centres can be instrumental in this, as can schools and faith communities.

Second, and perhaps oddly, an understanding of what separates communities can often build bridges between them. One person's difference is another person's diversity. An appreciation of differences can lead to an enriching co-operation.

It's useful to do a check on areas of importance to your company or organisation. Are these matters that are also important to the ethnic minority communities in your neighbourhood? If so, is there duplication of effort that could be turned into joint projects? Is the wheel being re-invented and are expensive resources being duplicated?

Areas worth looking at include *schools and education*. Initiatives are needed that are designed to bring levels of literacy and general education in the ethnic communities up to the same standard as in the majority community. Such initiatives should be incorporated into entry procedures for immigrants, developed in consultation with faith schools and other ethnic education facilities, and offered to applicants for recruitment to majority community careers (our interview with Nik Shah, p. 75 ff, has some excellent pointers). This strategy would call for major investment in language and basic citizenship skills designed to equip members of the ethnic communities to be comfortable in Great Britain plc.

Allied to this is *training*: strategies should be developed to help highly qualified people to overcome the barriers that often prevent them from gaining appropriate employment. This could mean, for example, job clubs to explain job applications, CVs, where various types of jobs are usually advertised, professional recruitment agencies and similar organisations.

Thirdly, *unemployment management*. The LSFU report (p. 57) shows that periods of unemployment in the ethnic communities are shorter and more frequent than in the majority community. This suggests that there is need for employers to examine hiring and de-hiring practice and review their policies on length of employment.

Deepak Mahtani was asked by a director of the UK division of an electronics media multinational to advise in a de-hiring situation. A large plant was to be closed down. It employed 70% ethnic minority staff. How could this be handled in a culturally sensitive way?

He stressed the importance of staff leaving on a positive note. Even though they were no longer employees, they would still be needed as customers and friends. And staff in the ethnic communities who become redundant are often lost to the skills market from which they were dropped. So there was a need for a programme of re-skilling, so that these people could become employable and re-enter the job market.

The skills pool from which all companies draw their staff needs to be maintained, even if those who contribute towards maintaining it are not always the ones who at a particular time benefit by recruiting staff from it.

Other areas to be considered include:

- The need for community facilities
- Civic amenities
- Employment
- Youth issues such as drugs and adequate recreation and sports facilities
- Language teaching and learning
- Cultural exchange, such as ethnic restaurants, cinemas and retail outlets
- Arts and media

For some people, even contemplating co-operation and bridge-building of this kind demands a radical shift in thinking of seismic proportions. But the results will be substantial and will pay dividends in improved and more productive business dealings.

Communicate Across Cultures

What does one do with the bridge once it is built?

Primarily, one communicates across it. We suggest that there are three key components of successful communication.

The Purpose of Communication – what are you trying to say? Are you sure that what you are saying is being understood? We provide substantial material in this book on effective communication and we have already discussed the crucial role of language, because we believe that it is central to effective communication and, in cross-cultural situations, it is often an early casualty.

The Credibility of the Communicator – Much communication fails at the outset because the person communicating doesn't realise that his or her credibility has been destroyed.

For example, leaders of a company trying to launch a diversity initiative need to be very sure that they themselves demonstrate (not just subscribe to) a commitment to diversity. This should certainly include examining their own corporate structure. If the only recruitment from the ethnic minorities is to the shop floor or to the secretarial level, that hardly constitutes a paradigm shift in thinking. A right approach to diversity recruitment can still create glass ceilings just as much as the old attitudes to ethnicity did.

In too many boardrooms, the faces of the directors are all the same colour. Too many executive teams are all male, all from the majority population, all with similar education, experience, nationality and social background. Many organisations affirm the need for diversity, and up to a certain establishment level they practise it. But because diversity has not been made an explicit company value, and the company has not committed to an effective policy of diversity management, at the top of the company diversity simply gets crowded out by other priorities.

As we have already seen, it can be the silent communication that speaks most loudly. During the months following the Eastern European revolutions, Western relief and other organisations sent representatives to discuss relief and aid projects with local people in those impoverished countries. It was not uncommon for an organisation to wonder why its proposals were not taken seriously, and to not understand the offence caused when the local leaders were invited to breakfast meetings at their representative's hotel, where they watched the visitor consume the equivalent of a month's salary in that country all in a single meal. Sensitivity allied to cultural awareness would have prevented such problems.

The Context of the Communication – this brings together what we have already said about unspoken communication. In Section 3 we provide information about the signal systems and signs and messages that can destroy communication and wreck a promising business meeting. To this should be added the danger that mass communication often fails to contextualise itself into the culture of the listener.

For example, a disproportionate number of patients on the waiting list for organ transplants come from the Afro-Caribbean and Asian communities. However too few organ donations are made, from the blood groups to which most of them belong, to keep pace with the demand. The Department of Health and other agencies were for years unable to persuade more members of the ethnic communities to donate organs. It was eventually realised that the publicity material being used was culturally irrelevant to most of its intended readers. It was not available in Punjabi, Urdu, Gujarati or other ethnic minority languages. Its posters showed Mum and Dad, two children and a nice dog – quite unlike the average extended family in the ethnic communities. The people portrayed were white, middle class and smartly dressed.

A change of approach, discussions with the Muslim leaders to obtain endorsement of the appeal, and consultation with community and faith leaders of all kinds resulted in a heightened awareness of the need among the ethnic communities, and a corresponding rise in donations.

Develop Your Organisation, Develop Your People

Successful awareness, bridge-building and communication will inevitably lead to change. This change requires key people to be identified and helped to develop and contribute effectively.

We discuss this topic throughout the book. Here, we want to focus on one aspect of development. We suggest that just as effective maps of ethnicity are important, so are effective measurements of change.[5] Changing practice in dealing with ethnic business communities needs to be measurable, especially if incentives are being used to achieve results.

Measurement is necessary in all areas of business. For example, *personnel.* What percentage of your current establishment is from the ethnic communities? How many members of the ethnic communities were you employing two years ago? Five years ago? What is the rate of change? On what basis were those people recruited: solely to satisfy a doctrine of equal opportunity – or to recognise skills and abilities that presented at interview? When you interview, what percentage of those short-listed is from the ethnic minorities?

This is not a matter of positive discrimination, which tends to focus on addressing problems and the needs of the applicant. It is a matter of diversity management, which looks at all employees together, to ensure that all maximise their contribution.

There is an urgent need for greater involvement and inclusion of ethnic minorities in mainstream business. One way is to appoint ethnic minority members as non-executive directors of limited companies, NHS Hospital Trusts and business support agencies; also as school governors, prison visitors, and members of police advisory boards. Such appointments can achieve major shifts in thinking, just by the very presence of ethnic minorities in decision-making contexts: and having made a start with non-executive appointments (thus ensuring that expense will not be a further barrier to change), in our experience it will often lead to executive appointments and greater inclusion.

Measurement will reveal whether recruitment and personnel policy has succumbed to tokenism: for tokenism creates a static personnel subset, with little incentive to grow once a quota has been achieved. Diversity, however, leads to growth; for if the contribution of everybody is recognised and maximised, every employee's contribution will count.

Another example is *business transactions.* What proportion of your contracts are made with the ethnic minority business communities? In a business that is celebrating, and managing, diversity, a significant percentage of trading partners and orders for goods and services will come

---

5. Some material in this chapter is drawn from a presentation by Deepak Mahtani, one of the authors of the present book, delivered to an NHS Trust under the title 'Investing in Diversity'.

from the ethnic communities. If there is no substantial increase in that percentage it's safe to assume that the level of diversity management in that company needs to be looked at.

In the same way, it's helpful to have some measurement of the extent to which local ethnic resources are being used in a business. Has there been a shift from old expensive sourcing to take advantage of competitive local ethnic business sources? Has use been made of local expertise, local knowledge, local contacts, to open up new areas of business? In a business that has begun to manage diversity, you would expect to find such developments.

Go Forward

At the beginning of a new millennium Britain stands at a crucial point. A great deal has already been done to maximise the contribution of the ethnic minorities, but time is not on our side. The continuing loss of skills, either under-utilised in Britain or exported to other countries; the continuing social problems in areas of large ethnic communities, so that local business suffers setbacks it can ill afford; the continuing lack of incentives for majority businesses to change their views on inclusiveness and multi-ethnic business; the continuing problems experienced by ethnic minority businesses in breaking out into the mainstream, so that they are forced to fish for staff and orders in a local ethnic pool of diminishing returns – these and more factors are fault-lines threatening to destroy the structures built upon them.

The good news is that it doesn't have to be like that. The agenda for change that we have outlined is based on initiatives that are already being developed. Change is happening, even though it is happening too slowly and in too uncoordinated a manner. The Government is committed to action, even though the 2001 election was widely understood as, to quote Tony Blair's victory speech, 'an instruction to deliver'. The presence of ethnic minorities in business and government is increasing, despite certain well-publicised cases where things have not gone entirely to plan.

Given a commitment to diversity and to develop the rich resource that is the ethnic minority business communities of Britain, plus the talents and motivation that so many in those communities possess, change is not only possible – it's inevitable!

Section 2
Encountering Diversity:
The Interviews

Though we have aimed for a wide spread of age, career, gender, ethnicity and geographical background, the people interviewed in this section are not intended to represent proportionally the numbers and distribution of the UK ethnic communities. We have not tried to achieve that kind of balance; to do so would require a much larger book and many more interviews. But the selection *is* intended to show – as much by juxtaposition of one interview with another, as by what is said in the interviews – the qualities of the ethnic minority business communities, and to provide some insight into how those minorities view themselves and their adopted country.

1: Levelling Playing Fields, Opening Doors
Hampshire Constabulary Positive Action

Positive Action: Employers may encourage employees and potential employees to provide training for members of a particular sex or race and who have been under-represented in a particular area of work in the previous 12 months. However selection must be made on the basis of merit and Skills/Abilities irrespective of Sex or Race.

Positive Discrimination: Unfair selection based on a particular Race and Sex whether under-represented or not.

DO NOT get confused with the lawful selection of Positive Action.

(National Police Training,
Workshop on Understanding Cultural Diversity,
Pre-Course Workbook p.14)

One of today's media buzz-words is 'the glass ceiling', meaning an invisible barrier. Invisibility is the only quality glass ceilings share with glass. They don't shatter when you come up against them unexpectedly.

The term is often used about minorities, for example ethnic minorities and the disabled community. It means the way that their members discover that progress in, and sometimes entry to, certain jobs and professions is closed to them beyond a certain point. So far as the ethnic minorities are concerned the problem in many industries and professions can be masked by the fact that they are often very well represented at entry level and middle management. Consequently it's not always immediately obvious how few, if any, there are at boardroom or senior executive level. In other jobs and professions recruitment of ethnic minority people is either extremely minimal or non-existent.

There are many reasons, in both cases, why this should be so.

Sometimes it is because the higher levels of employment demand skills and education that members of the minority communities lack opportunities to develop. In some cases it is because there is no tradition of ethnic minority entry into the job or profession. In other cases (probably most) the reason is that there is an ingrained unwillingness by the majority community to consider the ethnic minorities when promotion or even recruitment is occurring. They simply don't enter into the equation. Such attitudes, when an entire management and administration hold them, are called 'institutional racism'. It's a problem often found in Britain.

Institutional racism was much in the news in February 1999 with the publication of the long-awaited and devastatingly critical report of a committee of inquiry headed by Sir William Macpherson. The inquiry concerned the death of a black youth, Stephen Lawrence, and the subsequent investigations by the Metropolitan Police. Its report catalogued 'a combination of professional incompetence, institutional racism and a failure of leadership by senior officers'. Its seventy recommendations were far-reaching, and its final summary voiced the possibility that out of the tragedy might come 'genuine partnership between the police and all sections of the community.'

> The gap between Police Services and local communities may seem to be great, but early steps welcomed and encouraged by both sides will surely lead to confidence and co-operation. This may then be the start of the beginning of change.[1]

Implementing Change

'Macpherson' became a metaphor for radical change in several areas of public life. Many groups outside the police service took Macpherson as a prompt to review their own practice and to scrutinise their own attitudes to ethnicity, not least in the business sector. The report found that there was need for an 'immediate review and revision' of racism awareness, including recruitment targets from the ethnic minorities, positive preventive strategies including educational policies of emphasising the

---

1. Macpherson, William (Chair), *The Stephen Lawrence Inquiry* (The Stationery Office, 1999), 46:40, 42.

value of cultural diversity, and much more.[2] These are the same problems that confront business and industry; how to break down mistrust of ethnic minorities, how to combat ignorance, and how to enable people to value the contribution that each ethnic group is able to make. So the experiences of the police are a useful test-bed of possible ways of promoting good practice.

Although there has been a great deal of emphasis on training and education in racial awareness since Macpherson, much of it is the continuing of thinking and of programmes that began before the report was issued.

For example the National Police Training (NPT) Workshop on 'Understanding Cultural Diversity in Britain Today' includes a substantial summary of the report in its *Pre-Course Workbook*[3], but its origins are in discussions following the introduction of a new Probationary Training Programme in 1998.

Indeed the present tranche of government action really began in October 1997 when Tony Blair addressed the Labour Party Conference, calling for 'a country in which every colour is a good colour, and every member of every race able to fulfil their potential'.

This objective was developed further on 4 February 1999 when Government and Civil Service trade unions launched a joint 'Charter for Action to Redress the Under-Representation of Ethnic Minorities in the Senior Civil Service'. It promised racial equality in the respective workplaces and a non-discriminatory working culture in the Civil Service, and undertook to encourage ethnic minorities to apply for senior Civil Service posts, and make sure that ethnic minority staff would have the opportunity to succeed. Several months later Keith Vaz, at the time Parliamentary Secretary at the Lord Chancellor's Office (and the first person of Asian origin to serve as a Minister in the UK Government), commented that,

> Able and talented workers from ethnic community backgrounds should be encouraged to apply for positions at all levels in the wider public sector, central and local government; the Police,

---

2. Ibid, sections 48-54, 64-70.

3. National Police Training, Workshop on Understanding Cultural Diversity in Britain Today: Pre-Course Workbook (Home Office, 2000).

Emergency Services and Armed Forces. The Public Sector must be representative of all sections of the community. Britain's ethnic minorities are an integral part of society and should therefore play a full role in all aspects of public service life.[4]

Macpherson clearly accelerated a process that was already in place, but now there was massive public interest in the issue and a considerable public demand to see improvements. On 14 April the Home Secretary Jack Straw set new targets that required more than 8,000 black and Asian police officers to be recruited in the next decade, 5,662 of them to the Metropolitan Police. Straw's intention was that by the end of the decade, every force would reflect the racial make-up of the area it served, with areas where less than 1% of the community were of ethnic minority background being expected to recruit at least 1%.[5] Targets were announced in other services too: by August it had been announced that the uniformed fire service was to increase its representation in England and Wales from 1% to 7% over the next ten years – resulting in more than 3,000 recruits; numbers of ethnic minority prison service staff were to increase from 3.2% to 7%; the senior Civil Service, 1.6% to 3.2% by 2004/5. And the rates of promotion and the numbers of employees leaving the service should be the same as for white staff.[6]

Positive action

In June, Professor Simon Holdaway of Sheffield University produced a Memorandum for the Select Committee on Home Affairs, on the subject of police training and recruitment. He noted that 'just over half of all constabularies had published an equal opportunity policy statement'. His first recommendation was, 'It is essential for the police to stimulate ethnic minority recruitment rather than wait for people from an ethnic minority to apply to a force as a matter of course.'

The issues raised by Macpherson had naturally heightened sensitivity to

---

4. Keith Vaz, 'Promotion of Public Sector Ethnic Recruitment' (*The Source: Public Management Journal*, 18 June 1999).

5. 'Straw sets new ethnic minority recruitment targets for police', Press Association (14 April 1999).

6. 'Current announced targets for ethnic recruitment', (*The Source: Public Management Journal*, 2 August 1999).

ethnic issues in the police force. For example, the report's recommendation that racial insults and racism in police behaviour should result in disciplinary action, which in turn should normally lead to dismissal, brought a number of cases into the newspapers, such as the case of a constable in the Met who was fined £500 in June 2000 for making racial insults and gestures to a black colleague. The case was duly heard by a disciplinary body. In another much-publicised case a police officer was discharged from the service for using abusive racist language to a youth he had arrested (despite the fact that the youth and his family were disposed to take a rather more lenient view of the matter).

Positive Action

PC Nik Shah is the Positive Action Officer of Hampshire and Isle of Wight Constabulary. Born in India, Shah was brought to the UK when two years old. He had already been a police officer for ten years before he was appointed to the Positive Action post.

'It was a brand-new role in the force and my first placement out of the front line and out of uniform. I'm starting from scratch, building up a structure and developing it.'

Hampshire Constabulary serves an area with a relatively low ethnic minority population. Over the years there has been a trickle of recruits from ethnic minorities. 'If you walk through our training headquarters at Netley you'll be quite likely to see some trainees from the ethnic minorities. If you want figures, Hampshire has roughly 3,500 police officers. Out of those, 1% are from the ethnic minorities – and about 19% are women. One percent may not seem a lot, but the 1991 census put the ethnic minority population of Hampshire and the Isle of Wight at just under 2%. It's probably 3% now, and that is the proportion of ethnic minority police officers we're aiming at. We are not doing too badly. We could do better; obviously we recognise that, and we're working towards the full 3%.'

A model for the private sector?

Government in the UK has not yet gone so far as to set ethnically-based recruitment targets for the private sector, but many businesses are currently reviewing their ethnic representation for reasons we have already discussed in this book, and are looking to increase their recruitment accordingly. There are useful ideas to be picked up from programmes such as Hampshire Constabulary's, just as the public sector has in turn borrowed from the private sector in this area.

Both face similar problems, which can be summarised as one double problem: that of overcoming employer ignorance and prejudice, and that of overcoming suspicion and lack of confidence among the potentially employable.

Attracting new applicants

The first problem is the easiest to deal with. Most training schemes designed to educate police in ethnic awareness resemble group training programmes of the kind you find throughout the business community.

The NPT Cultural Diversity *Pre-Course* Workbook, for example, which we have already mentioned, applies standard group learning methods: announcing objectives, placing the course in the context of the work of the police as a whole, and supplying a pack of resources which students will use on the course – in this case definitions, a history of current legislation, a section of information on cultural, religious and traditional beliefs of ethnic minorities, and a comprehensive summary of Macpherson. Each section of the workbook ends with a page for notes. The course uses the popular 'Mentor' technique. The student is required to sign a statement, which is countersigned by his or her Mentor, to the effect that he has completed the section and asked for any necessary clarifications from the Mentor. Material of this kind has been used for some time in the private sector, perhaps more so under the present government where ethnic issues are more conspicuously on the table. For example, the Race for Opportunity-endorsed training booklet *Welcoming Ethnic Minority Customers: A Brief Guide to Cultures and Major Religions* was produced by staff of the retail chain Marks and Spencer. It is introduced in largely commercial terms by the Company's Managing Director Lord Stone of Blackheath:

> Marks & Spencer work hard to build on the Company's reputation for meeting our customers' needs. The retail marketplace is changing faster than ever and it is vital that we identify even more closely with what specific customer groups

want from us ...7

He continues,

> This simple guide will help you build on your customer
> knowledge, as part of ensuring that each store's catalogue truly
> reflects the community in which it trades. Also, a greater
> awareness of different cultures helps us continue to treat each
> other with respect and fairness.

The booklet was produced by members of a Staff Development
Programme in early 1999 but the second paragraph above could easily
have been taken straight from Macpherson.

In both public and private sectors there is a legacy of deep distrust from
the ethnic minorities and often there are good reasons for it. We asked
Nik Shah whether, in attempting to attract more recruits from the ethnic
minorities, he had found they were suspicious of the police. Was it still the
case that the police were often seen as the enemy – or were things getting
better?

'I would hope that it is more positive. We don't for example recruit
ethnic minority people to be police to the ethnic minorities. All recruits
enter on the same basis. At interview they are asked if they are prepared to
relocate within Hampshire and the Isle of Wight and they are posted to
where the vacancies are. If an applicant has children at school or similar
local commitments then obviously that's a consideration, but as a rule
applicants can be allocated anywhere.'

The small but increasing number of ethnic minority background
officers is already proving a useful resource, however. When a container
lorry arrived at Dover with over fifty illegal Chinese immigrants concealed
inside, almost all of whom had died on their journey, two of Hampshire's
Chinese police officers were seconded to Kent to help them with their
investigation. In another high-profile case, Hampshire's Punjabi-speaking
officers played an important part in investigations into the death of an
Asian whose body was found in a shallow grave in a field.

'The presence of officers from all sectors of the community is vitally
important. After all, we are a civil police force, not a military one. At the

---

7. Staff of Marks & Spencer, *Welcoming Ethnic Minority Customers: A Brief Guide
to Cultures and Major Religions* (Marks & Spencer with Race for Opportunity,
1999), p.3.

end of the day we only police with the consent of the community. Unless we have a workforce that reflects the community, we won't be able to police it effectively.'

Community policing is very much at the heart of the Hampshire philosophy. 'It's all about what perceptions people have of the police. And that has very much to do with where you live and the type of relationship that the police have to the community there. Maybe it's because Macpherson is so much in the news, but people often say to me, "You've got canteen culture in the police." It's a phrase the media bandy around, but actually I'm not sure what they really mean by it. I've spoken to some ethnic minorities about the phrase. They think it means white officers sitting together in the canteen and the ethnic minority officers sitting at different tables while their white colleagues talk about them behind their backs. As an Asian I haven't encountered this behaviour much in Hampshire. I know that in some parts of the country the perception of canteen culture in the police force is a real barrier to police recruitment.

I joined in 1990. I didn't know anybody in the police. I graduated in science, then did temp work for a while considering various jobs. I decided I wanted something more varied and challenging than office work or working in a lab.' He was attracted to both the fire service and the police. He chose the police.

Most of Nik's Asian friends accepted his decision. Many thought it a very brave one. 'Partly because it is a tough job, and partly because they thought I'd be exposed to racial abuse both inside and outside the workplace. I was told I'd be called a "Paki" and "Coloured" when I was in uniform. I'd have racist colleagues – "It will be harder for you to be a policeman than it would be for a white officer on the same beat." But quite frankly, I've not found that to be so.'

In fact he is often told he made a wise choice of career: 'People see it as a good job. They tell me it pays well, it's secure, you don't have to worry about being made redundant, you have a good pension scheme. But people from my community tend to wonder if it's for them. They aren't sure they would be welcome, or even whether they'd be allowed to join, however much they want to. Much of the Positive Action agenda is committed to assuring potential applicants that they will be welcome regardless of ethnic background, and that selection is entirely on the basis of merit and ability.

Hurdles and stepping stones

From the point of view of the business sector, there is a lot in common between recruiting into the police and recruiting in business. There are similar hurdles to be surmounted. Many candidates who are highly motivated are poorly equipped. To be successful, applicants must be able to handle a training course and must possess a certain level of numeracy and literacy. Police recruits need a minimum ability to articulate clearly, because the job will sometimes require them to give statements in court, and poor language skills could lead to disastrous consequences. The parallels with business are easy to see. Business executives, interviewing ethnic minority candidates for jobs, often face similar dilemmas. They recognise the capacity of an applicant to do the job, but they are also aware that – for example – the level of telephone skill and conversational grasp of English that the person possesses are inadequate for the tasks involved.

These are problems for which Nik Shah has had to provide solutions.

'There's a procedure called the Police Initial Recruitment Test that assesses basic competences,' he explains. 'For example I have a Chinese colleague whose accent is very strong, but he passed the test and got in. On the other hand there are otherwise promising candidates who fail the recruitment test because they don't have one or more of those basic competences. Part of my job is to monitor applications from the ethnic minorities. If I spot somebody who failed just because his or her command of English was poor, I don't let it stop there. I contact the applicant, explain why they failed, and I offer them help.'

He hates to lose people, especially good people. 'We've had applications from Bangladeshi people in their mid-twenties who have worked as waiters or chefs since they left school. But now they want better. They want a career; they want a job. But because they've always worked in restaurants, they've spoken their native language much more than they've been speaking English. So they want to be police officers; they've got no convictions and a clean driving licence; but their English isn't up to scratch. That's where I come in. There are various multi-cultural organisations that have been set up to help persons from minority ethnic backgrounds with interview skills, CV preparation, English, basic IT skills and so on. So if the applicant is willing to try again, I introduce him or her to one of those organisations, "These people will help you to get that competence you didn't have before. I'll contact you in six months or a year to see how you're getting on, and we'll try again." And that's what positive action is ...'

'Positive Action' is defined in the Police Training course-book as helping people to get to the starting line so that they start equal with everybody else.[8] It's a process that has enormous potential for implementation in business contexts, where it could be a way of bringing into companies people whose skills are needed, and whose communication abilities will not be expensive to upgrade.

The Task

Southampton's ethnic minority population is predominantly Asian, mostly of Sikh background with some Punjabi, Hindu and Muslim residents. Afro-Caribbeans are numerically the smallest group. Portsmouth's ethnic minority community is smaller, with Bangladeshis forming the largest group. In the Constabulary there were, at the time of our interview in August 2000, about 33 ethnic minority community police officers of whom around 20 were from the Indian sub-continent. The rest were mainly Afro-Caribbean with two Chinese officers.

'Hampshire Constabulary intends to have a workforce that reflects the community it serves. It's as simple as that. My job is to try to help the constabulary achieve it. I'm the positive action officer of Hampshire and the Isle of Wight. At the moment our worst recruitment statistics are from ethnic minority backgrounds, and that's what I'm currently working on exclusively.'

There are four aspects to his work. One is his input into the careers advisory departments of higher education establishments. He lets it be known in colleges and universities that he is available to advise students of ethnic minority background about a career in the police force. (At present this doesn't extend into schools, which are included in the work of the schools liaison department.)

Another aspect is building links with community organisations, for example religious and community leaders. He talks to them about how he feels about the job, as a member of an ethnic minority with ten years' police experience. He also works with multi-cultural organisations of the kind mentioned earlier, which provide help such as teaching literacy and communications skills.

---

8. National Police Training, op. cit., p.14.

Recruits

The third aspect is organising recruitment initiatives (the fourth is monitoring applications and policy decisions, looking out for ethnic implications). In June 2000 he ran the first Awareness Day seminar, a groundbreaking project for Hampshire. It was open to all from the ethnic minorities, and was designed to give potential applicants a realistic idea of what it would be like to be a police officer. The first session was held behind closed doors, an opportunity for potential applicants to ask serving officers from the ethnic minorities any questions at all. Then followed more conventional informational workshops, explaining various aspects of a career with the Constabulary, and the day ended with another session with serving officers from the ethnic minorities, to clarify issues raised during the day.

Sixteen people attended the seminar. Eight were invited guests and eight potential applicants. Of the latter, three had applied to join the Constabulary at the time of our interview. In Hampshire terms, that is quite a step to fulfilling the ethnic minority target. Not surprisingly, Nik is planning further seminars.

Serving officers

Macpherson, Nik Shah agrees, has been a huge force for change in some deeply ingrained attitudes. Under its influence Hampshire has launched a number of new initiatives for serving officers. One he is particularly enthusiastic about is the proposed mentoring scheme, an extension of the common management technique: 'It will be open to all serving ethnic minority police officers and civilian staff, and it will address matters like career progression. They will have a mentor, who will be able to help them in making the right directions and the right choices. It's a brand new scheme, a huge step forward. We're talking about recruitment, retention and progression – in terms of rank, or sometimes lateral progression.'

So much of the Positive Action programme is presently about recruiting, that relatively little has yet been done about instituting racial awareness practice among Hampshire's majority community background officers. However, the process has begun.

'An equal opportunities programme started over a year ago. It's a two-day course and all officers have to be trained on it. I've known colleagues who have begun the course saying, "I don't need it, I'm not racist." And they wouldn't behave in any glibly offensive manner towards anyone. But they come out saying, "I didn't know a lot of that, I've learnt a great deal." There's been extremely good feedback from those who've been on the course. As so much of police work is about relationships and dealing with the community, it's obviously important to be aware of these issues; then you can understand the potential for offence and embarrassment, and work to avoid it.'

But Hampshire's Positive Action agenda is currently dominated by the recruitment programme, which is likely to transform Hampshire Constabulary within ten years.

We asked PC Shah to say what he would most like to have achieved in five years' time.

'I'd like to have done my job well. And that means achieving the targets that have been set – 3%, over the next ten years. That would be fantastic for me and for my colleagues. Policing is about providing the community with better, more efficient and more professional service. That will happen if we get our workforce right, and I'd like to see it happen.'

Postscript

We have placed this interview first because it both confirms and amplifies several key points in Section 1.

- ❑ **Ethnic communities don't want special treatment; they just want to be treated like everybody else** – hence our title of 'levelling playing fields'. Positive action is a better way forward than positive discrimination.

- ❑ **Many members of the ethnic communities have the skills to do the job: they just need help to develop literacy and similar skills to a point where their expertise and skills can be used.** Giving this help is a good investment in the local and national economy. Nik Shah's co-operation with local education and training agencies is a good example of how potential employees with good skills and experience, held back by a lack of good language skills, can be brought to parity with applicants whose mother tongue is English.

- ❑ **Helping the ethnic communities usually works better if communities are empowered to help themselves.** Training trainers is a better way forward than sending in trained taskforces from outside to do the job. In this context, Hampshire Constabulary's use of mentoring schemes is especially interesting. Mentoring schemes are being used by organisations of all kinds throughout the UK.

☐ **Training people from the ethnic minorities so that they can be stationed within the ethnic minorities tends to perpetuate the 'us and them' syndrome.** Of course there will always be occasions when members of the ethnic communities will be the best people to deal with issues directly involving those communities (Nik Shah mentions cases where knowledge of ethnic minority languages is necessary for effective police procedures). But the main thrust of training should be to bring people into the mainstream community, to contribute to and to benefit from the diversity of multi-ethnic British society.

A timely footnote to the above is the report in April 2001 that the Metropolitan Police had decided to allow Muslim woman police officers to wear *hijab* – headscarves – on duty, and were considering allowing male officers to have dreadlocks, thus allowing Rastafarians to join.[9] These moves, which police authorities in other parts of the UK were widely expected to follow, were a result of a Home Office directive (post-Macpherson) that the Metropolitan was required to increase its ethnic minority recruitment from 4.1% to 25% within eight years.

---

9. Dipesh Gadher, '"Ethnic" Met May Allow Dreadlocks', *Sunday Times*, 22 April 2001, News Section p. 5.

2: The Asians of Bradford
Abdul Kader and Mohammed Ali

'If you are in business in a place like Bradford where every second child leaving school is of Asian background, and you're looking for a workforce, obviously you have a vested interest. And as the proportion of Asians in the city's population increases and their disposable income increases, you have an increasing customer base there too. For good business reasons, businesses are beginning to recognise that they can't afford to ignore this very important sector.'

Dr Mohammed Ali, QED UK

From the outside there isn't much out of the ordinary about Bombay Stores in Shearbridge Road, Bradford 7 – a car park fronts a long low warehouse-style building, and that's it.

Neither is there much in Shearbridge Road to show that Bradford has a high concentration of South Asians and that many of them live in Bradford 7. There aren't many pedestrians and most of those you see are Asians, but beyond that you could be in an industrialised district of any large British city.

When you step inside, you immediately enter a different world. It's like an Eastern bazaar located in a rabbit-warren. Crowded twisting walkways lead between dozens of stalls and counters, taking you ever farther into a fascinating world of fine fabrics, exotic ornaments, haberdashery stalls piled with sequins and buttons, clothing, bric-a-brac and fragrant cosmetics – and just as you think you've mastered the lie of the land, an unexpected corner reveals a bookstall, a music department, a stock of sitars and other Indian musical instruments and even a café where you can rest your feet and nibble a samosa.

Abdul Kader is a youngish sixty-something who frankly admits that he should be thinking about retiring but can't resist coming into work. He started Bombay Stores in 1967 with £100 in his pocket. In those days the business was a corner shop that he bought for £1,400. He raised £300 as a deposit and a further £100 to get going. Today his turnover is around £6 million a year. The store is managed by his son; Abdul keeps an eye on things and helps out at the check-out counter. He speaks about his store with pride and a note of mild surprise. 'My hard times are past now,' he says. 'It was very difficult when I began. I had no staff. Now over sixty people work for me. But starting something when you have no money is very hard. Our takings were sometimes as low as £2 a day. And even when our children were small, my wife worked in the shop with me.'

Like many Bradford Asians, Kader has never had much to do with the city's Chamber of Commerce or agencies like Business Link. 'I use my own resources,' he explains. He means the resources of his community and extended family. He's benefited from Bradford's situation: unusually for the UK, it receives around 500 new Asians every year, many of them arriving from the Indian sub-continent to be married in Britain, and all looking for somewhere to purchase familiar goods. 'Also some of our customers come from two or three hundred miles away. They can't get what they need in their own town so they come to Bradford. They'll stock up with groceries in Bradford, buy clothes and fabrics here. I do my research, you know. When I go to other towns where there are Indians I go into the shops and ask, "What are the Indians buying here"? And we have several established Asian communities here in Bradford – Bengali, Punjabi, Gujarati, Sikh for example – and we provide them with what they need. We look after their needs from birth to death. They can buy baby clothes here, and they also come to us at the end of their time; when they die their family buys the necessary fabrics and burial garments from us.'

Indeed, as he speaks, rites of passage are being enacted all over the store. A young Indian teenage boy is being fitted with one of the store's more expensive lines, a formal linen coat with colourful trimmings and elaborate embroidery. His mother adjusts the shoulders critically and stands back to assess the effect: the boy squirms unhappily and is told to stand still. Over in a beautifully draped and upholstered alcove, Abdul's son is deep in animated discussion with a group of glamorous Asian women standing round huge bundles of fabric samples, perhaps planning a wedding.

'All the communities are different,' Abdul observes. 'We provide the Sikh *rumala*, the Muslim *burqa*, Hindu wedding garments – we keep everything for them in stock.' However, the Bombay Stores' customers are not all Asians. Forty per cent of them come from outside the minority ethnic communities, drawn by the exotic products on sale and the low prices. Half the staff work in the warehouse built on to the back of the store, where clothing and fabrics imported from abroad are processed. 'We make small profits and have a high turnover,' says Kader. 'We don't have many competitors.'

Like several other large Asian retailers such as Mumtaz' Paan House, the Haq Supermarket and the Al-Halal store (where you can buy Basmati rice by the sackful and choose from a wide range of gleaming stainless steel cooking pans), the Bombay Stores is a name known throughout Bradford to a wide range of its residents. Perhaps because so many of them shop in his store, Abdul Kader sees the city as a small place. 'You can go anywhere you want, you can cross the city easily. You can't get around Birmingham or Glasgow like that. Last week I was down in London and I spent about two and a half hours looking for the motorway. I was with my wife in the car – we asked everybody, and they said "This way – that way – " That doesn't happen in Bradford. Bradford is a very small city.'

QED

On the other side of Bradford, in the inner-city suburb of West Bowling, Dr Mohammed Ali heads the charitable organisation Quest for Economic Development (QED UK). Known to everybody as plain 'Ali' he is a softly spoken man in his forties, whose friendly relaxed style conceals an impressive record of achievement in Bradford and also, these days, much farther afield. He arrived in Bradford from Pakistan as a thirteen-year-old and has lived in Manningham (the centre of major ethnic riots in 2001) ever since. In the multicultural tensions that currently dominate Bradford, QED is one of a number of small organisations dedicated to bringing lasting social change.

'You could illustrate the situation in Bradford by drawing two circles representing the Asian communities and the white majority ethnic community. Over the past thirty years, those circles have been moving apart. Today you could probably be a Bradford-born Asian, spend your life here, and hardly ever see a white face unless you got into trouble with the police or had to go to hospital. Asians have their own shops and their own economy, their own doctors and dentists, even their own graveyards. From birth to death it is all very self-contained. There is little interaction between the two circles. A lot of rhetoric is uttered about trying to improve the situation but in reality it is getting worse. What we are striving to do is to bring those circles closer together – not by assimilating minorities, but by respecting differences.'

Many of the findings of the report of Bradford's race review – 'Community Pride Not Prejudice', chaired by Sir Herman Ouseley and published in July 2001 (several months after our first interview with Ali) – confirmed what QED has been saying (and doing) for many years. Ali represents a constituency whose views might surprise those who form their opinion of Bradford's ethnic communities from some of the more alarmist tabloids or from racist pressure groups. 'Eighty per cent of Bradford's Asians have said that they don't want special treatment. They want to be treated equally, with their differences recognised and respected by other communities.'

A ghettoisation of services

QED was set up as an inner-city economic development agency in 1990. In 1995 it published a substantial report on Asian retailing and wholesaling in Bradford.[1] Its findings were that Bradford was home to 3,000 Asian businesses – around 25% of the city's business population, mainly concentrated in the lowest sectors of the economy. There was very little training of employees, and almost no interaction between the Asian business community and its majority business counterpart. Success stories like Abdul Kader's Bombay Stores were blips in a generally deteriorating situation. Ali's two circles were drifting ever farther apart.

'We used to offer advice on business start-up. We even translated business plans into English where needed. But a few years ago we stopped. Black business people looking for help were being referred to QED, and white business people were being referred to Business Link or similar agencies. A ghettoisation of services was developing.'

In the light of the report, QED identified three factors that were holding back the development of Asian business in the context of the overall Bradford economy.

ASIANS NEEDED TO USE EXISTING BUSINESS NETWORKS

The combined turnover of the 2,500 Asian businesses was an estimated £1

---

1. QED, Asian Retailing and Wholesaling: Perceptions and Realities and The Way Forward (QED, 1995).

billion. They employed around 9,000 people. But 86% of those Asian businesses never used Business Link, Training and Enterprise Councils or similar agencies.

The reason might have been that Asians were simply unaware of what was available. If so, there was clearly a problem in how services were being promoted. Secondly, they might be aware of the services, but the services might not be meeting real needs. If so, service providers needed to have those needs explained to them and the services needed to be adapted. Thirdly, staff of the services might not be properly trained to meet the real needs. If so, new training programmes were urgently needed.

So the priority became promoting existing services, helping to improve them, and directing Asian businesses to them for help and advice. It is still an uphill task. 'There's lots of government funding available and it looks very nice on paper,' observes Ali. 'But there's still a frustrating lack of help available for many who look for help, and a great deal of bureaucracy. We're hopeful about proposed new agencies, but at present it's sometimes hard work.'

ASIAN BUSINESSES NEEDED TO BE ENCOURAGED TO DIVERSIFY

Most of the city's Asian businesses concentrate on a very narrow range of interests. A 'me too' syndrome operates: successful business inspires imitators. There are plenty of Asian taxi firms, restaurants and corner shops – all businesses in which Asians have traditionally done very well. New businesses have joined them: for example many Asians have succeeded as driving instructors, so now there are Asian schools to train driving instructors.

Some new businesses are launched because they are easy to get into, in particular by older people looking for a new business venture, preferring the tried and tested. Younger Asians, however, often go for 'role-model' businesses, where the same entrepreneurial niche skills are called for, but in new and different business contexts. QED has invited young entrepreneurs to events aimed at encouraging the Asian business community as a whole to diversify in their business activities.

ASIANS NEEDED TO RECOGNISE THE IMPORTANCE OF TRAINING

Very few Asian businesses appreciate the importance of training in the development of a successful business. Out of 60 representative businesses interviewed, not one was operating any formal training scheme or taking advantage of training programmes provided by outside agencies.[2]

In one sense, training 'on the job' has always been a factor in Asian business success. Most successful entrepreneurs tell of the hours they worked as children in the family corner shop after school, and mealtimes listening to the extended family talking business (Ram Gidoomal, one of the present authors, has described his own experiences in a previous book[3]).

But such informal training is no longer enough. Everything is changing, and quickly. Businesses need to be trained in new technology and new legislation, not merely to be competitive but to keep within the law; and Asian businesses are very far behind. QED has run several aggressive campaigns to promote training. They have also produced a video of business case studies from major South Asian communities in Britain, showing the benefits and advantages of formal training.

Cultural awareness

If Ali's two circles are to approach each other rather than diverge, the ethnic minority communities must be equipped to play their part.

'For example, I don't believe in extensive translation into Indian languages except perhaps literature intended for new arrivals. Anybody who can read a leaflet in well-written Urdu or Punjabi would probably find it just as easy to read an English leaflet. Some supermarkets and other outlets go to some trouble to produce printed matter in the Asian languages, but it's mainly a gesture, a signal that the majority community welcomes South Asians. The problem is at a deeper level.'

People, businesses and support agencies need to be trained in cultural awareness. In some strongly Asian areas of Bradford – and in some other cities – you can still walk into a post office or other service point and find that though the queue is entirely made up of Asians the staff are all from the majority community. 'Society is changing,' says Ali, 'and that change needs to be reflected in the way things are done.'

A bank employee attended one of QED's training programmes on cultural awareness. 'She had worked in the city for the last twenty years. There was so much that she had wanted to ask over the years. Why was

---

2. Ibid., p. 55.

3. Ram Gidoomal with David Porter, *The UK Maharajahs: Inside the South Asian Success Story* (Nicholas Brealey Publishing, 1997), pp 17ff.

that Indian woman walking a few paces behind her husband? What does that item of dress signify? Why do Muslims do this and Sikhs do that? She had felt unable to ask about any of these things because she didn't want to seem racist. But it's all to do with understanding and respecting differences, and there's a lot of training to be done in that, in all sectors of society.'

The training that does exist in these areas is often limited, restricted to training in anti-racism. 'In the Asian community religion is extremely important. We need to train people in the difference between various religious observances – what is celebrated at Divali, why people fast during Ramadan, and so on. Business people need to know these things because they need to know when employees might ask for a day off.'

The two circles, at this point, barely touch. 'Asians work in the city centre and then they go home. We ran a training session with one company and asked the eighteen or so people present whether they actually knew any Asian people socially, on a personal level. Not one of them did. Most people who work in banks or the big institutions form their perception of the ethnic minorities from what they read in the newspapers or what they read fifty or twenty years ago. There is very little real understanding of the multi-cultural society in which we live, or of the implications for business.'

The role of education

One example of QED's 'bridge building' is a woman's group, in which Asian women can talk freely about being women in an ethnic minority community. Another is the Homework Club, where Asian children who struggle with such problems as simultaneous equations or English grammar can have extra coaching from qualified teachers from their own community.

Ali passionately believes that in Britain the role of education is critical; it is one of the main keys to economic development. 'We want to encourage Asian parents to take a practical, rather than a rhetorical, interest in their children's education. Many of them say they want their children to do well at school. But when you ask them what they are actually doing about it, they're sometimes not doing very much. There can be good reasons, such as the language difficulty between generations. We have a campaign we call *Tahleem Ki Baatein* – 'Talking about education'. It's based on a short video in Urdu, featuring well-known people like Imran Khan, with English subtitles and documentation in both languages. It gets people talking about how parents become involved in their children's education. Over 50 schools in Bradford are using it.'

About 200 parents are trained by the campaign each year, discussing issues such as enforcing sensible bedtimes, instead of staying up to watch videos and Indian cable TV; the importance of Asian representation on school governing bodies; and the wisdom of buying a computer for your children rather than more gold bangles for your wife.

Yet parental involvement is only one aspect. It's important to talk also to the education authorities. The Bradford OFSTED report for 2000 was a very gloomy one; the inspectors described it as one of the worst they had produced. One of its most damning criticisms was that schools were failing to communicate with the Asian community and other minority groups. 'Which was surprising,' Ali comments, 'because a huge amount of investment has come from government into this city partly to address exactly that problem. Yet after all that they have failed to communicate.'

He sees it as another training need. 'People are recruited into the education system, told to communicate with the Asian communities, and thrown in at the deep end with neither training nor support. There are exceptions. But usually support and training just aren't there. This too is an area in which we are talking to the majority community.'

A changing city

Between 1996 and 2011, the Pakistani population of Bradford is predicted to double from 70,000 to 140,000. One reason is a rising birth rate within the resident community. A second is the 500 or so South Asians who arrive in Bradford annually because of the tradition of marrying within extended families. In around half of Bradford Pakistani marriages, one partner has come from overseas, usually from Pakistan.

QED has pioneered a support mechanism for these new arrivals. It recognises that around 30% of them have good qualifications in their home countries; but the communities in which they settle are usually unfamiliar with professional appointment systems. As unemployment benefit is not available immediately on arrival, the newcomers often take the first job available, for example low-paid work in restaurants and workshops. That causes immense frustration and considerable emotional stress.

Some new arrivals are referred to local colleges, for English language courses. For most, 'a quick introduction to "Bradford plc"' is offered – 'teaching how a city works, how the education system operates, what a local authority is and does, what banks, police stations and health centres do. Because their minds are already trained, they pick up things very quickly.'

The limitations of focusing on minorities

Both Ali and QED have been given awards and honours (most recently, Ali was awarded an OBE in the 2001 Queen's Birthday honours list), and the projects and services launched in Bradford have been watched closely by other British cities. Ali is currently involved in projects in London and other regions. Many of the new initiatives repeat successful Bradford projects and have similar objectives. Ali is seeing one of his main ambitions come true: that Asians should be encouraged, trained and enabled to use existing structures and resources.

Nevertheless, the numbers are not encouraging. 'However much work we do in the ethnic minority community, at best we will be training 200-300 people each year out of 70-80,000. It's not going to make a big impact. If we really want to make a significant, long-term difference to Bradford as a whole, we have to work in the other circle as well. We must bring about change in the majority community.'

So there has been a shift of emphasis, targeting the majority ethnic community. 'We haven't abandoned our work in the "other circle". We have developed methods and our staff is very respected in the minority community. We could just concentrate on that – there's plenty to do; and though I believe our focus now should be on the majority community, we won't pull out of the work we've already established. We would be creating a big vacuum.' Not least because Ali identifies a lack of leadership in the Pakistani community, whose leaders, he feels, seem more committed to international issues like Kashmir than to local issues – such as youth, employment, housing, drugs and crime – that demand their time and energy.

On-going projects in the minority community include SAVON (South Asian Voluntary Organisations Network), a project to identify and help develop small infrastructure organisations working with the ethnic minority communities. Thus QED gains partners, and the small organisations are helped to overcome many of the problems caused simply by being a small organisation.

Majority appeal

Ali wants to demonstrate to the majority business sector that if the ethnic minorities and their businesses flourish, the Bradford business community as a whole will benefit. He wants to change how majority businesses think. 'Policing' agencies like racial equality councils and statutory bodies representing minority communities are not attractive to majority businesses, who tend to see them as an institutional arm of the Race Relations Acts. The private sector gives some funding to such bodies but in general dislikes dealing with them.

What's needed is an acceptable, broadly based agency to promote understanding and co-operation between the two circles. 'We're well placed to help. We have a trained, respected staff, and we know the business world because we've had business experience ourselves. We have the confidence of the private sector – leading companies are now coming to us for help. Yorkshire Water, the Bradford and Bingley Building Society, Abbey National, Barclays Bank, the Environment Agency and National Parks are just some of the organisations that have understood the importance of cross-cultural understanding and have asked us for advice and support – because they want to do something.'

Help offered includes a half-day 'Community Awareness Programme', covering demographic changes in society, current legislation, and the importance of religion in the life of the ethnic communities – largely secular majority white Britain often barely understands that Asian communities revolve around religion. The programme is designed to encourage genuine questions that would normally be left unasked for fear of seeming racist. Ali runs the course with his deputy, Adeeba Malik. The time they can give it is limited and places could be filled many times over, even though the programme is not publicly advertised. However, Ali – always adept at extracting quarts from pint pots – has offered QED's expertise to other organisations planning similar projects. For example, QED runs Abbey National's Diversity Programme, set up to help Abbey National recruit from the local communities.

Networking

Every city has its networks and inner circles, fast tracks and business clubs. Bradford is no exception. As in other cities, these facilities are dominated by a white majority and often controlled by cliques.

The reason is partly the ethnic minority business community's reluctance to get involved (due, in turn, partly to the fact that they have support networks and inner circles of their own). But it's also true that members of the minority communities feel conspicuous and isolated in such environments and often leave very quickly. It's hard to blend in when you are the only black face among twenty white ones.

'LIFE' – 'Leading, Influencing, Facilitating and Enabling' – is an infrastructure support network of people of influence and leadership in the ethnic minorities, for mutual support, comparing their experiences of participating in majority discussions and of taking part in decision making at city level.

'There's a gap here for training. We want to train groups of people to influence and bring about change. There's no shortage of government programmes – Sure Start, Excellence in the City and the like – yet there is very little Asian involvement in them. Which is strange, because most of those programmes are working in city areas with large South Asian populations. There's a huge amount of work to do.'

Educating for understanding

You can't talk long to Ali before the topic of education comes up. The press-cutting albums that visitors can browse through in QED's waiting room are full of news items about initiatives in education, events in local schools, competitions for children and much more of the same. Few topics so effectively demonstrate the kind of society that QED would like to see – a degree of integration that few cities can realistically aspire to, and which fits very well with the City's promotion of itself as a vibrant multi-cultural city of the twenty-first century. It's a vision of Bradford in which the ethnic minorities possess not only equality of opportunity, but also equality of contribution. The events of the summer of 2001 show that the vision will take a long time to become reality; but it will not happen at all if the foundations for change are not solidly laid. The 2001 Ouseley Report correctly identified Bradford's young people as the city's best hope for the future.

For example, 8,000 Muslim children between the ages of five and thirteen attend supplementary schools in Bradford, six days a week. QED has been talking intensively to the Education Department, the Director of Education, the Chair of the Education Committee and others, urging them to establish links with the supplementary schools. Much could be done to improve the quality of teaching, relying less on rote learning in the classroom with more time given for homework. Ali accepts the need for religious schools, and believes religious education should be rooted in the child's everyday world rather than expounded as academic religious principles taught identically in Huddersfield and Islamabad. 'But the textbooks need re-writing in good English. Children's reading and writing skills need to be improved. One of the commonest criticisms of South Asian schools is that they teach English language skills very badly. If the quality of teaching in the supplementary schools were to be improved, fewer days' attendance would be required and pupils would be much better placed to have an impact on their city when they are older.'

It is extremely unlikely that Ali's two circles will ever completely overlap. 'But I believe in the 80/20 principle. Eighty per cent of human experience is much the same for everybody. Whatever our race, religion or the colour of our skin, we have the same financial pressures, we all need to eat, we have similar experiences raising our children. The other 20% concerns how we differ: religious values, social attitudes and so on. I believe that we should recognise and respect the 20% differences between us – but spend most of our time acknowledging and celebrating how much we have in common. If we can crack that, I think we will be able to solve all our problems. And that's largely a matter of educating people very precisely about each other.'

Educating public perceptions

QED works with the South Asian population, seeking to be an agent of transforming economic change, with the hope that economic change will impact on other problems such as crime and housing issues.

A common problem, when presenting QED's work to the local and national majority population, is that the UK South Asian community is seen as economically successful and high-achieving. 'South Asian' to many people conjures up thoughts of millionaires, corner-shop entrepreneurism, academic and professional success (especially in the medical professions), and more. It makes people less interested in helping: 'They're doing very well on their own, they don't need any help from us.'

It's a damaging perception. No community, regardless of disposable wealth, is capable of maintaining the support systems and services that even a moderately achieving city demands – still less a thriving business hub like Bradford. But in any case it's a faulty perception. There are indeed some astonishing success stories in the Asian community, but most of them come from the Indian community rather than the Pakistani community, to which 75% of Bradford's Asians belong. The few Pakistani successes do not improve a largely depressing picture. Sixty percent of the Pakistani and Bangladeshi community in Britain is economically 'poor' (earning less than half the national average wage), as opposed to around 20% in the Indian community and 22% among the African, according to a study by the Office of National Statistics published in 2000[4]. Low education, high unemployment and poor economic activity among Bradford's Pakistani and Bangladeshi communities obviously contribute to this poverty. Rising crime rates and bad housing also play a part: though home ownership is not uncommon, houses are usually badly maintained because of poverty. In winter people heat one room and live in that, with predictable consequences for the rest of the building.

'Look at the health problems. My father is buried in Bradford. When I visit his grave I am aware of the dates on the other Asian gravestones – people dying in their fifties and sixties, very rarely in their seventies. There are many reasons for a mortality rate younger than the average. The ethnic minorities suffer disproportionately from high blood pressure, stress, diabetes, strokes and several other ailments, and that too contributes to their poverty.'

Ali set up QED ten years ago. He still has the press cuttings that quote him as saying that the organisation should last only ten years. He believed then that larger institutions would take on board the issues raised and that change would happen. Some change has taken place, but Ali knows the size of the task better now. He still thinks QED should aim to become redundant eventually, but even before the unrest of summer 2001 he recognised that it would take another twenty years. For example, communities' awareness of each other is still limited, and that has perpetuated a lack of mutual respect. Ali feels that more needs to be done to address this, especially within the leadership of the local authorities, where the issue has not been taken seriously enough.

What do all these social issues have to do with business?

Ali is convinced they are the key. The majority community is the only source of real lasting change – change of attitude, change in social welfare,

---

4. The Office for National Statistics publishes a regular *Report on Poverty and Social Exclusion*.

change in social demography. Bradford's Internet site focuses on the rich diversity of the city; the well-being and the effective mix of all its communities is essential if the city is to prosper in this way. Correcting inequalities in any of Bradford's communities is the only way to ensure the continuing success of this twenty-first century, modern, thriving city. The riots of July 2001 have undoubtedly set the course of progress back, but QED has no intention of abandoning its work.

But there are other good for the majority business sector to invest in the kind of programmes in which QED is engaged. Out of the growing ethnic minority community – growing at such a pace that the word 'minority' is already the wrong word in several parts of Bradford – will come a large part of tomorrow's workforce and tomorrow's customers.

It's something to work towards and celebrate. 'Fifty years ago, the first wave of South Asian people came to Britain, my own father among them. I hope that next year we can celebrate the half-century of Asian immigration to Britain. We should celebrate what has been done and recognise achievement: I'm already talking to national television about celebrating this anniversary.'

But Ali doesn't see it as mere back-slapping; there is an agenda. 'I want to show people in various communities and various walks of life what has been done and what the ethnic minorities have contributed, so that future generations can learn how we did things, and go on making similar achievements.'

Postscript

Abdul Kader's Bombay Stores is a classic example of entrepreneurism within the ethnic communities, a success story that is repeated in many parts of Britain and in many of its ethnic communities. It contains, in its few pages, all the hallmarks of immigrant entrepreneurial flair, such as:

- ❑ **Family commitment**. When the children were too small to help in the shop, Abdul's wife helped him behind the counter. This is typical of the sacrifices that many ethnic minority business founders have made to get the business started. It has a benefit, in that children grow up familiar with business issues, hearing them discussed at family gatherings and watching at first hand how business is done as they help after school and at weekends. Abdul Kader's son manages the shop today but his training started at a very early age.

❑ **Opportunistic market exploitation.** The large numbers of Asians arriving in Bradford every year are a market that Bombay Stores has accurately targeted. They are in a strange country and want to shop with people who talk their language and understand their culture. This business did not drop into Abdul Kader's lap but was developed by carefully evaluating the market and going for a specific sector.

❑ **Niche marketing.** Bombay Stores' primary market has needs that are met by very few mainstream stores: hence Abdul Kader's proud and justified claim that he provides all his customers' needs from the cradle to the grave. Note that this requires travelling (to inspect the opposition) and getting involved in manufacturing what can't easily be sourced. Diversification into items like books and music is also logical; these, too, tend to be difficult to find elsewhere, and there is a convenience factor in having everything under one roof – so that you can buy cut-price sitar CDs while purchasing Indian costume jewellery and fabric for formal dress.

❑ **Economic isolation.** Bombay Stores' success has been achieved without using the help and services available for small business and start-ups. Abdul has not used the services of Business Link, Training and Enterprise Councils, or other government business support services. This makes it an impressive success story, but also makes it much more difficult to survive. **Small businesses funded and supported almost exclusively from local ethnic community resources have, as we have seen, a built-in limit to growth and a question-mark over long-term prospects of flotation, merger and the like.**

Our interview with Mohammed Ali puts the impressive story of Bombay Stores into a wider perspective. For every Bombay Stores that makes it, there are numerous small businesses that fail or struggle to survive.

Certain key themes emerge from the interview that are worth summarising here:

❑ **The popular media view of Bradford's Asian community is a distorted one, built on untypical facts.** Most Bradford Asians are not looking to take over the city or to found a fundamentalist state within it (though it would be naïve to deny that groups exist who do have such agendas). They do, however, want to be given parity with the majority community. Organisations like QED represent a large cross-section of the city's Asian population and the overwhelming thrust of their programme is to achieve parity. Parity of respect would be a good start; Bradford will be associated for a long time with the protests against Salman Rushdie's *The Satanic Verses*, but few reports of Muslim reaction against the book attempted to give even a simple version of the complex theological issues involved. Dialogue between faiths and faith communities can make progress only when each side has some basic understanding of the other's position.

- There has been local media distortion, suggesting that all government resources go to ethnic minorities. For example high media coverage was given to the award of two Single Regeneration Budgets (SRBs) to ethnic minority groups, whereas the giving of three larger SRBs to white areas received no comment. Consequently many in the majority community resented what they perceived as favouritism towards ethnic communities. **The media must not be allowed to fuel misinformed speculation.**

- **Diversity within the ethnic communities must be acknowledged.** The Ouseley Report of July 2001 saw them as a single community – black. Policies have only been geared to one community, and certain groups have been excluded: 'one-size-fits-all' models do not work.

- **Practical steps towards a 'level playing field' such as The Homework Club, the women's group and other initiatives should receive the public funding and support they require.**

- **Assimilation is not the goal.** The ethnic communities will never be assimilated and absorbed into the majority community. It's not desirable that they should. In a response to the Ouseley Report sent to Home Secretary David Blunkett, Ali rejected the Report's identification of 'self-segregation' as the main cause of the problems. Societies all over the world tend to segregate by race and religion, he argues. It's a natural phenomenon. 'The way to address it is to improve people's socio-economic circumstances' – leading to new values and aspirations and the desire for dispersal and integration. He also quoted the 80/20 principle mentioned earlier. Thus Ali's model of the two circles presents one way forward to **a society of diversity, of rich resource and skills, to which all contribute and from which all benefit, while still retaining their unique identities.**

3: A View From the Far East
Kiku Horinouchi

'The Japanese way of managing people and companies is different from many others because it is based on harmony, on agreement and consensus ... Japan is changing, and I haven't lived in Japan for twenty years, so I shouldn't say categorically "This is the Japanese way." But traditionally, Japanese management is based on the consensus of everybody, including the workers and the management.'

Ask any non-Japanese person in the street what UK Japanese business is all about. They'll probably mention products – cars, cameras, computers – and go on to talk about management style: inspirational, lots of exhortation to corporate commitment, a distinctly non-Western approach to the shop floor. There's a certain mystique to the Japanese business culture. For many in the UK business community the Japanese are key players, yet little known. So we were delighted when our invitation to interview a senior UK Japanese executive was accepted.

We interviewed Mr Kiku Horinouchi on his home territory – not Tokyo, but the City of London. He is an associate director of one of the largest banking groups in the world (in asset terms) and his main responsibility there is IT. He has lived in Britain for twenty years – 'Which is a good thing in some ways and a bad thing in other ways, if you want to talk to me about the Japanese. I feel almost British now! Sweeping generalisations are dangerous in any case, but you'll get a British-influenced view of Japanese business from me.'

He came to Britain in the early 1980s to work for Quad, a long-established company in Huntingdon founded by one of hi-fi's legends, Peter Walker. Walker had created a range that included the Quad amplifiers, famed for their neutral quality that amplified but did not alter the original sound, and the innovatory Quad Electrostatic loudspeakers that were to be found in recording and broadcasting studios all over the world. In Japan, Kiku had been manager of a trading company importing hi-fi goods. When he met Peter Walker's son Ross in Tokyo and asked for a job at the Huntingdon factory he was well aware of Quad's reputation. He was accepted immediately. Ross Walker successfully applied for a work permit for Kiku and he left for England.

For the few months while he was waiting for his family to join him he was somewhat lonely. He was the only Japanese on the staff of 150, and twenty years ago there were no other Japanese in Huntingdon. Today there are more. Many are in Cambridge, fourteen miles away.

Kiku worked for Quad for six years. He left because during that time he had become a Christian (a remarkable story in itself: he had been a habitual drunk in Osaka, and claims that during one of his binges he heard God telling him to go to England. Shortly afterwards he met Ross Walker). Now he wanted to study theology in London. That meant evening classes, for he had a wife and four children to support; and that meant finding a job in London.

The history of Japan as a nation is remarkable for its ability to make radical changes in its national direction: the main example of which is the way in which a primarily agrarian country transformed itself in the later twentieth century into a major international source of technology and finance. Kiku likewise took a major career change in London. At Quad he'd been trained in computer skills, both programming and systems maintenance. He decided to apply for a job in the IT department of the IBJ International Bank, working as a programmer and systems analyst. He and his family continued to live in Huntingdon and have lived there ever since.

The Japanese in Britain

The Japanese population of Huntingdon is not large. Had his priority been to find a Japanese community in which to settle, Kiku could have chosen several areas of London. Most of Britain's Japanese citizens live in two areas of London – Acton, where a Japanese school is situated, and the area round Golders Green and Finchley in North London, because it is suburban, with a middle-to-upper class community, but has easy Underground access to the City. There are also pockets of Japanese people scattered throughout London. Outside the capital, Japanese factories attract Japanese workers in cities like Reading (Honda, Technics), and Sunderland (Nissan). There are Japanese factories in Scotland, Wales and Northern Ireland, all of which have some Japanese workers.

Where there are significant numbers, Japanese amenities have established themselves. The Japanese government funds the Japanese school at Acton for the families of expatriate Japanese workers. There are also a number of private schools in different parts of the UK. In Durham and Reading there are Japanese colleges within the university.

Such amenities are relatively modern. Twenty years ago, there were not so many support and training facilities available. How easy was it then, and is it now, for a new arrival to adjust to English-speaking community life? Does Britain provide adequate training, adequate language teaching facilities? Are there Japanese-speaking people available at key public information places so that things like writing a cheque, or going to the chemist with a prescription, can be explained to immigrants in their own language?

'Japanese people are good at reading and writing English, though not so good at speaking or listening to the language. So writing cheques isn't an issue. And most people coming from Japan are quite highly educated. British culture and way of life aren't problems either. People want to stay here. But, though there isn't perhaps the need for special language and orientation facilities, the British do give good help. When we brought four children into Britain, the local school provided extra tuition for them once a week, which was invaluable.

But the kind of problem you find in some ethnic communities, where people are disadvantaged in job applications and interviews because they haven't been able to get a good education or improve their language skills, doesn't apply very much to the Japanese community. The "playing field" is not completely level, but it's not a major obstacle.'

We put it to Mr Horinouchi that the image of Japanese business in the media, and probably the impression most in the majority community have, is that it is very much an import. Factories are run in ways unfamiliar to the British: there is a great emphasis upon order and correct behaviour, and also a type of corporate commitment to the company that is very Japanese. We asked him whether this image was a true one, and if it was, whether he had seen any changes over twenty years.

'The whole way in which Japanese people integrate into British society has changed. When we came here twenty years ago, we found it difficult to find Japanese food. People didn't know much about Japanese cuisine. Now you can buy sushi and tofu (bean curd) in the supermarket. People accept Japanese food, perhaps because Japanese products are so familiar in the shops. I realise that's not what you were asking, but it's part of it. More and more Japanese items are available to the general public, besides the gadgets, cameras and computers.

You asked me about business. Well, unlike some other ethnic minorities, the Japanese are not a very entrepreneurial community. There are three categories of British Japanese. The first is the ex-pats, who are seconded here from Japan to work with their company's British operation and after three to five years will go back. The second is those who have come here by marriage and are adapting to living in the country of their husband or wife. Third, you have those like myself – Japanese residents of Britain who live and work here. Now, the first group is purely here to do a job for their company. They don't start their own businesses. The second group is adapting, they are learning the ways of their adopted country. The third group *could* start up businesses of their own – but usually they don't. Generally speaking, the Japanese are not pioneers of new business in foreign countries, at least in the West – though it does happen in the Far Eastern countries. Most of us are here working for established companies.

As regards banking, in investment banking there are no borders. It's in the nature of investment banking that you are dealing with New York, Singapore, Hong Kong, London, Geneva ... and that shows. The bank I work for has a universal culture, neither Japanese nor British nor American but a mixture.

In regional business Japanese traditions and methods do survive longer. Many large companies use Japanese production techniques and technologies. I was invited to visit Dell Computers in Ireland recently. They are using the *Kanban* system. You don't hold stock, you buy parts in as you get your orders and you build your computers to order. So there's no risk of accumulating a large back stock of rapidly depreciating items. One company I know had a lot of stock, and I know that's how most traditional British factories operate. The trouble is that if you hit a parts delivery problem you have a factory full of half-finished products, an inventory problem and a lot of money wasted. With the Kanban system this shouldn't happen. Another Japanese technique is *Kaizen*, which means 'improvement'. The European version is called 'Total Quality Management'. Firms are keen to implement it because they want to improve quality, productivity and profit.

So there are a number of ways in which Japanese factories are run that are beginning to impact upon British manufacturing business. In America they use Kanban and Kaizen, and in some ways their productivity improvement is now better than the Japanese.'

The Shop Floor

Management style differs from culture to culture. Some management is dictatorial: 'OK, here's the target, and if you don't meet it I'll want to know why. Now do it.' Some is inspirational: 'Guys, we can meet these targets if we really go for it. Let's give it our best, right?'

We asked Mr Horinouchi what the typical Japanese management style is in 2001 Britain.

'There are some obvious differences from the British style. For example, take the decision-making process. The Japanese way of managing people and companies is different from many others because it is based on harmony, on agreement and consensus. A meeting could be just a ceremony, because underneath the decisions have already been made. Before the meeting, people who want to promote their ideas will canvass the key people, to convince them that theirs is the best way to go. Otherwise in the meeting they'll hear the proposals and think, "I didn't hear anything about that before the meeting." Japan is changing, and I haven't lived in Japan for twenty years, so one shouldn't say categorically "This is the Japanese way." But traditionally, Japanese management is based on the consensus of everybody, including the workers and the management.'

On that basis, decisions are usually made not by the bosses but by middle management after carefully listening to and weighing the opinions of all. Kiku regards this policy as the outworking of a philosophy of life, and quotes the views of Isaiah Benderson regarding the difference between Japanese and Jews. Benderson explains that Western people were originally hunters, but the Japanese were agriculturalists. They had a farming mindset, and they looked to each other as they planted together and harvested together. In the West, hunters looked not at each other but at their common quarry.

'In the early seventeenth century, the Tokugawa dynasty began, and Japan's doors were closed to the outside world for almost 300 years. During those centuries, salaries were paid to everybody from the Shogun down to the warriors. They were all paid in rice. The common currency and the shared isolation created an attitude of looking towards each other, of being involved with each other, that has carried over to modern times. It was a time of interdependency in many ways. For example, during the Tokugawa era Christianity was outlawed. Everybody had to register at the temple. The government grouped the population into groups of five people, and if somebody was found to have converted to Christianity, the others in his or her group of five were punished and persecuted as well. You can imagine, this also meant that people looked at each other a lot! It went on for almost three hundred years and it influenced how the Japanese look at life. They are reluctant to leave the comfort zone and depart from tradition. People are expecting a certain type of behaviour and way of thinking, from kindergarten to university, and there is no alternative value system – just one way. If you want to do things differently you are a drop-out: not an outcast, but out.

That is Japanese society, until very recently. Now it's changing. Young people are travelling all over the world. But they still carry with them some of the mindset they have inherited from middle-aged and older people. My parents used to warn me, "Be careful of behaviour that would harm the face and name of the family, and bring shame upon it." So again, we were looking at other people, watching to make sure they didn't disapprove – and that's changing now too. But those are some of the reasons why Japanese decision-making is consensus-based. It's safe. Do you know, there is a Japanese proverb that says if the traffic light is red and you are on your own, you stop. But if you are with other people you cross, unafraid. It's exactly the same idea. If we go across together then we don't care, we don't mind. In Tokyo you often see somebody waiting patiently at a road crossing. The road is empty, there are no cars, but the pedestrian will not cross because the lights are red and he is on his own. There's no individual decision making. But if a group forms, they cross together – even thought the lights are red.'

One of the authors of this book, Deepak Mahtani, lived in Japan for many years. As a trainer of companies working in the Far East, he often tells his clients, 'Things are changing all the time. But one thing doesn't change. You won't ever see a Japanese tourist on his or her own. There'll always be a group of them with a flag.'

Mr Horinouchi agrees. It's less of a characteristic of modern young Japanese people, but the general principle still applies. 'In Cambridge, if I issue an invitation to a group of young Japanese students, I ask one and he or she looks at the others. If they seem interested the invitation will be accepted, but if they are shaking their heads that's it, none of them will come. If one says yes they all say yes. If one says no they all say no. In restaurants, a Japanese group will tend to all order the same meal. If five English people go to a restaurant they will usually each have a different idea of what they want to eat. It's different with the Japanese.'

It is a collective oneness, which is very comfortable. But it is also a reflection of the fact that the Japanese are not very entrepreneurial. As a group they feel very strong, but as individuals they feel weak and vulnerable. They are probably not weak, but their mindset makes them believe they are.

The Japanese at Home

We wondered how small or great a part Japanese families play in business: is there any equivalent, for example, to the role of the extended family in the admittedly much more entrepreneurial South Asian business community?

'The extended family was much more of a factor before the war, and the head of some large families had enormous power. But after the war, all that changed. Now, like Britain, we have many small families. In the past there has been great respect for older relatives, and they would have an honoured place in the family. But I feel that respect is tied to success or failure, and how useful and successful you are. If you lose your skill or your earning capacity you are seen as a burden to the family. I would have to say again, it's dangerous to generalise. But I have found that elderly people, if they can't contribute financially or in other ways, are very often seen as a burden to the family.'

Riding the Wave

So is Japanese business adapting because of local laws, conforming to an alien business ethic only because it has to? Are not the changes in Japanese business practice the result of enforcement rather than the adoption of more enlightened policies?

'No. I think it's flexibility, a willingness to adapt to local requirements. Japanese companies working in Britain are happy to adapt to anything they are required to adapt to. In Japan the story is different, but we are talking now about the Japanese ethnic minority business community in Britain. I think many British local middle managers, however, are frustrated that all the major decisions tend to be made in Tokyo. There is not enough delegation of power. My own bank has a lot of autonomy, so it's not a typical example. Other Japanese banks I know are Tokyo-orientated, and everything waits on Tokyo for a decision. It's frustrating and de-motivating, and there can be business implications. But British people working for Japanese companies may have to understand the way a Japanese company operates.'

This has been a particular problem in joint ventures between Japanese and Western businesses. Deepak Mahtani recalls that several years ago Honda and Rover set up such an arrangement. Honda's penetration into the UK market has been much greater than Rover's into the Japanese market, where Rover has hardly any presence. The reason was that Rover found it extremely difficult to understand the Japanese distribution system and also the Japanese business philosophy. The Japanese success was yet another example of the ability to be flexible and adapt to local situations.

The Japanese Contribution – and the English

We asked Mr Horinouchi the question that we asked all our interviewees. If the UK Japanese community decided to emigrate tomorrow, and Britain woke up to find that she no longer had any Japanese residents, what would we have lost? What are the particular gifts, skills and business abilities that the Japanese particularly possess? He responded to our hypothetical question rather cautiously.

'That's a difficult question. In one sense you could say that there wouldn't be much difference; it's not as if we were as numerous as the South Asian community or as familiar as the Americans. I suppose that there would be financial consequences, because we'd presumably take our financial capital with us, and that would hurt the City. But I think you are asking about the people, their skills and abilities.

I think what I most observe in the Japanese business community is commitment to work. Japanese people tend to work long hours and to work harder during those hours. It doesn't necessarily make us more productive, but it enhances quality. British people have commitment as well, but for them commitment needs to be linked to ownership of work. Where British workers do have that sense of ownership – "It's *my* work, *my* problem, *my* project" – they work very hard.'

We mentioned the common experience of management buy-outs. Productivity and profit usually go up because now there's a sense of ownership and the workers aren't working for the bosses any more – they are the bosses.

'Yes, that's certainly so. But Japanese people tend to work and to commit themselves regardless of ownership. Given a task they will say, "I'm not enthusiastic about this task – but because the boss says it has to be done, I'll respect that and try to do my best." It's partly to do with personal pride, a sense that they wouldn't feel good about themselves if they gave less than their best effort. Japanese people, given the parameters within which to work, will usually work very hard at any aspect of their job, even if they do not actually accept or agree with the company's product or service. The object is not the product itself, but the doing of the job well. That philosophy has been a positive element in the Japanese contribution to the UK economy, and it would be missed.'

He turned the question round neatly on us. 'May I make a comment about the British? When I came here all those years ago, one of the first things that impressed me about Britain was the sense of fair play that is part of the culture here. I suppose cricket is an example of what I mean. But let me give you an instance from my own experience. Shortly after we arrived in England, we went along to the local evening class centre to enrol my wife in the pottery class. We waited in a long queue until it came to our turn. The lady dealing with membership applications wrote down our details. Then she discovered that because we had only recently joined the community and were not British citizens, we fell into a different category and had to pay a different fee. According to the rules, the fee for us was three times the normal fee.

The lady was very angry. "It's not fair! This class doesn't make your wife any more employable. It's not as if it were vocational training. It's just a hobby. So why should she have to pay three times more than the British?" She went off to find the organisers and protested that we were being treated unfairly. And they agreed, so my wife paid at the British rate.

I was stunned. It would never happen in Japan. There, "A rule is a rule, and we have to obey it." But here, there's a strong sense of justice that runs through the whole community. I was very impressed by it, and in my business experience I have seen it operating many times.'

That prompted us to ask Mr Horinouchi about such quintessentially British customs as queuing. In certain countries it is expected that if you are an important person, or simply possess more confidence than most people you will go to the head of any line of people and expect to be dealt with first; and most of the people in the line will put up with it. But in England, we pointed out, such behaviour would be greeted with great protests – perhaps even physical violence. Did the Japanese queue?

'I don't know why the British people like queuing, unless it's an aspect of that sense of fair play I mentioned. In Tokyo we are very civilised. People queue up to board a train, and when the train arrives they wait for the passengers to get out before they get in. It's all very orderly. But then, of course, it has to be: Tokyo trains are very crowded, and there are so many people squeezed onto the platform that there have to be some rules for the sake of safety. Again, you can see the impact of this on the way we do business and relate to business associates. It's similar when you're driving in the UK: when two lanes merge, people always give way to allow the next person into the traffic flow.'

One of the striking things that Kiku observed in Western management is the difference between Japanese and Western managerial personality.

'Western management tends to be hands-on; the manager knows what is going on in his company. In Japan, it's different. The management tend to ask their subordinates to write speeches and papers for them to deliver as if they were their own words. And in Japanese business, a successful manager is one who looks at the big picture and doesn't worry about details.'

Always anxious to avoid making absolute generalisations, he nevertheless sees Japan as only slowly changing its centuries-old mindset. 'The son of a very close friend came from Tokyo last week. He's a student, and goes overseas quite often. He told me that he can't stay in Japan, because it's a somewhat "crazy" society. Maybe that's not the best word he could have used, but what he meant was that having stayed in other countries he recognises that Japan is different, in pressurising people to behave in a way that young people find unacceptable. There's a pressure on them. And he told me that when he first arrives back in Japan he feels frustrated and uneasy, but after a few weeks he stops feeling that way. And that's why he doesn't like living in Japan. He doesn't want to lose his perspective.'

Our interview had been held in the offices of a major IT company where one of our authors Deepak Mahtani is an Associate Director. It is itself a good example of inward investment and ethnic minority business success. The interview over, we made our way through crowded city streets to Liverpool Street Station. It was mid-evening, and most of the office windows we passed were dark; but in the banks the staff would be perusing the VDUs, studying the faxes and teletext, analysing the financial news from Tokyo, Hong Kong, New York, Singapore.

Postscript

We chose Mr Horinouchi as an example when in Section 1 Chapter 3 we discussed members of the UK ethnic communities who had been living in Britain for some time, and had absorbed some aspects of British culture. In such cases the handbooks on global commerce and cross-cultural etiquette are only of limited value; clearly a man with a Japanese heritage and a strong sense of Japanese culture, Mr Horinouchi was nevertheless, as he warned us at the outset, a resident of the UK who had been living in Britain for twenty years.

It would be easy to mis-read such a background, however.

The Japanese are not a strongly localised community in Britain, but where they have settled they have developed infrastructures and services for their needs. However long they have lived in Britain they have not become invisible and non-Japanese. **We wondered whether enough notice is being taken of this small but potentially valuable resource within UK plc.** Generations of Japanese children are growing up in the UK, fluent in their mother tongue and educated in the culture and traditions of their mother country. While the Japanese community as much as any other experiences the tendency of the young to abandon much of their traditional culture, they are still very much of Japanese background.

Whatever the fate of the tiger economies of the Far East, Japan will be a significant global player in finance and technology over the next decades and is likely to remain a major exporter to Britain. This may be reinforced by Japan's current isolation within Asia:

> The eclectic, culturally confused Japanese, with no friends in Asia, are survivors ... The Japanese usually do not think of themselves as Asians at all. They have virtually abandoned learning classical Chinese, and are in denial about the Korean

affinities of their culture. Polls regularly show that their favourite countries are Italy, France, England and America.[1]

The fact that the Japanese community is less visible in Britain than are, say, the Chinese and South Asian communities, might make British business overlook the fact that home-grown translators, cultural advisors and Japanese experts are available, and look overseas for the same resource.

The consequences might involve rather more than British business spending more than it needs to on cultural advisors: **failure to make use of this valuable resource could mean that many of those young Japanese will leave Britain altogether and look for work in Japan or elsewhere in the global marketplace, where they are better able to 'add value'.**

As a business model in our midst, Japan is a particularly strong resource. **Japanese management skills and expertise that were frowned upon by the West twenty years ago have provided the stimulus for much of the economic growth of recent years.** Techniques such as JIT ('Just in Time'), Kaizen, and Supply Chain Management are just a few of those that have become international. UK plc has much to learn from the Japanese living in this country.

Similarly, if the UK wishes to become a leader in high-tech, it may need to tap into this rich available resource. Additional exchanges between the UK and Japanese institutions (schools, universities and management schools) would be a way forward.

---

1. John Casey, 'Understanding Japan – the World's First Genuinely Postmodern Society', *The Independent*, 30 May 2001, Wednesday Review p. 4.

4: Linking Up
Bedfordshire and Luton Business Link

Business Links and other business services are failing to support start-ups, and small and medium-sized enterprises run by minority ethnic business owners.
          'Wrong Colour of Money', *The Times*, 14 August 2000

If you leave your car in Sainsbury's car park on the edge of Luton's Bury Park shopping centre and walk along the main street, what strikes you first is how quickly the urban landscape changes. From the typical red-brick low-pitched structures of Sainsbury's you pass a few anonymous brick walls, turn a corner and are immediately in an Indian shopping street. The Victorian semis that line the streets leading off the main road look much as they must have done forty years ago; the architecture of the shops is English. But the stalls spilling out on to the pavements are loaded with boxes of exotic spices, fruit and vegetables; the shoppers are almost all from the Indian subcontinent or Afro-Caribbean; and even the Oxfam shop is stocked with Indian dresses and bric-a-brac, among which the occasional visitor from the majority community can be seen picking hopefully among the goods looking for an ethnic bargain. It's a bustling area, where you are as likely to hear Urdu or Punjabi spoken as English, and the cafes with interesting items on the menu are packed with people glad of a chance to rest their feet after a morning's shopping. Business looks good in Bury Park.

Go for a walk around those side streets and other, subtler signs of how large is the ethnic minority community in Luton become evident. Over a trim row of shops, the minaret of a mosque points skyward, and through open windows you sometimes catch glimpses of distinctly Asian or West Indian interiors. Twenty years ago these houses were mainly owned by the majority ethnic community, but now that community has become a minority community in Bury Park. The area has acquired an atmosphere entirely its own.

The process of change has been rapid and for many in the town has been met with some suspicion and fear. But there have also been consequences for the business community. Luton is, like most towns and cities with a large ethnic minority population, a town divided between a long-established business sector and a relatively newly arrived, highly entrepreneurial ethnic minority business community, which by tradition and also out of necessity has been largely self-contained and self-supporting. While the achievements are admirable, the consequences of ghettoising business are bad for those ghettoised and bad for the community in which the subculture develops. The future holds two possible scenarios: movement towards a ghetto community surviving on declining resources and increasingly badly faced to cope with aggressive competition, or integration, as part of a multi-ethnic community.

Integration is an alluring prospect on many grounds. The community as a whole benefits from an exchange of experience of culture, of outlook – and of very strong business values. For example, most of the ethnic minorities, because they are people in diaspora scattered across the globe, have cash-flow facilities between countries that the majority business community can only dream about. An example is Kirit Patel, who founded the multi-million turnover Day Lewis pharmacy chain:

> [He] said that the Asian network allowed him to acquire his first pharmacy in 1975. He was given loans by friends and family, stock credit from another Asian business, and an Asian business-man served as a go-between ... 'Ours is a networking culture,' he said.[1]

Ethnic minority networks have been built up through family and extended family links that make borrowing money, say, from a relative in Dubai or Durban very easy. It is a community that has become highly skilled at transferring money between countries, in legal but often innovative ways, reinforced by a system of cultural accountability and trust that makes borrowing from, or lending to, some of the minority ethnic communities a much less risky venture than it would be with the majority community.

The cultural benefits that some ethnic communities can contribute to the mainstream economy are therefore considerable. But to make it

---

1. Saeed Shah, 'Stereotypes Block the Road to Success for Asian Businesses', *The Times*, 4 November 1998.

happen, inter-relation between the communities has to happen. If for example a supplier of Asian food in Birmingham has built up a successful business and wants to now break into the mainstream and begin selling to the major supermarket chains, a potential very fruitful co-operation can fail to get off the ground because the minority business person doesn't know how mainstream business works and the majority business community doesn't know the minority business person exists.

These are issues that the Business Link network has been working with for several years in the majority sector. In recent years there has been an increasing focus on the needs of the ethnic minority business community: how can it be drawn into the mainstream, and how can its contribution be maximised and the difficulties it experiences be minimised? To discuss this and more, we visited Business Link (Bedfordshire and Luton).

Building Bridges

Shoukat Mohammed is Market Research and Evaluation Executive at the Bedfordshire and Luton Chamber of Commerce, Training and Enterprise, an umbrella organisation incorporating Business Link. He was born in Pakistan and spent much of his life there. Analysing the difficulties of bringing business communities together in Luton, he feels that one of the main issues to be dealt with is identification. 'Look at Bury Park, for example. It's a predominantly Asian-oriented community, mainly Pakistani and Bangladeshi. The people living nearby also tend to belong to those communities. They have a common interest, a common understanding – they can communicate at the same level. But when small businesses such as retail shops cross over to the mainstream business community they don't have that shared background and there is a communication problem.'

He also believes that one of the biggest issues that prevents the ethnic minority business community from being involved more in the life of the mainstream business community is the generational issue. 'Young people are growing up with little commitment to the corner shop that created their family's financial security. They are moving away into other things.'

And a third factor, Shoukat suggests, is the language problem. 'One of the problems with the kind of translations that are provided for the ethnic minorities is that what you get is a very English mindset and way of looking at things. It's translated into a foreign language but it's still very English in flavour. The images and examples that are used often don't mean very much to the people who read them. If you go into a Housing Benefit office, you'll find that much of the paperwork is available in various languages. But when somebody reads those documents in their own language they often still can't understand them. So translation doesn't then bring cultural understanding. It doesn't bring any sense of ownership of what they are reading. We need to do effective communication, and I think one aspect of that is developing a view or understanding of the community that is not developed by sitting in an office and expressing opinions, but is based on the kind of understanding that comes with being able to relate to issues faced by local communities.'

But to what extent do the minority ethnic communities want to get involved in the majority community? Would the various Asian travel agents in Bury Park, for example, who advertise very competitive fares to a wide range of destinations and seem to be doing very well, have any interest in joining a national travel agents association – or are they doing very well on their own, thank you?

'I would think they would definitely be interested if the opportunity was there. After all, they're business people and a business person is usually interested in investing in anything that brings a good return and positive benefits. What holds them back, I suspect, is a lack of awareness, a lack of vision. Obviously that's a matter for both sides, but it really comes down to whether the ethnic business community is being given the information in the first place. Once you've got the information, if you have the intelligence you can develop the vision.'

He is reluctant to blame anyone. 'You can't pinpoint any organisation or person who's doing it wrong. But there's a lack of understanding of each other and that needs to be put right. It's obviously easy to identify with somebody with whom you have a lot in common, but it becomes difficult where barriers exist. I think the government is taking that into account, and there's a lot of mileage in current discussions about social inclusion and exclusion.'

Social exclusion can be as simple a matter as an old lady of ethnic minority background going shopping in the city centre, deciding she'd like a cup of tea, and seeing a drop-in centre. Would the staff have the resources, in this town with many Asians, to speak to her in her own language or even be sufficiently aware of her everyday cultural background to chat with her beyond generalities?

'People used to assume – and probably some still do – that the ethnic minority community had some kind of in-built support system and they didn't need access to information or resources. But I think that's all changing, that in Luton we really are beginning to see a multi-cultural society, we are seeing diversity. Go to the Arndale Centre for example and you'll see a lot of Asians and Afro-Caribbeans shopping there. Some of the shops are taking this on board, hiring staff from the black and Asian communities who can speak the various languages. It's a service driven by need: in Luton ethnic minorities comprise an average 20% of the population, whereas in Bury Park, which is quite near the town centre, the majority of businesses are owned by ethnic minority groups. So it makes good business sense to provide for people coming from there into the centre. It's a large market.'

It could be argued, however, that the black and Asian staff working in the town centre have had to cross over and be assimilated into the majority culture. The majority population enjoy ethnic food and ethnic restaurants. They are very happy to have the occasional kebab house. It's foreign and it's glamorous. We asked Shoukat to comment on the alternative view: that what was happening was not ethnic integration, but simply the majority buying into the minority culture. Is Luton's shopping mall, the Arndale Centre, a place where many cultural communities contribute and share in – or is it a predominantly majority cultural place which includes a few representative ethnic minority elements because that's what the majority culture buy from time to time?

Shoukat countered by questioning the whole concept of a divide between societies. 'There is a new British Asian society evolving. Of course it centres on the young Asians, who are living in the flow of Western culture so their needs are similar to the majority population as well as to their own culture. Of course the facilities in the town centre can't cater for all the needs of the ethnic minorities. If they could there wouldn't be a need for the shops in Bury Park. But it's changing. Many Asians need halal meat or spicy food and so on, and that's available in Bury Park. But if you go to the Arndale Centre you'll find shops selling halal meat there as well, and they must be making money or they wouldn't be able to have a shop there. So the old boundaries and divisions are beginning to blur.'

After many years of not having a particularly large share of the town's funds, Bury Park is looking well-worn; the vitality and bustling life of its streets can't conceal the fact that those streets are often uneven, and the buildings often look neglected. But that is changing too. 'There's a great deal of investment going into Bury Park,' explains Shoukat. 'A great deal of improvement is going on or is in the pipeline. Luton Borough Council is fitting seven closed circuit TV security cameras, for example, and Luton and Dunstable Partnership is also contributing improvements. Of course it's sometimes difficult to get it right when you're delivering a service; sometimes it's hard to get the will of the people, and all of that is made more so when those who are delivering are from a different ethnic background – for all the reasons we've discussed: not understanding community needs, dynamics and orientation; sometimes making unwarranted assumptions, or not recognising that the recipient is not empowered to express his or her real needs. But as I said, it's changing.'

Communities in Change

As well as its offices in Kempston, some miles out of Luton, Business Link Bedfordshire and Luton has offices in Luton itself. There is limited literature available for the use of ethnic minority businesses. However, much needs to be done. A research project to identify the real business support needs of the ethnic minority communities is actively under consideration.

Business Link Bedfordshire and Luton is well aware of the fact that many ethnic businesses are threatened by mainstream interests seizing the niche markets that the ethnic minority business pioneered. Supermarkets and large stores are taking over small retail shops or driving them out of business, a problem that is not local to Luton but is a national, even global issue. The small business outlet can still provide a measure of personal contact and even pastoral care to its customers and those who own them often have a role in the local community that goes beyond shop-keeping. But the lure of the loss-leader bargain and the sheer variety of product available in the larger stores is a growing threat to small retailers.

The vulnerability of this sector, Shoukat feels, is partly due to the disintegration that is beginning to take place in the social and family structures that were the backbone of the classic corner-shop entrepreneurial economy. 'For example, old people need care. But the burden of care isn't always acceptable in the wider community. In my community it is expected. I would not like my parents to live in an old people's home because I think they deserve the best and I can offer the best; I don't think an old people's home would be able to offer that. But on the other hand, families are getting bigger. Our ethnic minority communities live among the majority communities and because there's an impact on the minority communities, the dynamics are changing. And the needs are changing too, and so is the lifestyle.'

One consequence is a type of dual personality. 'The second and third generations don't accept the ideal of a close community as our parents did. For example, people of my age who like me came to Britain from Pakistan having grown up there, or from India, can accept the idea that we live closely together. But those brought up here are more involved with the individual, making decisions for themselves, not to be dependent on their parents to make decisions or being able to come home at this time or that sort of thing. They want their independence; they probably want to live in a more liberal lifestyle compared to their parents and family. That is becoming an issue. We have among British Asians two different types of generation. The divide is such that, for example, when a young person goes out for the evening he is going into a wider Western society: into modern liberalism, into individualism – you enjoy your life. When he comes home he probably returns to a Muslim culture. His mother will say, "Sit down there, don't wear those clothes, don't wear tight clothes, go to prayers." So that young man is experiencing a cultural clash. Outside, he's seeing a different side of the world and learning different morals. It's very difficult for him to focus on a single ideal. And I believe that the reason why some young people in Bury Park are involved in crime and drugs and such things has to do with this.'

The other side of the coin is that there are some very successful people who have benefited positively from their contacts with the mainstream culture. Shoukat is in some ways a traditionalist – 'I come from a very cultural background, I respect my family, I live with my parents.' But he is also British and outside his immediate family circle he gets on well with friends from both communities. 'So I find I can retain my ethnic identity and also relate to my friends whatever their background. But there are two sides to the coin. A strong upbringing does produce a positive outlook on life. A good job and a secure family system do engender a positive outlook in your children. On the other hand, a father who has a large family, as many Asians do, and who is the sole breadwinner, can create problems for his children because he has less time for them, and in such situations they may drift into drugs or crime. So in that sense the Asian culture can be a negative factor. But there is also a richness to the Asian culture that is rarely understood. They come from one culture and are adapting to another, so they have the benefit of seeing both sides. Those in the majority community live in a multi-cultural society but usually don't see both sides because they don't understand the ethnic minority culture.'

The Multi-Cultural Society

Diversity, Shoukat argues, must be positive. It must contribute skills and provide understandings. In the business field it can contribute a great deal – for example entrepreneurial flair, as seen in companies like the Asian-owned Watford Electronics, a major computer and electronics retailer. 'Such successes should give us a positive message about diversity. But we need to explore ways of utilising it, and we need to have properly developed systems of identifying and utilising these skills that are on offer.'

The nature of the ethnic minority business community is changing. The first, immigrant, generation arriving in Britain in the mid 1960s came for economic reasons and as refugees. Their priority was to make money and that money was needed for survival. Today, few enter business for those reasons, because the first generation usually secured adequate financial security. Today there is an emphasis on quality of life, moving up the social ladder, and so on. Young Asians are developing their own potential and moving forward. On the other hand, Pakistani and Bangladeshi academic performance at college level is below average, though a different kind of training is available to most Asian children: working in the family business after school, hearing family members talking business, watching their parents at work. Thus the strong-knit family and entrepreneurial expertise confers another benefit on the children, who even if they do not go on to work in the family business acquire an unrivalled understanding of intuitive business flair.

A valuable service that Business Link can offer, Shoukat believes, is to pull all these strands together. By providing a source of business information to feed the vision of the young Asian business people, by helping the innate business skills to flourish even more, young Pakistanis and Bangladeshis can be helped to develop themselves in even more positive ways, and thereby enabled to contribute their skills and abilities to the business community as a whole.

'To sum up: there is a role for Business Link and other organisations in helping this process along. There's obviously more that could be done, and one step forward will be the development of Learning and Skills

Councils which will target social inclusion. I think the future is bright. And as the Asian community flourishes and is helped to flourish, we'll see changes within business.

But that depends on take-up and implementation, and that's something we always need to be working on. Which brings us back to where we started: communication is the issue.'

Putting it into Practice

But how does one achieve communication and how do you persuade a reluctant and sometimes suspicious ethnic minority business community to make that first contact with the mainstream? Shoukat's colleague, Israr Jan-Parker, has wrestled with this problem in her post as Membership Officer of the Chamber.

She has found that business co-operation can sometimes be hampered by lack of understanding between ethnic groups. She once tried to persuade an Asian post office owner in Bedford to act as a collection centre for recyclable discarded packaging from the numerous Asian shops in the area, but he was unwilling to be involved, mainly because he was unaware of the recycling movement and couldn't see the point of collecting old boxes. Another member had a thriving catering business. He wanted to expand into the mainstream catering business, but lost interest when he realised that though Business Link was happy to provide him with lists of potential clients, he would have to approach them himself. It was not laziness, but a combination of misunderstanding the type of help Business Link was able to provide, and of being reluctant to cold-call people from another ethnic community. He was afraid of being rebuffed.

An area in which Business Link could have been of great help to him was in helping him prepare presentations and giving him some training in how to sell his service, but he declined the offer. Like many similar organisations, one of the frustrations Business Link has is that having developed effective programmes there is often little take-up.

Some organisations even find it difficult to give away money, because available grants go unclaimed. When we visited Kempston, Israr was working on a project in which a three-day workshop on business start-up was being offered free of charge to a range of businesses. There had been an extensive mail-out, but she knew that there would be very few applicants. Many ethnic minority business people have had bad experiences of attending mainstream business functions and being ignored on the fringe of the event – while delegates from the majority community who obviously knew each other well exchanged greetings and news.

But for Israr the challenge is to secure the attendance of those few. Experience has shown her that once somebody attends such an event and realises the benefits for their business, they make the most of what they have learned and they tell other people about it. A process of networking begins, and one person attending one event can lead to significant representation from the minority community at future events.

Luton is in the heart of the '£5 billion corridor', and some of the ethnic minority businesses are extremely successful. The need that Business Link is targeting, however, is to identify and work with those for whom the self-contained world of Bury Park is not in fact the ideal environment in which their business can prosper. Yet for many in that position the move towards the mainstream business community is fraught with difficulties and uncertainties. Organisations like Business Link can do a great deal to ease the transition, but, as Shoukat and Israr both pointed out, the task that is of highest priority is to build bridges of understanding, remove practical impediments, and create a two-way flow of information that will harness the skills and abilities of both communities and reap the economic and social benefits that success will bring.

❖

Postscript

Shoukat's first-hand account of living in an ethnic minority community is particularly interesting. As somebody who is not a second-generation immigrant and has come to Britain relatively recently, his view is perhaps more objective than many and less likely to tolerate thing things that could be changed.

There are several points made in the interview by implication, that are worth identifying as they touch on some central issues.

□ **The ethnic communities are not homogenous and should not be treated as such.** Shoukat's point that Bangladeshi and Pakistani college education levels are below average contrasts with the high levels generally attained by the Indian community. Yet all three are commonly lumped together as 'South Asians' when discussing education. Similarly, as Roy Hattersley pointed out in an article in

The Times in May 2001, the Muslims of Bradford encompass groups that have very different backgrounds, histories and religious affiliations. All-embracive generic names can serve a purpose – we have sometimes used them ourselves in this book – but they can be too unfocused in some contexts. The ethnic minority communities, even when they share a country of origin or a common world faith, do not all have the same and they do not all want the same. **This is why a one-size-fits-all approach tends to fall short in most cases. Government initiatives, business support agencies, the police, schools and hospitals must ensure that they tailor their policies to the needs of the communities in which they operate and serve.**

❑ Israr's experiences show an aspect of cross-cultural misunderstanding that can have serious implications for business. The man who declined to join the salvage scheme did not know about recycling, but his refusal could easily be read as an unwillingness to join in community schemes or to work with initiatives from local Business Centres. This is an important point when evaluating take-up of schemes and response to surveys and questionnaires.

❑ A key factor in both of the above is that they involve invisible barriers. Much has been done in recent years to attack the visible barriers of housing, employment, health and the rest. **Ways need to be found to tackle invisible barriers: the lack of common ground in business dialogue, the tendency of the majority to over-simplify and generalise what are actually complex issues, and the silent processes of change that are taking place within the traditional structures of the ethnic communities: the extended family, respect and care for the elderly, the role of faith in everyday life, and much more.**

5: Through Polish Eyes
Alice Dabrowska

'Young British Poles ... have to deal with fact that their parents came from Communist Poland, and the Poland of today is a different country. So they have a feeling of alienation from three different communities ... We aren't quite sure what we are. Most of us would say we are British, which is true: I was born in England. But we have such a strong Polish cultural background. Yet we don't relate to the Poles of modern Poland. We relate much better to the English here in England. When Poles come over from Poland, there is a barrier between us, even though we're of the same age.'

The Polish community in Britain is in many ways typical of the UK's eastern European communities in general. There are three main groups of Poles. The first came to Britain immediately after the Second World War, as war refugees. The second group have arrived since the rise of Solidarity and the coming of democracy to Poland in 1989; suddenly it was possible to travel to the West, which for most Poles had been almost impossible before 1989. Some of these visited Britain simply because they could travel, and stayed. Others became refugees. Camps were set up in Germany to receive them, and eventually they settled in America, Australia, Britain and some other countries. Because the economy of Poland was unstable and the quality of life poor, Poles were attracted to the democratic way of life in the Western countries and many became economic migrants.

The third group comprises those who have come to the West more recently. They come because they would rather live and work in the West than in Poland. A proportion come through the black labour market, and some others marry British citizens thereby acquiring residency rights. It is a slower trickle of people than the first two groups represent, but it is typical of the new Europe: like most eastern states, communist Poland placed heavy restrictions on travel and required citizens to be invited by a sponsor in the proposed countries. Today Poland has a thriving tourist industry and its citizens can cross frontiers much more easily.

Alice Squire, born Dabrowska (she uses the Polish name at work), lives in a quiet suburban house near Hampton Court with her English husband John. Her parents both came to England from Poland after the war ended, though at that time they were not married. Mieczyslaw, who was later to be Alice's father, had been a soldier, rising through the ranks and seeing action in Monte Cassino and other European battles. Her mother was a schoolgirl in Africa during the war. She was placed in a camp at High Wycombe, later settled in Ealing and there met Mieczyslaw who was working for Macalpine's construction company. They married, and seven years later Alice was born. She went to London University where she obtained a degree in food chemistry, then went to Harrods as a trainee. After four years at Harrods she took an MSc at Cranfield University Business School and went on to work for Meyer International (at the time, the owners of Jewson builders merchants), finally moving to her present post at Kurt Salmon Associates.

Ealing is the home of the largest Polish community in Britain, though the presence of so many Poles is not immediately obvious: the community is well integrated in most respects. Like every Polish community of any size it has a Polish church, which looks to most passers-by like any other Catholic church: 'You'd walk past it a million times and never know,' says Alice. 'But it's a Polish church and the services are held in Polish, nothing else. Some of the bigger communities have a cultural centre attached to the church but again, it's not really visibly Polish, there's no flag or anything like that.' One indication that there is a large Polish population, however, is the Polish delicatessen shops, like the one in Ealing Broadway, and the occasional Polish restaurant.

Like the Muslim community, Poles maintain special schools. They are held on Saturday mornings. 'Only Polish is spoken. Here in London I know of schools in Ealing, Putney, and Chiswick. They have very strong connections with the Polish church but they're run by individuals. They are separate from the English schools and don't integrate with them at all. They *do* integrate with the Polish Boy Scout and Girl Guide movement. Nearly all Polish immigrant youth belongs to it. It works closely with the Polish schools. And there is also a number of Polish youth groups affiliated to the church.'

Polish identity is particularly expressed in the graveyards, like the one in Gunnersbury by the Hammersmith flyover. The roar of London's traffic is muted among memorials carved in the elaborate sombre continental Catholic style and polished slabs of black marble simply inscribed in letters of gold. In such places the British Poles bury their dead, and here too they remember the dead of past tragedies. Gunnersbury has a memorial to the dead of Katyn, a notorious massacre of Polish officers by the Russian army in 1941. Recently the Russian government has accepted responsibility for the massacre and has for the first time permitted memorials to be erected in Russia. The setting up of the British memorial has deeply moved the whole UK Polish community.

Poland has always been a strong influence in British arts and culture. There are few if any equivalents of the Indian-language cinemas that are found in the large midland towns, because the giants of Polish film are regularly featured in mainstream general and art cinemas and on terrestrial TV. There are Polish-language bookshops, and some large stores in districts with large Polish populations have Polish book departments. Poles get TV in their own language from the satellite channels, and newspapers like *The Polish Daily* have good circulations.

'Polish people integrate very well,' Alice says. 'They don't stand out; you wouldn't notice most Poles in the street. But go to the Ealing Broadway shopping centre and if you have an ear for Polish you'll hear it all the time. It is like a little Poland – if you know what you're looking for.'

Alice was born in Ealing and spent her childhood and most of her adult life there. 'Of course there are Poles outside London. For example there are quite a few in Scotland. Traditionally there has been a community in Edinburgh since the war, because there was a Polish army base there. Now they have built a Polish school and church in Edinburgh and I have friends who've moved north to live up there.'

We asked how much the British authorities were doing to help Poles for whom English is a difficult second language.

'In the large Polish areas all the local government information is translated into Polish. When you get leaflets about Council Tax, for instance, and the same information is given in different languages, one of those languages will be Polish. Similarly the high street banks would have a Polish speaker on the staff.'

Native Skills

In what areas of work, we asked Alice, do Poles excel? And do they have opportunities to do those things in Britain?

'A lot of Polish immigrants went into medicine and engineering. Their children – second-generation British Poles like me – were expected to work very hard at school and get good examination results. They have gone into 'hard' subjects – not so much into the arts, but into the traditional professions, medicine and engineering again, for example – where they are pretty well integrated so you don't think of them as a Polish group to be treated differently to any others.'

As in all the eastern European countries, Poland's work ethic has changed dramatically with the fall of communism. 'During communism Poland was not an entrepreneurial culture; but now it is. Everybody wants to start their own business and make a quick buck – that's the prevailing attitude. But among British Poles it's a different matter. There aren't many Polish-run small businesses. We aren't very entrepreneurial, we mainly work in the professions.'

Etiquette and Family

Alice tends to adapt her way of relating to people according to the culture to which they belong. Appointments, for example, are seen differently by different communities: some like you to be early, some like you to arrive on time, others like you to be late. Poles traditionally belong to the third group. 'Nevertheless,' explains Alice, 'in Britain I would try to be on time for a business appointment. And if I had a meeting in Warsaw I would turn up on time. Western ways have been a strong influence on Polish culture, and many Polish business people would try not to turn up late for an interview because that's not the norm in the West. But Poles as a people aren't known for punctuality.'

As in many business cultures, Polish business meals have their own do's and don'ts. 'If you are offered a drink you must accept, it's considered rude to refuse, and you will often be expected to help to drink the whole bottle. You mustn't refuse food, either, and it's a good idea to compliment your host on the quality of the food. In England it's quite acceptable to leave part of a course unfinished on your plate, but at a Polish meal table you have to finish it. Otherwise you're insulting your host. And gifts are very important in our culture. If you are invited for a meal you must take a present – maybe flowers, or chocolates – you mustn't arrive empty handed. If you are given a present, you have to open it there and then, never put it on one side and say you'll open it later. It all stems from the fact that Poles are very generous and very hospitable.'

Another convention of Polish etiquette that is not much observed in British circles today – nor even in the new Poland – is that which says that at meetings or meal tables, the most important person present must be given the most important seat. 'It's dying out, except in the very few businesses which remain entirely run by Poles. So many Western businesses are moving into Poland that business is becoming more and more integrated; the Poles are increasingly changing to the Western way of working.'

In common with most of the eastern European countries, Poland has black and grey markets and a thriving back-hander economy. 'If you went to Warsaw you would still need to go with a very open mind to cut a deal. To get things done, you'd have to give and take back-handers. The reason that one large retail chain, when they went to Poland, consistently failed to secure the prime out-of-town sites is that they refused to go through the back door and wouldn't pay any bribes.'

It's an after-effect of the years of communism. So is the typical Polish attitude to work that prevails in Poland today: 'It's a very relaxed attitude to work. In the days of communism they didn't have to work hard or work very long hours, and initiative and hard work weren't significantly rewarded. Today it's changing, of course, like everything else in Poland. Poles are not lazy, and they are good labourers, but they're not grafters, they won't readily work long hours to get a job done. Western companies moving into Poland today are having to struggle with the problems of making workers follow real rules, protocol and procedures to go through the necessary red tape.'

Much of the foregoing is seen most strongly in Poland itself. However, because a sizeable percentage of Poles resident in the UK have come since Solidarity and have settled here in recent years, traditional attitudes are still often encountered, especially when making first business contacts with a Polish company that has not yet done much business with the West or with British mainstream companies. Such companies have not yet begun the process of rapid integration that is characteristic of so many Polish companies in Britain – and in Poland – as the new century dawns. In that, Poland is typical of most of its eastern bloc neighbours. 'Eastern

Europe' is a dangerous generalisation, but these countries have some strong similarities deriving from the effects of long years of closed markets, economic isolation, and a work ethos that hardly encouraged entrepreneurial excellence and innovative thinking.

We moved on to the topic of the extended family, which for many ethnic minorities is the heart of the home, business and community. We asked Alice whether Polish society was based on the extended family model, or whether it was more nuclear.

'It's much more nuclear. You don't find the extended family system in Polish business. Poles aren't big entrepreneurs, they usually work for other people, so you don't find the kind of inter-generational family business framework that you do in some other ethnic minority communities. I know of only one family, out of all the Poles I know, where the son has gone into business and the business has been handed down the family. It's not common. For the same reason there isn't really an issue of whether the Poles get a fair share of business start-up funding and that kind of thing.

Of course we are an invisible minority; we don't look different to the majority community. Whereas if you're black or Asian, you are categorised as a minority as soon as you walk into an office. For that reason many in those communities won't apply for what they're entitled to, and they run into a lot of business difficulties. But the Polish, the Dutch and other communities that look Caucasian avoid those problems.

On the other hand language is a big problem. As a management consultant I'm sometimes brought into situations where my knowledge of Polish can really sell a project, because so many Western companies are moving into Poland to do business, they want Western-educated people who speak Polish. A number of my friends who are working in Warsaw work for UK companies, and in my own job I have sometimes been called into sales meetings because I speak Polish. I work as a retail logistics management consultant specialising in retail and distribution logistics, the supply chain side, for an American company called Kurt Salmon Associates. Recently universities in Poland have been contacting our company because it's a front runner in category management and efficient consumer response, and I deal with all those queries. That's happening more and more now that Poland needs to be far stronger in commercial and business knowledge. Also a number of companies are expanding into Poland and my knowledge of Polish comes in handy there too.

Generational Identity
Young British Poles have a bigger generational identity crisis than do, for example, British South Asian young people, who feel that they are not Asians, because they were born in Britain, and are not British because they are of Asian background. The Polish situation adds another dimension: for them, they have to deal with fact that their parents came from Communist Poland, and the Poland of today is a different country. So they have a feeling of alienation from three different communities.

'It's something I often discuss with my friends. We aren't quite sure what we are. Most of us would say we are British, which is true: I was born in England. But we have such a strong Polish cultural background. Yet we don't relate to the Poles of modern Poland. We relate much better to the English here in England.

When Poles come over from Poland, there is a barrier between us, even though we're of the same age. In fact there's a rather disparaging nickname that we British Poles give to those coming from Poland. We call them "imports". So when you hear that somebody is marrying a Polish girl, the first thing you say is, "Is she an import?"

Many Poles have gone to back to Poland, just as many Germans living outside Germany have gone back to the new unified Germany. People like me are going back, though the reason is usually not love of Poland but the fact that British companies offer very good salaries and promotion prospects over there. They live in the best parts of Warsaw. There's a street called Nowy Swiat that's the equivalent of the King's Road in Chelsea – it's the trendy part with the fashionable shops. You wouldn't know you were in Warsaw; it's more expensive than London. That's what's luring them back. Not particularly patriotism for Poland or their country, but a business need and opportunity that they see.

On the other hand, the Poles who come to Britain come because they can't afford that kind of life in Poland. There's a big class divide between the rich and the poor. So the poor are coming to England looking for the kind of life they can't afford to have in Poland. They see more opportunities in England for people in their situation.

Something that is particularly noticeable to Poles born in England is that young Polish women come over here and head straight for the English-born Polish bachelors. The sad thing is that most of the girls don't have a profession and a career and they dote on these men who are all engineers or doctors. Then they get married, which is why they came over. But two or three years later the marriage breaks down. That's why there is such a negative view of "imports". Sometimes they target English men; Polish girls are very attractive and they sweep the boys off their feet. Again, people say, "How long has he been going out with her? Six months? Oh, right ..." They are getting married because she needs a visa.

I know this all sounds a bit pompous. But it really does happen.'

Mieczyslaw Dabrowski

Alice's father, Mieczyslaw[1], is from one of the first generation of post-war Polish refugees. We had the opportunity of talking to him, and conversation ranged over many topics not related to this book. We are including some of his comments, however, because they show in a very intense way the fact that the ethnic minorities in Britain all bring with them memories, and some of these memories are painful. Issues that profoundly affected Mieczyslaw's attitude to working in England are still very real to him, and awareness of such feelings is an important part of understanding many of Britain's ethnic minorities. So we include this footnote from Mieczyslaw Dabrowski for those reasons – always remembering we could have easily interviewed an Asian from Uganda, a Greek from Cyprus, or anybody from dozens of similar backgrounds.

'After the war we faced an awkward situation. We didn't know which way to go. Nobody wanted to talk about atrocities like the Katyn massacre because there was such a high level of friendship between Russia and the West. England and America treated Russia as an equal and a friend, as the victors of the war. But in reality they deserved to be treated like Hitler. By rights they should have stood trial at Nurnberg. They started the war; Hitler wouldn't have undertaken that big war if he hadn't made a pact with them, so they started it.

Right through the war I was fighting in the British army. I was living with the hope of going back to Poland. But this hope vanished because when I came to England they said, "Go back to Poland." And what happened to people who went back to Poland? They were sent straight to Siberia. The West knew what happened then, they knew what was happening; they knew about wartime atrocities and about atrocities that happened before the war. But they did nothing, they took their time. And

---

1. 'Dabrowski' is the masculine form of the surname: the feminine is 'Dabrowska'.

I can understand, because after five years of war it wasn't worth starting another one with Russia. It was bad. But it was also good, because the war was over.

I came to England at the end of the war and I was very disappointed because we were not allowed to take part in the victory parade. Only the Polish Air Force was invited. I fought in Italy for four years. I was an officer and there was fighting all around. I had to deal with that problem personally. I had to send people to death in good faith, and I was twice wounded. I think I did my job well there. We were told by Churchill that the Poles were an inspiration to the nation. Then to be told by Bevan, "You've done your job, you may just as well go, you've got your own Poland." But we never had Poland. 1989 was the first time we rediscovered Poland. In 1945 we had no Poland to return to.

Those were the kind of feelings I was left with in England. It was hard. The English and Americans were our friends during the war but as soon as the war was finished I found myself on the other side. I was even accused of being a Communist or a Fascist. I was being accused of the two things against which I had been fighting!

It was hard to live with the knowledge that the Russians had massacred Poles, like in Katyn. The Red Cross told us that the Russians did it, but everybody was saying the Germans did it. Now, very recently, the truth has come out and everybody knows the truth. The Russians gave the Poles a big stupid palace of culture in Warsaw, a kind of present to the Poles. It was the silliest thing to do, to build rubbish like that in a beautiful city. But if I had my way I would bring back those Poles who died on Russian soil and I would bury them in Poland, where they should be. I would build a monument to the Holocaust there, like the Jews did in Jerusalem.

So the first few years in England were very hard. It took a while for me to find myself and build my house and have my family. They were wasted years because I was disappointed. We'd done the job, we saved a few British lives doing it. I would have thought people of good will could have found a better solution for us. Lots of Poles left England. I stayed and started working for London Transport. I worked thirty years for them.'

We asked Mieczyslaw if the bitterness of his first years in England still affected the way he thought of the British.

'No. I think we are all evolving. We don't think it so important that we should be Polish or English or Scottish or American any more. We are going a different way now, with democracy and globalisation. Europe is a different Europe. And I don't want to hate people for forty years. After all, Stalin is dead, Communist Poland is dead. I live here now, this is where my home and my family are and these are my neighbours.

During the war I had to move up with two of my men to an observation post on Monte Cassino, to observe activity on the German side of the line. The enemy guns had bombarded the post and it was wrecked, and when we got there we found the bodies of four British soldiers. We spread our blankets out over the bodies. There wasn't any room, we had to lie on them for an entire fortnight. We couldn't bury them, we couldn't repair the observation post in case the Germans saw us. We had to stay awake at night in case they came in the dark.

The soldiers had written goodbye letters to their families. I took them. I hoped that one day I could take the letters to the families and tell them exactly how their men had died. It was my first English lesson, trying to read those letters. One solder was from Glasgow, one from Belfast and two from Manchester. Unfortunately the letters were blown up with everything else when my armoured car was blown up later in the war, so I was never able to deliver them.

But those were the kind of people alongside whom I fought. It was disappointing when I first came to England, it was very disappointing. But it is a different world now, and this is my home. This is where I live.'

Postscript

The Poles are a community with very low visibility; you can't immediately recognise them in the street and unless you are close enough to hear them talking, you don't even recognise them as a separate ethnic community. So we were particularly interested to know what sense of identity if any the community possessed.

Though the interviews in this book express differing views about cultural identity and the desirability of merging ethnic communities (the interview with Kim Tan, for example, makes an interesting comparison with this one), the Eastern European communities are a special case:

❑ Many are economic migrants, driven to look for work by years of a depressed national economy and a situation in their home country of economic instability. Such an economic climate has sometimes created a work ethos that is hard to motivate and is liable to produce low incentive and low output. **In Britain, such workers will need help to bring their job skills up to a competitive standard.**

❑ Many are, in effect, sightseers, enjoying the freedom to travel after being forbidden to do so for many years. If they join the British workforce they are unlikely to have long-term ambitions, and where they possess skills these will not always be utilised.

❑ **Some are highly educated, skilled and trained and have come to the West to find professional opportunities. If successful they are likely to be highly motivated.** Problems can exist where professional experience and training in their home country is not accepted by the appropriate professional body in the UK. Hungarian dentists, for example, have to partially retrain if they want to practise in the UK: perhaps the Health Service needs to work with other health authorities abroad to bring in a greater consistency of standards.

Alice's comments on the difference between Polish and UK Poles apply to many of the less visible communities, as assimilation is likely to have developed further in such cases. However, it would be a mistake to ignore the strength of community present even in small, scattered UK ethnic minority communities; and in business dealings it is important to remember this. That is why we included Mieczyslaw Dabrowski's interview, as a reminder that the political issues that brought many immigrants into the UK remain live issues many years later, and require sensitive understanding.

6: Keeping it in Britain
Dr Kim Tan

'The world is becoming increasingly homogenous. Look at the food we eat. The mainland Chinese are eating McDonalds and Kentucky Fried Chicken; in ten or twenty years' time that will be considered part of the Chinese diet. Whereas in Britain, British families eat stir-fries on a regular basis. There's a real mingling of cultures going on and I think it's a positive development. We assimilate what is distinctive and good in each other's cultures.'

Dr Kim Tan has been described as one of the foremost biotechnologists in Britain. We interviewed him at his Guildford home, a comfortable family residence with a décor that reflects both his own Malaysian Chinese background and that of his English wife. Appropriately enough he lives near the old Guildford Surrey Hospital, though his doctorate is not a medical one but a PhD; the companies he has founded have produced treatments for various cancers and a developing programme of products for treatment of osteo-arthritis.

'The business really grew out of the fact that I was a failed scientist!' reflected Dr Tan. 'I'd gained my PhD and had been awarded three post-graduate research fellowships – all funded by the Medical Research Council – but I came to realise that I wasn't good enough to be a first-division scientist; I lacked the dedication to be a first-division scientist; and there were too many other things in my life that were also interesting to me. I didn't want to spend the rest of my life in laboratory research.'

His background is typical of many members of ethnic minority communities. His father left China while still a teenager and settled in Malaysia, where Kim was born. 'He's had to work to build his little business up, to earn enough to bring up his family. Eight of his ten children have been educated in the UK. He made it possible by motivation and hard work. He sacrificed everything to make it possible and because we saw how he worked, we grew up with the same mentality.' He doesn't see it particularly as a Tan family trait. 'It's characteristic of immigrants. They had nothing waiting for them in Malaysia. There was no social welfare to look after them; if they were ill they were in trouble. That is true of immigrant communities around the world. You only have to go to New York to see the Jews from Eastern Europe who came with nothing and made their way – big time. The Italians have done the same. The Koreans in America have done remarkably well. So have the Vietnamese boat people. They arrived with nothing, so they had to work.'

He and his wife spent the next eighteen months in Malaysia. Like many Asian entrepreneurs he had grown up with the family business, living over the shop and helping after school, wrapping orders and learning the ropes of retail business. Now he was back. 'I spent a year and a half running around my Dad, watching how he runs his business.' Soon Kim made the decision to leave the world of research and use his scientific training in business. 'We came back to Britain and I started my first company. It was a medical diagnostics company supplying components for kits to detect various diseases.'

The company established itself very quickly, mainly because among the range of products that Kim developed was a kit for testing for salmonella in chickens. His company was the first in the world to offer such a test, and the disease was a high-profile one. 'I had no formal training in business. I was just feeling my way. I cut my business teeth with that company; it did well, and seven years later I sold it to an Austrian consortium. With the money, I set up K. S. Biomedics.'

K. S. Biomedics plc is his flagship company. It was founded with government backing. 'Again, the British government was very kind. We put a product together, approached the DTI and explained that we believed our product was going to be very important. "We would like it to stay in Britain rather than go to America. Would you consider funding us?" And the DTI said yes: they gave us a business grant, matching us pound for pound up to £250,000. No strings attached – no conditions – it was just amazing.'

So there was no need to go to America. 'We began with no venture capital in the company at all. Over time we began to take money from friends – and some angels! – then in 1995 we went on to the Alternative Investment Market (AIM). It was the first time we had taken public money from the equity markets. In December 1998 we went on to the main board of the Stock Exchange, so raising another injection of capital. So that's how we began. And the British Government has been exceedingly generous to me. I have not personally experienced any discrimination from them. On the contrary, even though I'm still a Malaysian citizen, they have given me grants for research and business enterprise. I've never experienced exclusion because of my ethnic background.'

But perhaps, we suggested, he had been given preferential treatment. After all, he had several treatments for cancer under his belt; maybe a company like K. S. Biomedics was inevitably going to be looked on favourably by the government of the day?

'Well – my brother runs a supermarket over in Egham, and he hasn't had any problems either! Admittedly, because all my businesses bank in Guildford, it was very easy to get the facilities to support him and help him start up. But I do believe that the UK Chinese community as a whole would be able to say that all in all there has been very little discrimination against us, and very few obstacles put in our way to achieving success. I personally have found the British environment extremely conducive to getting a good education and running a good business.'

The Chinese in Britain

We asked Kim Tan to describe the UK Chinese population.

'Outside of London there are centres of Chinese population in places like Liverpool, Glasgow, Leeds, Belfast and Cardiff. Guildford doesn't have a significant Chinese population. Those who are here are mainly students at the University or working in the restaurants.

The UK Chinese population is not a homogenous population: it's made up of several different groups with different characteristics. I think it relates to the two different ways in which the Chinese have arrived in Britain. The first wave of immigration has largely come from Hong Kong. These people, who are the longest-established here, have predominantly been less educated, less literate members of the Hong Kong Chinese community. They are largely restaurant workers living in the Chinese ghetto quarters. They don't need to be able to speak good English to get by, because they spend most of their time with Chinese-speaking neighbours. I would estimate that they form the bulk of the Chinese community in the UK.

Then a second wave of immigrants has come for other reasons, primarily wanting an education. These come mainly from South-East Asian countries – for example Singapore, Malaysia. Recently people have been coming from mainland China itself, to study at university. The mainland Chinese are a transient population who will return to China after graduation, and their economic and cultural impact is probably not very significant.

That leaves a Chinese population of South-East Asian background being educated here. These are highly literate, highly educated people who are being employed and working along in mainstream companies in mainstream industries.'

The same pattern is evident in many countries, he points out, most interestingly Australia. Australia's first wave of immigrants in modern times was European, including significant populations of Yugoslavs and Italians (the first immigrants of all, of course, being the British!). They were largely people of low income and low literacy who became manual workers. (It's very similar with the UK West Indian community, whose members were originally invited to Britain to work in menial jobs and among whom, consequently, education has not been a high priority.) But in recent years a wave of Asian immigrants has come – particularly Chinese people from Hong Kong, Malaysia and Singapore, and also some from Bangladesh and India. This second wave can only enter if they are highly educated, or have a lot of money to invest in businesses. This is a very different type of immigrant: educated, middle-to-high income bracket, highly articulate and very entrepreneurial. In Australia there is currently a backlash against the new wave of Asians who are perceived as taking over jobs and dominating a part of the economy.

'So the Chinese community isn't homogenous. If you meet a Singaporean Chinese who is educated and is working, perhaps in a profession, he will be quite different in many ways to a restaurant worker from Hong Kong. You find educated Chinese in the mainstream professions, in banking, accountancy and others. There's great diversity.'

Chinese Culture

We asked Dr Tan how strong the Chinese community's sense of cultural identity is today. The Chinese appear in British culture a very long way back, from the days of opium dens in earlier centuries, through such tales as the Sherlock Holmes stories and, in more recent times, the colourful Chinatown festivals that are celebrated in many Chinese cities. China has been through a long Cultural Revolution that destroyed much traditional culture and art, and folk culture was exploited by the State as a propaganda tool. Yet many British cities have highly visible reminders of the Chinese who live in them: the ornate gates in London's Gerrard Street, Liverpool's Chinese emporiums in the refurbished remains of the world's second oldest Chinatown (San Francisco has the oldest); the New Year festivals with paper dragons and street parties ... Is that mere window-dressing, or does it reflect a real sense of cultural identity?

'The world is becoming increasingly homogenous. Look at the food we eat. The mainland Chinese are eating McDonalds and Kentucky Fried Chicken; in ten or twenty years' time that will be considered part of the Chinese diet. Whereas in Britain, British families eat stir-fries on a regular basis. There's a real mingling of cultures going on and I think it's a positive development. We assimilate what is distinctive and good in each other's cultures. Project forwards, say twenty years, and even if you went to Singapore you would find that the Chinese community was completely Westernised.

If you went to Hong Kong, on the other hand, and visited the Chinese there, you might well see rather more of Chinese culture surviving. Of course it's difficult to define culture, but I think language is a very important part of it. In a sense language embodies culture. If you have a small Chinese community such as that in Trinidad, where the small number of Chinese has intermarried with the locals and Chinese is no longer spoken, you've lost everything that's distinctive to Chinese culture. So I think communities where Chinese continues to be spoken will still have some Chinese culture.

When the language goes, the culture probably manifests itself in other, less distinctive ways. I'm one of those who, while still able to speak Chinese, don't use it at home any more. My children were born and grew up in Britain and speak European languages more than Chinese languages. But there are still recognisable Chinese cultural features to our family. Food, attitudes, the whole aspect of the extended family who come to us, the notion of the open home with people dropping in and out all the time – that's very much part of our culture. We have loads of visitors staying with us, and many open meal times. In the summer we have barbecues with anything from forty to seventy people joining us. That's all very Chinese.'

Family and Business

The extended family is important to the Chinese, and its influence extends into business as well as social life. As in the Asian extended family model, there is support at various levels. 'For instance, I still have a responsibility to my extended family if they are in need or difficulty, even if they are not my immediate family. For example, my uncle's sons, daughters or sons; if one of them was in difficulty and approached us for help, we would be obligated to help. My younger brother in Malaysia is a surgeon. People he has never met arrive at his door looking for medical help. 'I'm the son of So-and-So, who's the son of So-and-So, who is your father's brother.' That's still the case, despite all the Westernisation that's gone on in Malaysia. And if any of us is unable to afford the fees for their education, which is for us a very high priority, we would all be there to support that. The same is true if anyone wanted to start their own business.

My own view is that Chinese businesses, like South Asian businesses, are usually designed to be Mom-and-Pop style enterprises. By that I mean that they do not include in their books the full cost of running the business. My father still runs his wholesale business at the age of eighty-three. If I were to evaluate it dispassionately as a business I would have to say that it is non-viable and has been so for a long time. How does he survive? Because he doesn't have to pay any rental, it's his own property. He doesn't have to pay for three members of staff, because they are Dad, Mum and my sister. If one were to add those costs into the company books one would see that the business is not viable.

That is why so many Chinese businesses cannot make the transition from being that one shop to being something larger. They are committed to a policy of self-determination. They don't believe in surrendering part of the control of the company, or in bringing in outside management. They don't believe in share options, they want to retain control over the whole of the equity. In fact they prefer to be self-proprietors even rather than limited companies, because they secure good tax advantages that way. The traditional Chinese company, therefore, is viable until it reaches a certain size and then, unless there is a good son available to take over, it collapses. Asian businesses rarely plan expansion and growth, and they do not know how to delegate control and management to other people.'

Westerners analysing Chinese culture have sometimes identified a prevailing influence of Confucianism on social and business life – a pragmatic and tolerant attitude that contrasts strongly with the Western mindset. Kim Tan isn't convinced. 'There are people who claim that Sun Tzu's *Art of War*[1] provides principles that you can use to run a business. Confucius, too. But I don't think so – I'm certainly not aware of such thinking in business. On the contrary, successful Chinese business has basically adopted western principles. *Time* magazine chose as their Entrepreneur of the Century not Bill Gates or Steve Jobs, but Li Ka-Shing – a Chinese man who started out making plastic flowers and built three different empires. He's the man behind Orange, the phone company. He didn't run his businesses as a Chinaman. He adopted Western principles. His corporations are very innovative and very Western. If Li Ka-Shing had wanted to remain a sole proprietor, he would never have got to where he is today.'

Kim Tan sees an increasing Westernisation of Chinese culture in almost all areas of life, but doesn't regard it as necessarily a bad thing. The decline in the use of the Chinese languages, for example, has led to increasing literacy in the English language among communities that have suffered low literacy rates in the past. It's also, he believes, an aid to tolerance. 'We probably discriminate on the basis of language more than we do on colour of skin. Somebody who is fluent in a language will find it easier to be assimilated and be a part of a community, but if their language-skills are weak they will always remain marginalised. So I think increasing the literacy rate of the next generation of Hong Kong Chinese born in Britain can only be good in terms of integration.'

He feels similarly about second-generation issues, which in other ethnic minorities (like the British South Asians) have led to a feeling of alienation among young people who feel they are neither British nor members of their ethnic community. Sometimes that has been turned into a positive result, for example the rise of the British Asian movement in popular music. 'It's difficult to generalise. But my view is that the next generation of Chinese, born in Britain, educated in British schools and speaking the English language fluently are going to be better integrated than their parents were and less likely to feel alienated. Education – that's the key. And also intermarriage. They're factors that are increasing the chances of better social integration.'

---

1. The earliest known treatise on the waging of war; its authorship is disputed. It was a sourcebook for much of Mao Zedong's tactics against the Japanese and the Chinese Nationalists.

He places a great value and significance on the new generation. 'That first wave of immigrants is disappearing. I believe their way of life will continue here for just one generation. Take arranged marriages, for instance. My parents' marriage was arranged. But none of their children had arranged marriages, nor did any of my cousins. The next generation is imbibing the individualism of the West and will not accept the practice of arranged marriage. Within a generation, because we have become "Westernised', it's all gone by the wayside."

Potential and Resource

As we have seen several times in this book, many members of ethnic minorities engaged in manual work are from professional and business backgrounds; they hold qualifications and degrees from their home countries, but as economic or political migrants – or because they do not speak English very well – they are not able to find appropriate employment. Current Government thinking therefore sees the ethnic minority communities as potentially a very valuable resource of untapped skills and expertise. We raised this with Dr Tan. Did he think that all those restaurant workers, for example, were doing that work because in China they would be restaurant workers – or were they unable to do any other kind of work because of language and financial problems?

'Many of them are people who have been in the restaurant trade before and are happy to continue, because their hope is that their children will achieve more than they have achieved and will leave the restaurant business and enter one of the professions. One of the great Chinese traits (and I think they share it with the South Asians) is the aspirations of parents for their children to be teachers, accountants, lawyers, and especially doctors. That's true of every Chinese and Asian family I know.'

But how secure are those restaurants, in the face of increasing penetration of ethnic niche markets by large companies from the majority community? And when you see penetration in the other direction, where Chinese restaurants, fabric shops and other businesses appear in the high streets and shopping precincts that have so far been dominated by majority businesses, is this real penetration – or just the majority community indulging its liking for the occasional Chinese meal and the opportunity to buy fresh ginger from a delicatessen? We wondered to what extent the Chinese community benefit from what might seem a promising economic expansion into the mainstream.

'I think you are seeing evidence that the minority ethnic communities are being entrepreneurial. Just look at the relatively short period of time in which all our corner shops have been bought over by the very sophisticated, entrepreneurial, educated wave of South Asian immigrants from Africa. Similarly the Chinese who are running the restaurants are very entrepreneurial and if they see an opportunity they will expand.

Usually that means moving the business into a mainstream site. Most of them own a single restaurant, though a few entrepreneurs in London run small chains. But most of the Chinese own just the one restaurant that they run themselves, for reasons we've already discussed – they are unwilling to hand over the reins. It's certainly so in Malaysia, where in all the Chinese businesses I know, people wouldn't dare to trust anybody else with their business. They are amazed that Western supermarkets survive, even with financial controls and reasonably trustworthy people at the check out counters who won't pocket money that doesn't belong to them.

Chinese people do find it difficult to trust others, which is why they employ their own relatives to run the business, on the assumption that the relatives are more trustworthy than non-relatives.'

Keeping it in the Family

K. S. Biomedics, on the other hand, is clearly not staffed entirely by members of Kim Tan's family.

'That's quite true. I dislike nepotism, and it's bad for business. In fact nepotism is one of the key problems for Asian businesses.'

We asked him how that squared with what he had said about the strong sense of obligation in Chinese extended families.

'Helping your family doesn't mean you have to practise nepotism. For example, a nephew might come to me and say, "I need a job," and I might know that he is quite unsuitable for any vacancy I have at that time. So I would phone up one of my friends and see if he had a suitable vacancy. Let me give you a real-life example. We were building a cancer hospital in Malaysia. My sister is a very talented interior designer, and she asked me to give her the hospital design contract. I said no. "What would I do if you didn't do a good job?" But she was very persistent! So in the end, as Chairman, I said to my fellow directors, "Put the job out to tender. Look at the design ideas, look at the cost, and then you guys make the decision without me." I encouraged her to apply and she got the job. She really is a very good designer, but I dislike nepotism. It's unhealthy for business, and it's why Chinese businesses never grow. They feel that they have to pass it on to a son or a daughter.'

Whether the business passes into incompetent hands through nepotism or by an unwise handing over (on death or retirement) to an ineffective family member, the result is the same. 'Wherever you have incompetent management, the company dies.'

Westernising Business

Kim Tan's businesses illustrate his views, both in approaches to funding and also wanting to have a global reach. 'Our industry is a sunrise industry, but it's also a global industry. To have that kind of global reach you have to have very, very deep pockets to bear the finance all yourself – and it's debatable whether it's wise to do so even if you have deep pockets. Access to the UK and European equity markets allows us to expand and grow the company, and to share some of the risks. I took many risks in the early years myself, but the risks became a little too large for me to take on, we brought other people in. Which is not the usual Chinese way.

I've also recently stepped down as the chief executive as well. That too would surprise many Chinese. "Why is he losing his company? He's the founder, he started it – why is he stepping down?"

Well, he's stepping down because he's not smart enough to run his own company, that's why! One of the problems in Chinese business is that if you are not competent at managing the expansion of the company, you still stay in there because you want the control. My father couldn't believe that I was going to step down voluntarily. I said, "Dad, I don't know how to manage this company's moving forward."

I could learn – but that's not what I'm good at. I've brought a manager in who's a far better manager than I could ever be in a hundred years. And I've given him all the responsibility to get in there and do it, with my support.

My interest has always been entrepreneurial. What I enjoy doing is looking for new technology, thinking how to commercialise it, forming a company around that, and then nurturing the company to a stage when we can take it to the stock market. I've done that now with three companies, and that's what I enjoy doing. I enjoy the excitement and buzz of turning ideas into reality, of seeing something being formed out of ideas in people's minds. I enjoy doing that and I hope am reasonably good at doing that. That's what I should be doing, not trying to manage a big company. I wouldn't know how to do it and I wouldn't enjoy it. I think enjoyment is a pretty important factor, when I consider what it is I do.'

For Kim Tan, Britain is a country that has treated him well, and he readily acknowledges that fact.

'The British government has now funded me in total with four grants plus a PhD, plus a DTI grant. I can't complain, they've been exceedingly generous. And I hope through their investment in me it's paid off, and we are creating something a bit more substantial as a result of their investment. Hopefully the growth will continue.

Growth in this industry, of course doesn't mean creating thousands of jobs. One of the new companies we've founded manufactures biotech drugs. We are siting the production in China, in the low cost countries such as South East Asia and South America so that the products are manufactured nearer the markets. We won't be building factories in the UK. And the research part of our business will not create large numbers of jobs. The high tech industry is so automated it doesn't require a large workforce. We will never be significant job-creating businesses, until you get down to the manufacturing end where the requirement is for pairs of hands. At the research end, you need to be in places where people want to live, so that you can hire skilled people. The biotech clusters are around Oxford and Cambridge and the key universities, so that's where the companies are, spilling out from the Imperial College, University College in London.

So what benefit will Britain get from its investment in my companies?

I believe strongly that one of the best ways to motivate business is with role models. Once you have a successful company with a high profile, others will say, "I can do something similar too." And I want my companies to be models for others, demonstrating by their success that the British Government has been supportive, that there's been no discrimination at the funding level, that we've gone ahead and done it, and succeeded. So hopefully others will say, "We'll have a go too."

There really has been no discrimination. When I told my father about the funding I was offered he said, "You mean you are not going to be bonded for five years if you take this money?"

"No, Dad! No conditions."

Britain has become more entrepreneurial in the last ten years, which may be part of the reason, but my discussions with DTI officials and others never touched on race issues, but were all about creating jobs in leading-edge technology based in the UK.

There are things still to be done, of course; Britain hasn't got it all right yet. I think Asians will make more of a contribution in the United States than in Britain, for example, because the US encourages foreign students to stay on and work when they graduate. But in Britain we get overseas students coming in, we train them; they are bright, hard-working and relatively cheap. Then they qualify and we say to them, "Sorry – you've got to go now." We should be saying, "These guys are so bright we should encourage them to stay, so that they can create new ideas and come up with new inventions and start the next wave of technological inventions" – which is what the US people do, especially in my field of biotechnology.

I think the government should review its policy about granting visas to students when they've finished their studies, particularly post-graduate students. If you go to the American National Institute of Health, the NIH, which is the Mecca of medical research, there is an unbelievable number of Chinese students there. Many of them stay on, and now if you look at scientific papers and patents in biotechnology you'll see lots of Chinese names. We have missed out on this, where the Americans, as a culture of immigration, are more used to handling such situations.

But things have changed in Britain. We've seen the pace of technology, and I think the Government realises that if we don't keep abreast of it we're going to be left way behind. Recent changes in the tax laws to encourage entrepreneurs, for example, will help. It is a more enterprising culture now – even the banks have changed. And if you look at the companies on the Stock Exchange you can see a large number of new companies. Also, the OFEX board[2] is increasing – they've three hundred companies there. AIM has four or five hundred companies now, all new companies, and the survival rate is good because by the time you've reached the public markets you've survived many of the danger periods already. So there's a thriving climate of entrepreneurism, Government awareness of change and opportunities, and, certainly in my own experience, a willingness to recognise and accept ethnic diversity and ethnic skills by treating them in the same way as majority diversity and skills are recognised and rewarded.'

---

2. The 'off-Exchange' list of companies trading, like AIM, outside the main board of the Stock Exchange.

Kim Tan's success is part of that climate of entrepreneurial activity, and ¡as given Britain a powerful cutting edge in a field that has traditionally ›een dominated by America. Quite a feat, when you remember that Dr Γan describes himself both as a failed scientist and as someone who could ¡ot run a large company! Which goes to prove that his story, like all ·uccessful entrepreneurs' stories, is all about maintaining a sharp focus, ·dentifying niche opportunities, and playing to one's unique strengths.

›ostscript

‹im Tan's story left us with two points to ponder.

> ב He suggests that in a relatively short time most Chinese culture will have been lost to a new generation of UK-born Chinese. But (a) Is this a good or a bad thing? Would we feel the same had he been talking about, say, the Pakistani community? (b) Is assimilation more likely to occur where, like Kim Tan and his companies, business has prospered – or, in communities that were struggling to survive and needed the community and its ethnic culture for strength and support, would the process be much more gradual? His experience would be countered by that of a large number of ethnic Chinese who operate on a smaller scale: corner shops, restaurants and small businesses.

> ב Dr Tan's discussion of the extended family in Chinese business is a good example of a 'fault-line'. Expansion, as he told us, has strict limits to growth, such as the family's unwillingness to bring in outside expertise and finance. This is common among the ethnic communities; major banks and financial institutions are beginning to target the problem: for example in the matter of succession, where tradition rather than business skills often determines who inherits the business; dependence on lateral thinking and flair rather than established avenues of growing a business; and (as we have already seen) a lack of familiarity with UK business procedures, how Great Britain plc works.

Action must be taken before businesses reach the crisis point that Kim Γan describes. By then, it will often be too late to rescue the situation. Business support agencies, chamber movements and the Small Business Service are in a prime position to assist in these situations.

7: The Dutch Abroad
Jaap van Klinken

In *When Cultures Collide*, his fascinating study of global management practice, Richard D. Lewis surveys the characteristics of the major countries and their people. However, he omits the Dutch. They don't even make an appearance in the index – despite the fact that Lewis acknowledges Dutch author Geert Hofstede as a major influence on the book. When we interviewed Dutch executive Jaap van Klinken, we mentioned this omission.

'He wouldn't have left out the Dutch if he'd been writing a few centuries ago, that's for sure,' he observed. 'The Dutch were the greatest competitors to the British once. They were far ahead of them in trade, not only in Europe but in other parts of the world, too.'

Van Klinken is a Dutchman married to a Scottish wife. He recently retired from the Royal Dutch/Shell Group where, as Vice-President for Corporate Strategy, he worked closely with the Chairman and other Board members 'to define and implement best practice in all aspects of strategy, business planning and appraisal'. He led and managed the annual planning and appraisal process at Group and subsidiary level which ensures that individual business strategies and plans are 'complementary, challenging and robust' – which meant that he was dealing with many of the issues that we touch on in this book.

The dual Head Office structure of the Group meant that his office was in the Shell Centre, London, but he also spent at least one day a week at Shell's office in the Hague, Holland. 'Around 30% of the staff in the Shell office is Dutch; in Holland it's the other way round. That's not always the case with Dutch companies. But Royal Dutch/Shell is highly mobile, more so even than a company like Unilever. When you join Shell, you join a truly international community. Most graduate staff in Shell have worked in several countries; I've worked for the most part in Britain, Holland and the States. Of course, my job itself has been an international one – for the last ten years, and especially the last five, I looked after Shell's international strategy worldwide. That strategy has to accommodate a global perspective, so I came into contact with many different cultures and many different backgrounds. In fact the place where I worked, whether it was Britain, Holland or somewhere else, was really a minor detail.'

When Jaap van Klinken came to Britain, though he had a number of Dutch colleagues, there was no ready-made Dutch community waiting for him. The Dutch are dispersed in the UK and tend not to gather together in particular localities: for example, though there are many Evangelical German churches in Britain there are very few Dutch churches. 'No doubt there are small networks of Dutch people who visit each other. But we were not a typical Dutch family, Lillian being Scottish, so we didn't get into that. Occasionally we meet with the Anglo-Dutch Society for various functions with our British colleagues, but that's only a few times a year.'

Jaap is one of an increasing number of Dutch people who have chosen to make their home in Britain, a move that's been made easier by the European Union. Many come as students, at both school and college level. The quality of British education is much admired – 'and English is considered a necessary language to have under your belt'. British independent and private schools have a substantial number of Dutch pupils, a tradition that is supported by no less than the Dutch royal family; the Crown Prince has attended a Welsh school.

'The Dutch have a natural affinity with the British that goes back a long way,' comments Jaap. 'They have much more in common with the British than with their mainland neighbours, the French and Germans. It goes back in part to the war, when relations between our countries were very strong. The Dutch get on well with the British, and UK tourists in Holland are treated very kindly and hospitably. It's not so with every European country. It's not so easy with the French, as a rule. The French get on better with the Scots. We named our chalet in France *L'Alliance* as a reference to the "Auld Alliance".'

The Ethics of a Multi-National

We asked Jaap whether the differences between the two countries were reflected by differences in the way that business is done in Britain and Holland. Shell, we already knew, had an impressive portfolio of ethical business policies, and was prominent in current debates about ethical business. We were aware that the Group had established an attractive track record for a variety of ethical initiatives. They are being considered appropriate business practice and were also designed to give something

something back to a society that was suffering ecological damage from the presence of the company. It is part of an ongoing discussion about the need to recognise the responsibility that multi-nationals have towards the communities in which they operate, on the grounds that simply by being there they are causing change that may be neither desired nor controllable locally.

'Yes, there is a lot going on environmentally, but we are also exploring business practices appropriate to a Group that operates all over the world. For example, Shell has uniform worldwide business principles, and everybody who works with us has to agree to be bound by them. If you aren't willing to sign, you can't be part of Shell. If you do sign and you then go against the business principles – if you pay bribes, for example, or accept bribes – you get sacked on the spot.

That's very tough if you are doing business in a place like China, where bribes are part of normal business dealings. And I'm sure that many companies don't have such a set of principles. When I went on long visits for Royal Dutch to destinations in the Far East it was quite common to be offered bribes. That was how business was done, how information was obtained. It was also so with the Japanese, who would present you with luxurious gifts or particular forms of entertainment. But we were not allowed to accept them and we weren't allowed to give them.

I must add that our business principles are widely known and accepted within the communities in which we operate, and this has not precluded us from doing business in the above-mentioned countries.

On the other hand, there were significant consequences for the kind of business relationship we were creating. We could never get back into Indonesia, because we wouldn't participate in the bribery system – and as you can imagine, that was a particular frustration for the Dutch. But without bribing, you would have no chance whatsoever. Recently things have begun to change, and maybe there is a chance now for Royal Dutch to go back there. It would be appropriate ... Of all people we should have been close to, we should have been close to the Indonesians. Shell started its non-Dutch presence there.

The British are not so easily bribed, of course, though from time to time it does appear to happen, in politics as well as business – cash for questions, for example. And when it does happen it's a big news story. I think this is reflected in the kind of business practices that exist. The examples I've given in countries abroad do set a very bad example and business in those countries certainly reflects that to a greater or lesser extent.'

Jaap came to Britain with a heightened sense of these issues because that was how Shell operated, and putting those values into practice was part of his job specification. Another way in which Royal Shell/Dutch works in the global context is its approach to ethnic minorities in the countries in which it operates. In the UK, for example, there is a graduate programme that has a high number of entrants from the ethnic minorities.

'That's so. And Shell has also always been in favour of equal opportunities. It's reflected in the policies adopted. In South Africa during the apartheid regime we were the last multi-national company to remain in the country. We didn't quit. Most British and US companies did quit South Africa because of the reaction in the West. They didn't want to stay and in some cases they were not able to stay. But we stayed, because we believed in South Africa and we employed lots of South African people.

Indeed, in the countries in which we work we usually put local people in charge. It's not out of charity or because we feel sorry for them. It's good business sense. We believe in the principle that you can only run good business locally with local people. International staff are used only as a temporary bridgehead, or because they have specific skills that need time to develop and can't be built up quickly enough in the local people.

So we invest in the local community. In some less-developed countries we have built hospitals – of course this is for the benefit of the expatriate community, but it's also a benefit for the local people. We set up training schools to train local people, and we send them abroad for further education and training. Again, it's not charity. It's adopting good business considerations. It shows a different attitude to many other companies. Some American companies (and to a lesser extent some British ones) will never discharge responsibility, certainly not senior management responsibility, to local people. They are always run from the centre. But Shell is a decentralised operation.

Much of the work with local people isn't relevant to the UK, because the same needs don't exist here. But if you want to know the thinking behind the way one major multi-national works in Britain, and its philosophy of its operation, these are some of the principles by which Shell works.'

Dutch Business Personality

But what about the individual Dutch business person? What are the characteristics of the Dutch that a business person from the majority community would find helpful to know, before having an important business meeting with a Dutch person for the first time?

'The Dutch are very straightforward, to the point of bluntness. We don't have such good manners as you British. We aren't gentlemanly! On the other hand we do have a sense of humour, and we get on well with the British because you have a sense of humour too. I'm not saying that we share the *same* sense of humour, however. You might not get the point of some of our jokes, or quite understand why we find something funny. But we appreciate humour and so do you, so we like that.

But we certainly aren't as well mannered as the British, and it is very obvious that we aren't. It can create problems in relationships and it certainly causes many frictions in meetings. In my work for Royal Dutch/Shell I was able to observe this first-hand; my main dealings for the last five years was with the Shell Board, which was made up of approximately half Dutch and half non-Dutch, mainly British. Over the years I witnessed quite a few cultural clashes there, due entirely to the way that different nationalities do business. Between the Dutch and the British it was certainly so. The Dutch would be very open and say immediately whether they were in favour of a policy or agreed with a proposal. The British would take a long time to come to a decision and even then you had to listen very hard to catch the nuances. Maybe they were not entirely happy with the proposal. But they often wouldn't come out and say that, and sometimes they wouldn't even vote against it. A very British caution, I think!

But you can imagine that, in any context, if you are a business person trying to close a deal or agree a strategy, and the other party isn't expressing their real feelings – or, from the other's point of view, is trying to rush things – it can make for a very tense meeting.'

We asked about contracts. Does a Dutch 'Yes' mean 'Yes' – bearing in mind that in some countries, like the Middle Eastern countries, 'Yes' can mean merely 'I'm prepared to go away and give this contract some serious thought'? Many British business people have returned from a sales pitch to another cultural market, in great excitement because they thought they'd got several contracts, and later found that the contracts didn't turn into real orders.

'When the Dutch say 'Yes', they mean it. For us a verbal contract means more or less what it means to the British. If a British business says 'I like it', I trust that even more than I would trust the Dutch.'

We asked Jaap what the status of women is in the Dutch business community. 'You do find women in Dutch companies, but not nearly so many as you find in British ones. The Dutch are even further behind you in that respect. There has been an increase in the employment of women, but we're still way, way behind. As a result there is a lot of inequality in pay. However, it's not characteristic of Dutch society as a whole. You'll see from the history books that Dutch women were liberated centuries ago, much earlier than British women. But they were liberated more in the sense of being in control of the household, rather like Asian women are in control of the household. But that hasn't translated into the business world. For Dutch women the household was their business and that was where they could call the shots. But outside the home, in the world of business, they didn't have anything like the same power.

Today Shell still has relatively few women in top positions in the company. Traditionally the Dutch have been less tolerant of women in business, less willing to accept equality of ability and status, than the British. But that's changing. I sense now a policy of positive bias, so they can catch up.

We do not give great respect to authority. We do respect achievement and skills. So you won't usually find people getting to their feet when the MD comes into the room – unless he has achieved something that people respect.'

What the Neighbours Think

The Van Klinkens' home in England is a large comfortable property in Haslemere, Surrey, deep in the heartlands of the Shires and surrounded by archetypal prosperous English society. They now divide their time between Haslemere and a home in France.

We put it to Jaap that he had settled in one of the centres of traditional British culture, and was living in commuter-land in an up-market area of Surrey where he was surrounded by people who were as British as could be – we had already learned from Nik Shah (p. 79), that in neighbouring Hampshire ethnic minorities make up just 3% of the population. Had he experienced any suspicion or mistrust from his new neighbours, because he was a foreigner and an immigrant?

'No. In general, I have found the Brits very welcoming. On the other hand, there are some significant cultural differences that come to the fore in many ways. First of all there's the different views about social class. British society is extremely aware of class; Holland is not. And it soon becomes apparent that your opportunities to meet people outside your social groupings are limited right from the start – certainly in my job. You meet your colleagues at your social level and it's not so easy to make contacts elsewhere. We have social class structures in Holland, of course, but they are not so strong and it's much easier to make contacts from different layers of society.

In Holland, we might live in a house like the one in which we live in Haslemere – where almost all our neighbours earn similar amounts of money and do similar jobs – and over there we would have a very mixed society around us. You don't find that distinction which you find in Britain, between people who are 'middle-class' and people who are not.

And I would say that by comparison with Britain, there is no poverty in Holland, there are no poor people. I'm making extreme statements, but here in Britain the poverty hits you in your face, even if you come from a neighbouring country like Holland. That's disturbing, because you don't expect it.

The same is true of racial differences, although they are becoming smaller. Coming from a relatively integrated society like Holland, it's disturbing to see the ethnic problems there are in Britain.'

Jaap worked in America during the early 1970s. 'I knew what I was going to find in America, and although the racial conflicts were much greater then than they are today, I was expecting them. But I never expected to find ethnic conflict in a country like Britain. I thought that by then such problems no longer existed.'

A Visible Presence?

The Dutch presence in Britain is significant but it's hardly a ghetto situation. There are no British cities with districts where you can see, as you do in Amsterdam, shops with shelves full of wooden clogs, or market stalls piled with Gouda and Edam cheeses. A recent advertising campaign for Grolsch beer features actors with attractive Dutch accents, but Grolsch has not been marketed as a Dutch product in the way that (for example) the Australian Castlemaine XXXX and Foster's lager have been promoted – those TV advertisements make plentiful use of Australian celebrities,

Australian settings and lots of references to how highly Australians think of the product.

We suggested to Jaap that the high level of integration that the Dutch appear to have achieved in Britain is a reflection of the exceptional level of ethnic harmony that Holland has achieved as a country with a very mixed society.

'Yes, Holland does have a very integrated and tolerant society. But that is our background – Indonesia, Surinam, our old colonial presence. And we not only had an empire, we traded with the world. We represent a minority because we really were a minority. All we had to begin with was water, and we couldn't do much with that except try to keep it out of the door! So we had to fight for existence. We had to struggle to survive and not to drown. Secondly, there was nothing to export locally. So we had to go outside our borders, and we did so – out of necessity.

In many ways we're like the Japanese. Like us, they have few local natural resources so they had to create the equivalent with something else. They had to develop a strength and exploit it, and that's what they did. They became big, which was also their downfall, but they may be recovering now.

But the Dutch have always been sea-traders. They were fishermen, because they needed more food than they could grow on the land. They also sailed all round the globe, not so much because they wanted to but because they had to. And so they came into contact with many different cultures. They had to get on with them, or their business ventures disappeared. Britain had a similar past but the British did not have the same need to get on with the cultures they encountered; they had enormous resources at home. There were people whose whole lives were bound up in exploration and sea trade but most of the British people had no need to be involved. In Holland, almost everybody in the country had to be.

When you encounter the Dutch in business, remember our history. It has affected the way we deal with people and our approach to other cultures in commerce. For example, when I was at school our education had an international orientation. I had to learn four compulsory languages: German, French, English and of course Dutch. On top of that, most people studied Latin and Spanish – which is no longer the case, unfortunately. But that is part of our culture and our upbringing, and it gave my generation an outward orientation rather than an inward one.

That makes an enormous difference and is one of the reasons the Dutch get on well with other cultures today. They still have to. It's one reason there are so many Dutch multi-nationals.

We Dutch trade in things. We have no basic Dutch skills. We sell 70% of the world's flowers. Not because we grow them in Holland – we used to, but that's in the past. The flowers we sell come from all over the world. They are flown in from California, Argentina, Israel; and they are repackaged and redistributed in Holland. They mix different flowers from different parts of the world and send them back. And they make a small trading margin (on the back of a large trading volume, however).

You should see the activity on the trading floor. If you ever visit Holland, visit the flower auctions. They smell beautiful! And it's fascinating to see where the jumbo jets full of flowers come from, and where they go to – back to where they came from, but with slightly different flowers.'

In the days following the death of Princess Diana, we reflected, it was said that every second truck arriving at Dover ferry terminal was bringing flowers from Holland.

'It could well still be the case … the vans are refrigerated. We have developed skills and techniques for this work. I used to think the flowers were ones we'd grown in Holland. Originally we had a huge market in home-grown flower bulbs and tulip blooms, but that was part of our golden era.'

The Dutch Contribution

So we came to the hypothetical question. If all the Dutch people living and working in Holland were to emigrate tomorrow, would we miss them? What would Britain have lost that we would find hard to replace?

'Technical skills! Yes, we are good at trading, we once dominated the seas, but the British are good at that too, so we wouldn't be much missed for our trading skills. In fact the trading arm of Shell is largely of British origin. But in Britain, technical skills are under-rewarded, under-utilised and under-valued. We have bridge-building skills, water control skills, working with the sea – Dutch expertise has been called upon in the proposed lifting of the Russian submarine that sank in Norway recently. We also have strong chemical engineering skills. We built all these skills, like everything else, from necessity.

The British have technical skills as well – look at Cambridge, for example – but their orientation is more managerially orientated than practical. In thriving companies the people who do the technical jobs are often the Americans and Dutch, not the British. In Britain the technical man is under-valued. In big business (I am generalising, of course) the technical people do not originate from Britain: or to put it differently, the good British technical people go abroad. Holland is one of the countries that highly qualified technical people go to. They don't stay in England because they are not paid enough here. On the other hand, lawyers are high on the list of highly rewarded people in Britain. They are not high on the list in Holland at all.

In a company like Shell, the job I did – international strategy – is in many ways highly politically, socially and financially orientated. Those were skills I did not have. My predecessor had more of an economics background. I didn't have an economics background at all; but they brought me in because they wanted someone who had a technical background and could give a technical perspective. I started out doing research and development in Shell. The British people usually don't have a technical background, they are lawyers, economists or political people and are very good at that.

That's the advantage of the marriage of the British arm of Shell and the Dutch arm. It's real synergy, because the skills they each have are skills that are really developed and rewarded. The Dutch really don't have much of a clue on political matters, we're clumsy and we make mistakes. We only cope with it because we have this alliance. Another strength of the Dutch is that they have ten parties in government. That's another alliance.

So if you talk about what Britain would lose if they lost the Dutch, I would say that she would lose the appreciation that we have, of alliances of different groupings coming together to make things work. In Britain the political left and right are more or less mutually exclusive, and that appreciation of alliance is not there. But it is in Holland. We realise that you can't run a company with only technical people, and you can't run a company with only political people. You need them all and you need them working together. For years the British have had alternating governments with opposite views – maybe that's going to change too with proportional representation on the horizon. But for years it's been the case that Labour gets in and carries out its policies; then the Tories get in and undo all that Labour did so they can carry out their policies; then Labour get in ... Leaders tend to become more and more arrogant and will not allow the slightest opposition, even within their own ranks.

That's a weakness of the British, and it's also their strength. But to make it work they need the alliance of others, and in business, the alliance of Dutch and British has worked many times extremely well.'

Postscript

There are strong links of history between the Dutch and the British, and they are links of a different kind to those between, say, Indians and the British, which go back to the Raj and beyond. But the Dutch had an empire of their own and competed with Britain for the mastery of the seas. Jaap van Klinken's interview takes full account of the history, but suggests a way of working together now that both nations have seen their empires drastically decline – an adaptation symbolised, perhaps, by the transformation of the Dutch flower industry, once a huge agricultural industry in Holland, into a floral shipping and forwarding industry.

❑ **Given the shared experiences of the UK and Holland, the UK should endeavour to work closer with the Dutch, as the issues they face are similar.** One of the authors has regularly suggested to the police forces that they should visit cities in Holland (such as Rotterdam, where 42% of the population is immigrants of 150 nationalities) to share and learn from best practice. Similarly, schools and hospitals in Holland have some positive examples of working solutions and models from which Britain can learn.

The Dutch are yet another invisible minority. Yet Jaap makes a strong case that such people are vital elements in the multi-cultural mix. Indeed, his summary of the Dutch contribution to British corporate life – native skills, which help synergy by complementing skills and characteristics that they do not have; and the understanding of the value of alliances – might be read as a prescription of how the multicultural society would work best: a prescription given even more value because it is offered by a multi-national executive. **The Britain of the future will have to deal with a world in which borders function very differently to the way they did when the Dutch and the British held the high seas.**

8: The Art of Food
Isidora Popovic

Popina Taste Sensations operates from the same building in which its founder, Isidora Popovic, lives. Isidora is a 28-year-old Yugoslav who set up Popina a year before we interviewed her in her apartment in London's Hackney. A relatively small space in a stunningly imaginative warehouse conversion, her home nevertheless has a spacious, sunlit feel, though everyday living has to share space with a large industrial refrigerator, plentiful evidence of some serious cooking, and the office paraphernalia of most small businesses. Isidora's husband Igor is a graphic designer; books on art and graphics jostle for space alongside volumes on terrines, sauces and the principles of interior design. We sat round the very large table that serves as her office, trying not to look too hard at the neatly packaged and mouth-watering boxes of chocolate truffles stacked at our elbows. 'I'm afraid I can't open them,' said Isidora regretfully. 'They're an order for clients.'

She cooks in the converted warehouse, employing helpers as she needs them. The ingredients are stored in the industrial refrigerator. She would like to move to a larger space in the same building so that she can increase production and focus on new products, but until funds permit this she is concentrating on making her brand name better known and attracting investors. Nevertheless, the flat made an appropriate setting for our conversation; like the business, it combines several creative disciplines, the skills of a number of people, and a variety of ethnic themes.

Isidora came to the UK ten years ago as an eighteen-year old. It was supposed to be an exploratory visit to explore the possibilities of studying in the UK, but she discovered that she could work as an au pair in London and save enough to cover her fees. She spent two years living on a shoestring and saving most of her wages – 'It was very tough' – then took lessons to improve her English, went on to gain 'A' Levels in fashion and art, and was finally accepted by Goldsmith's College to read Fine Art and Critical Theory.

After college she had several exhibitions, but before long decided that she wanted to work in the food and catering industry. Hers was a very specialised approach to food, however, and her Goldsmith's experience was an essential part of it. Popina provides 'fusion cuisine', drawing on Isidora's Eastern European background and on the cuisine of many other countries; and that is put into an entire context, so that she controls presentation, decoration of the allocated space, and concepts like 'all-day Popina'. A conference opting for the latter begins with delegates being offered intriguing freshly-squeezed fruit juices and fresh baked pastries; lunch is an interesting range of salads and sandwiches to fuel the afternoon sessions; and a themed cocktail reception or dinner party might round the day off.

There's a lot of art and visual content in Popina's product. 'I started while I was exhibiting my photographs and paintings. I was told by one venue that they didn't have any exhibition space available. But the organisers were friends of mine who knew I cooked, so they asked if I'd like to prepare food for a gallery function. I made original mediaeval dishes, but in sushi-sized portions, and I handed the food out during the exhibition, talking to people about the ingredients and recipes I'd used. There was a lot of interest and it created its own audience. Later a few people asked me to cater for events they were planning, and so it all began from there.'

Background

Isidora was born in Novi Sad, in northern Serbia not far from the Hungarian border. It's an area of considerable ethnic variety. Her family also has a mixture of ethnic backgrounds: her mother is Hungarian, her father is a Montenegrin and there are Greek connections too. It happens that her husband Igor also comes from Novi Sad, but they did not meet until they were both students in London.

The war that destroyed old Yugoslavia began after Isidora left. Since it ended, many residents of the worst-affected areas have become refugees and many of those have come to Britain.

'There are Bosnians, Serbs, Croatians – and there are a lot of Albanians here at the moment. I'm not in contact with many of them. I have a few Yugoslav friends but that's it. Some of them live in particular areas like Shepherd's Bush or Notting Hill. Here on the East side of London there aren't a lot, it's a very un-Yugoslav area, you could say. There's a Yugoslav Orthodox church just off Ladbroke Grove, and various centres. But the Yugoslav community, unlike some of the bigger ethnic communities like the Asians, is not a distinctive one. They tend to blend in with British society.'

So much so, in fact, that when Isidora started her business she saw herself as being in the same situation as any British citizen. 'I didn't consider myself marginalized or isolated and I was aware that there were places I could get help. I was living in Shoreditch at the time. I applied to several business centres that offered financial help, because equipment was expensive and I knew I couldn't afford to finance myself at the beginning.'

As a first step, she went on a course run by the Portobello Business Centre. 'It was a really good course. It covered things like how to write a business plan, how to do marketing, who to contact ... and they gave us the phone numbers of all the agencies prepared to offer help and financial support. That was how I found out about the Prince's Trust.'

The Prince's Trust

The Prince's Trust was set up by the Prince of Wales in 1976, 'to help young people to succeed by providing opportunities they would not otherwise have.' It has been extremely successful: at the time of writing it has a turnover of £32 million, employs a staff of 400 nationwide and over 11,000 volunteers, and has helped over 400,000 young people. The Trust helps people between 18 and 30 to start up businesses by making low interest loans, grants for test marketing and larger grants in special circumstances, and by providing a range of free advisory services and other business support. Among the young people the Trust has helped are thousands from the ethnic minority communities.

Isidora benefited from the Trust in several ways. The expensive equipment she needed (expensive, not just because cookery hardware is expensive but also because standards of hygiene have to be met) was paid for with a low interest loan repayable over three years, with a six-month interest-free starting period. The Trust also arranged an introduction to Hackney Business Venture, a local community business centre specialising in encouraging economic regeneration: they gave her a non-returnable grant. She had previously applied to them and had been turned down, but they have a special relationship with the Prince's Trust, so now she had a different status.

Talking to Isidora you get the impression that the money wasn't what she most valued: the advice and supervision the Trust gave her meant that although she had no experience of running a business, she was soon moving confidently around the world of accounts, business forecasting and much more. Key to this was the mentoring system, staffed by experienced business men and women who have volunteered to donate their services. Isidora was allocated a mentor when she contacted the Trust, and his first task was to help her to prepare her final application. 'He didn't do it all for me, but he told me what I had to do, that I had to draw up a business plan and a proper business proposal. It took me quite a few months.'

That mentor was one of a panel who had first assessed Isidora's business idea. After her presentation was accepted, a new mentor by the Trust became an essential part of her new business. 'You're appointed a mentor from your locality. Mentoring lasts for a minimum of a year and during that time you have monthly meetings with him when you can discuss your business and what's currently happening. And there are other specialists you can ask for help – marketing experts, lawyers and so on. It means that while you're learning a mentality that you don't necessarily have at the outset, you have help and advice in areas in which you're not yet comfortable. For example, I've been allocated an accountant for a year. He comes in once a month – I don't have to pay a fee for the visit – looks after my books and explains any areas I'm not sure about. And there are seminars to discuss aspects of running a business, which I find very helpful too.'

Popina

The business is Isidora plus a team of freelance helpers, whom she employs as she needs them. Four or five of them are graphic design and marketing specialists, some are waiters and waitresses, and for big events she hires extra chefs. We asked her to describe the work of Popina (the word is the Latin for eating house), and she showed us the brochure designed by her husband and written by a friend, full of photographs of sumptuous food beautifully presented. 'I prepare food for events of different kinds and I organise the music, decoration and interior, and anything else that is part of the environment of the food.'

In those areas, Isidora's art training is obvious. 'We organised a Christmas dinner for the directors of the Whitechapel Gallery. Ryan Board, who is now my business partner, created the interior. We had huge aquariums on the tables with fish swimming in them, and special lighting; the plates were decorated for the occasion and the music was designed to fit in with the overall theme. It was an environment for people to eat in, a setting for the food, which several different skills created.'

Quality is very important. 'Our Unique Selling Point is that everything we provide is of the highest possible quality – most of all, the food. For chocolate truffles, for example, I use the finest cocoa bean you can buy. It comes from South America, it's 70% pure cocoa. Nothing is added at all. The finished truffle tastes absolutely beautiful. It costs a lot of money to make, but I'd rather use those beans than go out and buy just any kind. That goes for everything I make. It is simply the highest quality.'

Isidora recognises that people tend to buy first for the image and worry about quality later. 'But it's important to get known for quality, so that when you're out there with your menu you stand for a certain excellence. People are wary when you first meet them because the product is quite expensive. So you have to show them that they are buying the very best quality available.'

Isidora is constantly looking out for opportunities to expand Popina into new areas. An acquaintance was helped by the Prince's Trust to start a theatre company. She suggested that Popina handle the catering for the opening show, and Isidora readily agreed, even though the theatre company could only offer to cover costs. 'We thought it would be valuable to make those connections and meet new people. It was a very nice job and I got to meet a number of people who came to the show and might be future clients. In this kind of business I need to meet new people all the time. You know what they say – "You don't sell products, you sell people." You have to be friendly. I tend to meet and socialise all the time, with people from all backgrounds and all minorities and majorities.'

Even the part-time job that she took to help the business through its early days is a source of future clients. 'I work part-time as a sales consultant for an up-market fashion and design company in South Kensington – Popina's bills have to paid even if the jobs don't always come in! I sell really nice designer wear. But also I meet a lot of my Popina clients through that job. The customers are very wealthy and include lots of celebrities.'

Cultural Mixes

We returned to Isidora's background in Yugoslavia. How much had it influenced her career?

'The reason I'm so into food is that it's a family tradition that food should be really beautiful to look at, as well as being really tasty. Both my parents cook, so I've been cooking from a very early age. My parents aren't obsessively health conscious but they made sure there were always fish and lots of vegetables on the table, so I was taught the value of good food early. That's a major influence, of course, but my food has lots of influences – Asia in the East, America in the West, France, Italy – I try to incorporate all sorts of flavours and I'm always searching for a flavour. I use cooking almost as a form of painterly expression.'

Isidora's background is a defining part of Popina. 'I don't have an ethnically clear background. My parents are from different backgrounds, and my home territory was under the rule of Communism while I was growing up; and Communism said that you must appreciate your neighbour, no matter what his colour or origins might be. So I was always brought up with an appreciation of different influences. That's what I'd like to nurture, and show people through my work: there's so much quality in different things.' She feels that in today's Britain people are very open to different cultures' food. 'Food is in a sense much more consumer orientated, it's much easier to get them to test and appreciate different tastes.'

What, we asked, are the particular qualities of Yugoslav people?

'We're very good at re-integrating – maintaining the culture in terms of family values and other things that are important to us. Yugoslav families are very close-knit, even our language shows it. Near cousins are called 'brother' and 'sister', so that we're very close and interconnected. We tend to eat together and be with each other as a family more than people do in Britain, I think. We stay living in our parents' home a long time; often after younger members of the family marry they will live in one of the parents' houses. Whereas in Britain young people often leave home as soon as they can, some of my friends in Yugoslavia are thirty years old, still living with their parents and often married. It's a common thing in Eastern Europe and I think it's probably because of the economy; accommodation is just too expensive and salaries too low to do anything else.'

The economic problems in the Yugoslav republics have had positive by-products, however. 'In England there is the opportunity to prove yourself. You can have an idea and the resources can be made available to you to make it happen. That's how I started Popina, whereas in Yugoslavia it would have been really, really difficult. I think it's characteristic of Yugoslav people that if they do get an opportunity to show what they are capable of, they work hard and achieve things.'

Perhaps because of her ethnically diverse background, Isidora was not aware of any distinctive points of Yugoslav customs and etiquette that would be important to remember in business meetings – 'You can definitely sit cross-legged!' And unlike some ethnic minorities, the close family background doesn't mean that the family is involved in the administration or day-to-day running of the business in the way that, for example, many Asian extended families are. 'I can only speak personally, of course, but although I am in good contact with my family, they are not helping me directly. It's partly because they are not wealthy, and partly because I'm so independent! There is a lot of support in other ways, of course. My husband's family are very involved in his business. It's not a financial or physical involvement, but they are there to talk things over and to help confront problems. They don't call him to ask, 'What have you been working at today?', but there is a bond, part culture, part family, which means they're always there to care for him. It's like that with my family too. I get the impression that British families aren't always so close.'

Bethnal Green (Popina's nearest Tube station) and Hackney (its postal address) were both, in times gone by, rural retreats for London's wealthy population. By Victorian times Bethnal Green had become the poorest district of London, and by the end of the twentieth century Hackney was wrestling with economic blight and the breakdown of community services.

Today the area is showing every sign of regeneration, whether you look at the rise in property values or the increase in small business enterprise and entrepreneurism. Agencies like the Prince's Trust are playing a major part in this, and organisations like Hackney Business Venture can be found in most British cities. Isidora Popovic and Popina reflect an emphasis on youth and on ethnic diversity that must be key to future prosperity.

We left Hackney and drove back along the Whitechapel Road – itself once the heart of London's Jewish community – and on into Fenchurch Street towards the City. It isn't a long journey in miles from economically challenged Hackney to the global financial giants of the City of London – if you weren't in a hurry, you could just about walk it. The economic distance is much greater. But with businesses like Popina arising from the combination of tapping the flair and enthusiasm of gifted minorities, and government and established business investing funding and advice for those fledgling enterprises, that distance is shrinking all the time.

Postscript

Isidora Popovic illustrates several themes that we have explored in this book so far.

□ **The importance of training.** The success of Popina is entirely due to the fact that a way existed for Isidora to find support and funding for her business idea. A number of agencies played a part: for example Hackney Business Venture and The Prince's Trust. The importance of such agencies is that they are not charities, but enablers, and the approval process that Isidora had to go through was designed not to assess her need so much as to test her business potential and the viability of the Popina project. **Such agencies fulfil the core requirement we have suggested for action on behalf of the ethnic communities: that help given should be designed to remove barriers to parity, that positive action should be taken to level the playing field and bring everybody to the starting line together, and that entrepreneurial potential should be allowed the greatest opportunity to be fulfilled.**

□ **The need for investment in training.** There is a continuing need to invest in agencies like The Prince's Trust, for by investing in trainers help can be multiplied beyond the immediate recipients. **Large corporations, banks and successful top 1,000 UK companies need to initiate similar schemes.**

□ **The contribution of the ethnic communities.** Isidora's background, in a particularly ethnically-mixed area of Europe, meant that she brought with her to England an innovative openness to draw on many cultures. Her willingness to explore different markets to source ingredients, and the fusion of her two interests art and food, have created a unique product and service that contributes to the culinary variety that Britain possesses. Note, too, that Isidora financed much of her own training by working as an au pair, so there is a sense in which giving her a work permit and residency in Britain was really importing skills for free: she was in effect underwriting the costs of her own training in business.

☐ **The fault-line that mends itself.** Had Isidora concentrated on producing Yugoslav food and selling it to the Yugoslav community in Britain, she would have been surviving on a market with limited growth and an uncertain future. But her project brings a Yugoslav product into a creative contact with the wider UK business community, and thereby overcomes the limitations that a purely ethnically focused business would have had. Investment in businesses of this type tends to preserve capital where rolling funds are involved, generating new funds to finance further projects, rather than 'topping-up' short-life and fault-line-threatened businesses. **We suggest that the majority of public funding should go to projects of this type.**

9: Divided by a Common Language
John Deacon

'When I first arrived in the UK I was very outgoing, I used to go up to total strangers in meetings and shake hands and say "Hi, I'm John Deacon, I'm from the States, I just moved over here ..." After a while, a colleague took me to one side and said, "Look, John, people really don't need to know you that badly."'

George Bernard Shaw is said to have remarked that America and Britain are two nations separated by a common language. It's a perceptive thought. Americans are a unique part of our experience; we share a common ancestry, and our modern media are full of Americana. Most British people have seen America second-hand through TV, film, music and much more.

When we visit in person, we often find that we have absorbed a media view that's only partially true. Our easy assumptions are challenged. It's not just the language that we don't have in common. Victorian writer Matthew Arnold wrote that America is just like us without the Barbarians. Maybe he was right, but the close relationship Britain has had with America over the centuries can lead us to think that we are more similar than we really are.

John Deacon has seen the relationship from both sides: an American citizen, he and his family have lived in Britain for eight years. His employer, an IT multi-national, sent him to work in the defence industry (John Deacon isn't his real name; we've changed it because of the sensitive nature of his work). He didn't expect to stay in Britain so long. He'd visited the UK several times and had enjoyed his visits, but making his home in Britain was a different matter. 'It's a very different matter living in a place to being a tourist there. When you are an American, you have the idea that the Brits and us are very much alike. We shared a couple of world wars together, we're very good friends, so things will be pretty much the same. It took a while to figure out that on the contrary, this is very much a European country. It isn't the same as our home town.

I came here expecting that we would all share the same assumptions about life, society, politics, the way things ought to be. And it was very challenging to find that it really is not so, and that there is a very different culture here. Take politics. I had the idea before I came that the Tories were just like the Republicans and that Labour was just like the Democrats. But that's not true at all.'

John is a company manager. 'I'm dealing with people a lot – meeting after meeting, group meetings and dealing with individual employees. A lot of my work is people-driven.'

Business and Personality

Did the differences between the two cultures, we asked, extend into the world of business? As an American working closely with British colleagues, had he noticed any major differences?

'I hope that in our office we've achieved a mixing of cultures. I certainly hope that we've taken some of the best of the British and some of the best of the Americans. In fact the office is becoming more British, numerically at least – when I first arrived, the Americans were in the majority, now it's the British. Maybe that's made me more aware of differences.

I think Americans tend to be much more action-oriented. If a problem crops up the response is. "Let's just do it." The only thing Americans won't forgive is lack of action. So long as you're seen to be doing something, even if it's bold and risky, that's fine. We're prejudiced towards getting things done. There are positive and negative aspects of that, but on the whole it's effective. I've found that my British opposite numbers sometimes like to think about things more, or study the situation in more depth: "Let's adopt a more gradual approach", or, "Let's set up a committee to look at this". The British have a real concern for not just making *a* decision, but for making *the right* decision. That's very obvious when contracts are involved. Americans take the line, "Let's get the basics down on paper and we'll work out the details as we get into the job." But my British counterparts want to have everything in writing. They'll spend six months negotiating the contract before we actually get started. Maybe it's part of the fact that the British have too much red tape.'

Contracts are, of course, an area of business in which different people groups sometimes adopt very different approaches. Another is the way business meetings are conducted. Some consider that a meeting that has not produced a decision is a failure, others see meetings mainly as an opportunity to sound out business partners, any decisions achieved being a bonus. Which is the American way?

'Oh, there certainly has to be a result. In fact it can make for some short meetings; if the result's reached quickly, the meeting has served its purpose ... One thing I have noticed. Americans tend to shout at each other more. It's almost a macho thing – lose your temper, make a big stir, get everybody riled up. The British tend to see that behaviour as crazy. They say that losing your temper is a sign that you've lost your self-control. It means you're doing very poorly and not making any impact. Frankly, I prefer the British approach.'

And dress code? For example – if a meeting were to be scheduled on a hot summer afternoon with the MD of another company and several members of both Boards attending, would they dress casually, or formally?

'If it's an important meeting people will dress up, though it's interesting you should ask, as our company has just adopted an informal dress code. People are allowed to wear sports clothes whereas until very recently they weren't. But for a high-level meeting they'd still dress up. Having said that, I would say that Americans tend to have more of an air of familiarity. There's an egalitarian strain right across America, even with important people. You say 'Hi,' to the guy who empties the dustbins, and you also say 'Hi, how are you doing?' to the managing director. Our systems are less hierarchical. Maybe there's less respect. I find that some of my British counterparts, on the other hand, are more deferential to authority.'

So what do you have to do for Americans to respect you in business?

'You have to get things done! British people tend to award respect according to seniority. If the MD or a director walks into a room they get respect regardless of who they are, because of *what* they are, the position they hold. In America you find people at the top level of companies who aren't respected because they don't get things done; whereas people at a much lower level, who are seen to be achievers, the guys with their fingers on the pulse – those are the ones to whom people tend to look up, regardless of level or rank.'

And punctuality – another aspect of business guaranteed to bring out ethnic differences? 'Generally people would prefer you to be on time for a meeting. There are exceptions in various circumstances, but time is important to Americans.'

We asked what part women play in the American workplace and in business generally.

'There is respect there, and I think there is genuine conscious effort to create a harassment-free environment. The same is true of minorities of all kinds. In the American business world in general, there has been an attempt to bring minorities in, and to ensure that those people have good opportunities and are not left behind. Of course these matters look very different in the context of American society, where we have a much more ethnically mixed society than Britain has. Maybe it's just the part of Britain in which we live; but because ethnic minorities are such a small percentage of the whole population, I'm not nearly as aware of them as I might otherwise be. Back home one is much more likely to encounter multi-racial, multi-cultural situations every day. In my situation here, I don't encounter them so often. We do have various people from different ethnic backgrounds in the office, but we tend to see them as individuals rather than as representatives of a particular group.'

Life in the Old Country

We agreed that John, who lives in a rural part of England, might have had a different picture if he'd lived in Liverpool, Glasgow, or Belfast.

'Of course, that's true. I've travelled round Britain quite a lot and have seen other aspects. Our travelling has been family holidays – I don't travel much in my job. We've enjoyed going to the North-East, and we're getting to know Cornwall, which we like very much. They are certainly two very different parts of Britain. But, you know, that's another aspect of the American/British difference. We see Britain as kind of monolithic – all the same kind all over. Maybe it's because it's such a small country by comparison with the USA. Yet there really are distinct differences between the various regions.'

John and his family decided long ago that rather than trying to create a little piece of American home life in England, they would adapt to English life as much as possible. 'I work with a number of other Americans; I'm in touch with Americans every day. But we don't feel ourselves part of an expatriate community, though I know quite a lot of Americans in Britain do. We've decided to immerse ourselves in the British community. It's worked out very well. Of course we meet with other Americans on Fourth of July and Thanksgiving – which are particularly American festivals without British equivalents. But we don't have television, so we don't see American entertainment, and unlike many expatriates we don't have boxes of supplies sent over from home.

We have three children. One was born in England; the other two were one and four years old when we came to England. The youngest hadn't taken in much of America and can't remember any of it, obviously. Our oldest child adapted well to the move, but he certainly remembers that he lived in America once and he knows that he is an American, in a way that the two younger children don't – for them England is all they have known.

We home-school our children, which is quite common in America but very unusual in England. When our new neighbours heard that we were teaching our children at home, they looked at us as if we had two heads.

That's actually another difference between America and Britain. Over there, you can be more of an individual. If you're not satisfied with your job you start your own business. If you're not satisfied with the local school you home-school. You start up things on your own, you do things on your own. Even if you *are* satisfied, you might want to try something different.

So for us it wasn't a strange thing to do at all. But our neighbours, I think, saw it as a rejection of their community. We don't go to the parish church, either, which is probably seen as another rejection. It's as if we were saying to them. "What you have isn't good enough." But in America, people are much more inclined to let you do your own thing '

Setting up home schooling was straightforward, and the local authority was helpful. 'We had to be inspected; various individuals came to our home to make sure we were doing things in what was deemed the proper way.'

Social Conventions

We asked about domestic and social life. What would be useful to know in advance, if one were invited to dinner with an average American family? Are you expected to take presents? Do you shake hands with your hostess, or give her a peck on the cheek? Are there things you shouldn't do at table? These can be difficult matters to negotiate.

'The main thing is to be friendly with each other, and to be informal. Up to a point, that is, for Americans aren't all the same in this respect. In different parts of the USA you have more of a culture of hospitality and of openness than you do in others. For example, in the northeast people are like the English. They are more aloof and quiet than the people in for example the Deep South. There, you meet someone in the grocery store and after you've talked to them for a few minutes it's as if they are your best friend. So Americans aren't all the same. Gifts? I don't think they're necessarily expected when you visit. But you must be polite and friendly.'

When we asked John his opinion of the British pub, he was enthusiastic. 'It's a social environment in itself, a separate community gathering place, quite unlike American bars. My impression is that your pubs are like extensions of your living room, a place where people gather and spend time together. In America, people go to bars to drink. I'm over-generalising, of course, and there is a social aspect to bars, but in America it all seems rather more hard core.'

Playing to Strengths

We returned to the theme of business. We'd begun by touching on the 'Special Relationship' that has long existed between America and Britain. Does it extend, we asked, to business? If an American needs to do business overseas to obtain a product or service that can't be found in America – looking for a place to build a factory or hire a workforce – do the English get preferential treatment, or is just an open market?

'There is more of a warmth towards Britain, and a corresponding slight mistrust of continental folk. The common language breaks down some suspicion. There's this general feeling, that the Brits are OK.'

John and his family are certainly enthusiastic about the cultural heritage of Britain. 'There's a much richer culture here, and having access to the continent has been wonderful for us. It's a bonus, that the children are spending so much of their childhood here. There are some things in America that we do miss, but on the whole we are quite happy. We are here because we want to be here, we chose to be here. We were actually supposed to be long gone, but we've been able to extend our stay.'

Most commentators on American business point out the difference between the entrepreneurial culture of America, where banks and other institutions are geared up to support, fund and even train entrepreneurs in the running of businesses, and the much more difficult situation that entrepreneurs have often faced in the UK.

'I think that's true. I don't have a deep knowledge of the banking industry, I just think in general terms. But this perhaps goes back to what I was saying earlier. If people want to start their own thing, American society is structured to be more supportive of whatever that thing is. In business, somebody has an idea. For the most part, for every ten good ideas maybe only one of them will succeed. But you read of fabulous success stories where somebody just goes and starts up a business, and runs with it, and my goodness! They are millionaires in three years. That kind of thing is much easier in the USA.'

He mentions a colleague with whom he worked in America. 'He was doing very well with the company and had very good prospects. Then one day, he'd gone. He'd decided to start up his own company. It happened very quickly because in America there are lots of resources to help you do it. There are lawyers in every town who are used to helping business start up, most of the banks have programmes to help entrepreneurs and new businesses, society as a whole is more receptive to such things. There's still an entrepreneurial culture. I'm speaking off the cuff, I can't give empirical evidence. But my impression is that in Britain somebody else is in control. Call it the Oxbridge connection, the Old Boy network ... somebody else is running things and we average guys don't stand a chance.'

Hypothetical Questions

Suppose, we suggested to John, you were putting together a management team, and you wanted to bring together the best qualities of the British and the best qualities of the Americans: where would you go for the particular skills you needed?

'I would probably appoint an American marketing guy and also an American technical director. I'd want a British contracts manager. For financial controller, either British or American would be good. The same applies to quality control, I'd be happy with either. On the other hand, for process control it would have to be British. Anything to do with procedures and the writing out of procedures is very well done here.'

And when he returns to America, what will John miss most about Britain, what would he most like to take back with him?

'There's a sense of dignity here, much more than in America. We can be incredibly silly and shallow sometimes. Yes, we're more action-orientated. But in much of America there's a culture of shallowness. Shopping often seems to be the main pastime. I think there's much more depth to the English culture, and the average person is more interesting, more articulate, and thinks about things more.

Of course that doesn't mean that we don't value our American culture. We do – we try to instil in our children some of the values that we believe are very important. I wouldn't want them to miss that spirit of, "You can do it! If you take matters into your own hands, work hard and have creative energy, you can really do something different. You can go where you want to in life." That's one very positive aspects of American culture. Over here I find a different attitude. Opportunities are almost grasped, but there's a sense that we're all stuck in a rut and we can get by without the opportunities.

Maybe Americans are sometimes foolish and optimistic, but that can be a strength as well as a weakness. America has more of a "can do" attitude. There are dark sides to American culture as well, but that's one aspect that I hope that the children will retain, however long we live in England.'

Postscript

The Americans are the community most like the British; even without a special relationship' the links of culture, language (Bernard Shaw notwithstanding!) and much else, are very strong. That might lead one to assume that the two nations thought the same way about business and business relationships. John Deacon's story is a useful reminder that assuming that could be a costly mistake; and he also reminds us that we should be careful, if our major impression of Americans is gained from TV and the cinema, to avoid allowing that to prevent us from forming more accurate impressions from our direct encounters with them – a principle that holds true for relationships with all ethnic communities!

There is a need for cross-fertilisation of ideas between the UK and the USA. Britain can learn much from the US culture of innovation, experimentation and entrepreneurship. The UK still lags behind (No.6 worldwide) in numbers of patents – behind the US, Japan, Germany, Taiwan and France – registered by the US Patent Office.[1]

---

1. Cited in: John Howkins, 'From Ragged Ideas to Riches' (MT, July 2001), p. 68.

10: Community Issues: Change – or Decay?

To present the ethnic communities of Britain as a shining success story is, of course, as much a simplification as it would be to suggest that everybody in the UK wants them here. On the contrary, every day the media reflect prejudice, antagonism, suspicion and fear harboured by some sector of the community against the ethnic minorities.

This has consequences from a business point of view. It places a question mark over issues like the viability of mixed-race workforces in areas where there is ethnic conflict; it makes it difficult to build mutual understanding between communities where there has traditionally been mistrust. In this chapter we explore some of the misgivings and fears that members of the majority community often express about the ethnic minorities. We believe that this is a necessary counterpoint to the many more positive themes discussed in this book – if only to show the size of the legacy of mistrust that most inter-cultural business enterprises have to overcome.

The chapter is based on conversations with two couples living in two different midland towns. Both are from the majority ethnic community. We have decided to change some names and certain identifying details, which is in part a sad comment on the ethnic violence that erupted in several UK midland towns in early summer 2001. Both couples are from the majority ethnic community and both have lived for many years in their respective towns.

Peter and Janet

Peter and Janet are a professional thirty-something couple living in a predominantly white area of a town in the '£5 billion corridor', where the majority of Britain's South Asians live. Peter works as a solicitor and has several Asian clients. These are the only Asians that he knows personally. Janet does know some Asians with whom she comes into contact through her involvement with the local school. Very few of their neighbours belong to the ethnic minorities, so when they look at the predominantly Asian and Black areas of the city they regard the situation as one impacting the city as a whole, rather a local situation. Peter and Janet, like many of their fellow-citizens, live in a town that has one of the largest concentrations of ethnic minority residents in Britain, yet they have very little personal daily contact with them.

Peter is concerned about two factors. Firstly he is aware of the increasing influence of Asians in local politics, which troubles him. Secondly, he is aware that the situation is not static. 'We are seeing a spreading out of the Asian community. For example, many of the shops we once used aren't shops any more – they've been turned into Muslim centres.'

Janet does not have much contact with the Asian community. 'The shops in the Asian districts tend to cater for Asians and there isn't much I need to go there for. We eat some Indian food, like most people, but there are Indian restaurants and take-aways all over town, and the supermarkets all have Indian food sections.'

They both feel that the influence of the ethnic minorities is growing at a disproportionate rate. They are not very involved with local politics and are worried that unbeknown to them the increasing number of Asian councillors might be affecting their lives in significant ways. 'Recently in the local newspaper it was being said that leading councillors were having to make decisions in particular ways to make sure of retaining the Asian vote.' Peter points out. 'That's quite a pressure on council business ... though I guess there's a similar pressure to keep the white population happy, too.'

Asked whether they felt the ethnic communities were treated fairly, Peter and Janet had mixed feelings. They pointed out that there are very poor majority ethnic areas of the town. 'The Asian community don't seem any worse off than some of the white people who live in the same areas.' Analysing further, they pointed to some of the qualities they admired in the ethnic communities: 'There seems to be a real strength in their community', observed Janet. 'They have extended families and I think they get more support in that way than perhaps some other communities do – they look after themselves a great deal.'

'It could be something to do with the priorities you choose in life,' added Peter. 'Quite a few of my Asian clients are very well off, but they don't necessarily live in houses that match their income and standard of living. Some of them are financially supporting members of their family abroad, and in some families four or five adults live in the same house because they are looking after each other – and of course in those cases there's probably not a lot of spare money around. But in some homes there undoubtedly is a lot of wealth, but it doesn't show in the fact they've got nice double-glazed windows, that they've got a well-kept garden. Different priorities.'

Social trends

In Peter and Janet's everyday experience there may be few personal contacts with the ethnic minorities, but even in their overwhelmingly white neighbourhood the presence of those communities is acknowledged. For example, in the local library (a small branch library by comparison with the main town library), besides the sections that contain English newspapers, magazines, reference, information on benefits and so on there are similar sections in the main ethnic minority languages. Council leaflets about recycling and similar utilities are printed in several languages.

For Peter and Janet these are good and necessary developments, but they are frankly apprehensive about the future for their two young children. They feel that there is an increasing segregation in the local schools, for example, and they're not wholly convinced by attempts at cross-cultural education. 'In our local school they have visits from the Anglican church and the Baptist church. An Asian priest comes in too. But they don't have a rabbi coming into the school, for example.' They wonder whether comparative religion is even being taught adequately. 'It seems rather token – a bit of this, a bit of that.'

In fact, the problem they identify is not primarily a perceived threat to the majority cultural identity from the growing Asian community. Asked if they thought that being taught about Hinduism and Islam might lead to their children being taught less and less about their own cultural and religious heritage, Peter and Janet felt that the main problem was of a different kind.

Janet explained. 'It is a healthy thing for children to grow up knowing that there are different cultures, and that other cultures are rich in their own ways. But I think the schools over-emphasise this out of fear, because they are aware that there is a high degree of racial tension in the town. There are a lot of gangs and a lot of gang warfare between different Asian religions, and obviously between white and Asian gangs. The situation is very sensitive. So I don't think that multi-ethnic syllabuses entirely reflect a desire to introduce children to the various facets of their society. It could well be more a case of the schools being desperately anxious to be seen to be fair – giving equal respect to all communities – so as not to inflame tensions.'

Part of the tension is caused by unfamiliarity. Janet comments, 'Shopping in an area of town that is predominantly occupied by the Asian community can be a bit intimidating.' It is a bit like shopping in a foreign country. 'The shops cater predominantly for the Asian community: Halal restaurants, foreign exchange shops, and clothes shops full of saris ...'

Change – and decay?

We asked Peter and Janet whether they felt that a growing ethnic community in a particular district was in some sense a social loss – did they feel that when the Asians moved in, the area went downhill?

'It shouldn't be like that. In a utopia a multicultural community should benefit from what all its members have to offer. But in reality our town might be multicultural, but it's not a community. There's one district that is really a ghetto and I'm sure that the Asian resent that in many ways – and the rest of the town seem to resent them spreading out of that area. How can you find a happy medium?'

'I'd like to discover more about the cultural contribution, and I would like to get to know some Asians socially,' says Peter. 'But there are real problems for us as parents and homeowners.'

Janet explains: 'Some of the lowest-performing schools are those with a majority of Asian pupils. I would be worried if my children had to attend them, simply because having worked in schools I know that for many pupils English isn't their first language so the emphasis is more on language teaching than on the general syllabus. Of course that's important when you have children who speak Urdu at home and only speak English at school, but it's a problem for children whose first language is English. I know of English-speaking Asian families who have moved away from strongly Asian areas so that their children don't have to go to Asian schools! I'm also concerned that there might not be enough RE taught, or school assemblies with a Christian basis, to make sure that Christian pupils were taught adequately.'

Peter does not find much hope in the notion that ethnic minorities bring diversity and skills into the business life of a community and that in that sense the local Asians are an untapped asset. 'McDonald's is mainly Asian-staffed. You'd probably see 80% Asian workers and 20% white. If

you go up to the hospital they are more or less equal. A lot of the servic
industries now are predominantly Asian. But there's a glass ceiling her
like everywhere else. If you are from the ethnic minorities you can onl
rise so far. And that will take a lot of time and effort to change and w
won't see a lot of advantages until then.'

Peter and Janet are not racists. They don't have any hang-ups about racia
superiority or inferiority and they aren't in principle opposed t(
immigration or the presence of substantial ethnic minority communitie
in Britain. If they meet people from the ethnic minorities they are warn
and friendly and they are trying to bring their children up free from racia
prejudice. They deplore any visible evidence of racial hatred or abuse an(
they believe that all human beings, regardless of race, are of equal wortl
and dignity.

Like many people caught up in the stresses of major social change the}
take many of their bearings from the past. 'I drive with my Mum througl
parts of town where the ethnic minority population is large,' says Janet
'And she says to me, "I remember when those houses were *the* place t(
live." They are the huge Victorian houses built for wealthy families witl
lots of servants. But they're really run down now. It's so sad. Maybe th(
residents feel they've been just crammed into ghetto accommodation an(
so they don't have an incentive to maintain the houses.'

Peter sums up his misgivings. 'Many of the local Asians I deal with ar(
very nice people indeed and there's no doubt about that. They are please(
to see you, they are very sociable and I like them. On the other hand
living in an area where the community was predominantly of ethni(
minority background and belonged to an 'alien culture' would definitel}
have adverse consequences for the well-being of myself and my family.'

Leigh and Charlie

Charlie and Leigh live in a comfortable Victorian villa with their toddle
daughter, Lucy. They are both from the majority white community an(
have lived in the town of Luton all their adult lives. Charlie works ir
computers and Leigh is a local government officer in the London Borougl
of Islington. The house is in what would be called a 'white area', thougl
they have Mexican, Asian and African families in the same street. 'I
haven't really thought about it before,' Leigh told us.

They moved in five years ago. Before that they lived in Bury Park, a strongly Asian area. 'It was cheap accommodation and it was a really nice flat. It was cheap because it was in a part of town that isn't seen as desirable – that was because it was fairly near the football ground and people were funny about living near the mosque. Actually the mosque was at the end of our road and there was a Catholic church halfway up. People used to ask me, "Don't you get disturbed by the Muslims' call to prayer every day?" But I never minded it. If I'd lived next door to a cathedral there'd have been bells all day … In fact we rather miss it. If you had certain ideas about people, that sort of thing might make you angry. But we quite liked it.'

The area had pluses and minuses. 'It was well located, we lived in a very nice tree-lined road with good amenities and it was really near to town. We didn't have a washing machine, for example, and we didn't have far to go to the launderette. It was a homely place to live. Bury Park is a mainly Asian area and we were definitely outsiders. But over the four years we lived there we got on well with the Asian community. We knew quite a few of them on good enough terms to stop and chat in the street.'

'We got to know the people who ran the launderette quite well,' Charlie commented, 'and it was very much like the relationship you'd have with anybody. You'd talk about the weather and your income tax and things like that. I got to know the little boy who helped his parents run it – we usually chatted while our washing was being done.

We hardly ever went into their homes, but then we don't do much of that where we are now. We have a wide range of friends from a variety of ethnic backgrounds, though it's fair to say they're predominantly white, as it happens (it wasn't by deliberate choice). But we don't visit our close neighbours so much. I think the days of neighbours dropping in and out of each other's houses are probably over in much of Britain.

Also, I was working at an arts centre at the time in the town centre and we did most of our socialising there, so we didn't spend much time in the local pubs in Bury Park, or other places where local people gathered.'

They enjoyed the Asian culture, especially Charlie: he likes curries, Leigh doesn't care for them because she doesn't like hot spicy food. There were plenty of shops selling Indian spices and herbs, and friendly shopkeepers to advise on their use. 'And there were good shops for fruit and veg and so on – we used them a lot.'

'There's a range of products you just don't get in supermarkets,' Charlie agreed. 'When we left Bury Park, I missed the food shops the most.'

We suggested that Bury Park must be a popular place for Luton people in general to get their Indian food from, but they were not so sure. 'Bury Park over the last few years has been increasingly a high crime area. The red light district's nearby and after a certain time of night there are roads you just don't walk down if you can avoid it. It was like that when we lived there. And that's a minus point. I wouldn't willingly go anywhere on my own after dark, and a couple of times I got some very nasty hassle from men hanging round outside a pool centre. But I honestly don't think you can say that they were like that because they were Asian. They were just a nasty group of people hanging round a rough area of town.'

Would they have stayed, we asked, if Lucy had been born there?

'That's an interesting question. I'm not sure we would. We moved here because it was a "better" area of town, better housing and so on, but you have to separate the question out. If you asked us would we move to a predominantly Asian area if it were a nice area, the answer is definitely "Yes". But it's a fact of life that in a place like Luton a lot of the Asian areas are not particularly nice parts of town.

Part of the reason, I think, is that they don't all get a fair deal from local government. Marsh Farm, which has a lot of black people and a majority of white people, has just got a substantial handout of public money. I think it would be a very fine distinction to try to say which area was actually more deprived. It would have been nice to see the money divided between them, really.'

Local culture

We asked Charlie and Leigh how the Asians first came to Luton. Charlie explained that the community established itself in the days when Luton was a major hosiery and millinery centre. The Asians are very successful in the hosiery business.

'However, Bury Park today isn't a notably entrepreneurial area. It's too run down. The road we lived in was very nice and there are a few other nice parts, but most of the roads aren't too nice. Some of the houses are beautiful, old Victorian villas, but some are just rows of horrible terraces.'

They don't feel that Luton would be better off without the Asian community. 'I like living around people from all walks of life,' says Leigh. 'It makes life more interesting, doesn't it.' We asked how easy it was for the majority community to access the Asian culture. If they fancied some sitar music, would they be able to find it easily?

'As it happens, the arts centre organised a concert by Ravi Shankar a while back! Although he didn't play in the middle of Bury Park. It was at the University.'

And restaurants?

'It's very interesting, because I know a woman whose background is Gujarati, and she says it's disgusting that 'all the so-called Indian restaurants in Luton are run by Pakistanis'! – she says it's not proper Indian food. So there's a kind of racism within the Asian community as well as outside it. In any case, I don't know of many Indian restaurants in Bury Park. There are a couple of Chinese and two Italian. The Indian restaurants are concentrated in the town centre. One of Luton's finest restaurants in years gone by was a Chinese one in Bury Park called the Man Ho. It got a lot of custom but I'm sure people didn't like going there, because it was in Bury Park.'

They liked living in Bury Park but didn't get deeply involved in the local culture. Leigh feels that when Lucy is older that might change. 'When she goes to school she'll start learning about festivals, and then it gets quite interesting. They look at Divali, for instance, which is a big local festival. We'll probably get into it more then because of Lucy – we'll have a reason to get involved.

The one big thing in Luton every year is the carnival. That's very much steeped in black culture, with Caribbean origins. Every year the rumour goes round that there's going to be a big old fight between the Asian population and the black youth population, and because of this the festival shuts down at six or seven o'clock. There's a huge police presence there too. But nothing ever happens.'

Getting on with the neighbours

We asked Charlie and Leigh how they felt about the size of the ethnic minority presence in Luton. Were there too many living there?

'No, not at all. In many parts of Britain you can go quite a way before you see anybody who is from an ethnic minority. Obviously Luton and Leicester have a quite high concentration and a more diverse population. But there's a huge Irish population in Luton, and nobody moans at them – because they're white.'

'So we've established that you don't mind the Asians being here,' we suggested.

'It's not that we don't mind. It's just not an issue.'

But, we said, Bury Park is clearly a large problem area with high crime and lack of facilities, so that you end up with a high street that looks like a badly-maintained street in Madras. Surely that wasn't good for the people who lived there and it didn't help create a viable city. Did Charlie and Leigh have any opinion on how matters could be improved?

'Obviously there needs to be a lot of work done with the local youth. That's not just in Bury Park, but in Marsh Farm as well. The police are now looking to recruit from the ethnic minorities but they struggle to get that recruitment. And in any case policing is not necessarily all of what it's about. Young people in places like Bury Park and Marsh Farm usually come from homes where there isn't a lot of money. And you need money for the kind of entertainment that is on offer in this town – ten-pin bowling, clubbing, whatever – it all adds up. It's quite expensive entertainment. So increasing youth facilities would probably combat crime considerably, but unfortunately they seem to be always being cut back. And also better provision of community centres, because people from the ethnic minorities have a great deal of respect for community leaders and community elders, if they have access to them.'

'Of course,' added Leigh, 'another thing that needs to be dealt with is drugs. I don't think the problem is down to the ethnic population. If an area is run down, prostitution and drugs move in; and when it's all on your doorstep and you're young and bored, it's a dangerous mix. Drugs cost money and higher drug use leads to higher crime.'

People are people

One reflection of the differential between facilities in the town centre and in Bury Park was the fact that few of the Asian community were seen at the arts centre in town.

'You did meet some. One prominent character was an Indian – I remember he was quite racist in his views about Muslims. And I met one man who was a successful singer, a Bengali. He came to the arts centre to record his music and was quite successful in selling it, not only in Bury Park bit also in the Indian subcontinent. You quickly learn that not all Asians are the same, there's a wide range of types, just like us. I think people forget that they come from different areas and they relate to each other as we, perhaps, might relate to the French – geographically not too far away but a very different type of people. That's only in terms of cultural background, of course. They're British Asians.

You get different attitudes among any group. When I was growing up in Luton my next-door neighbours were Sikhs, and at junior school my best friends were Asian children. And I think I can honestly say that I thought there was no outward difference. We all had the same kind of interests, the same hopes for Christmas presents, and so on. Obviously they had their religious festivals like Divali, which we didn't get much involved in. But we went into each other's homes and their parents treated me like the parents of any of my other friends did. Really there wasn't any difference at all.

I must say that that's one of the very positive things about living in a multi-cultural town like Luton and later spending four years in Bury Park. You learn that humans are humans. I know it sounds a bit crass, but people are people all the same. They want good things for their families, they want enough money to live on, they want material things, and we all have the same hang-ups. Everyone has people they dislike and people they have an affinity with. The one thing I realise is that on that level, everyone's the same.'

Postscript

We have included these two interviews because the whole picture cannot be told in terms of programmes and policies. A truly diverse, multi-cultural Britain will only happen in a climate of mutual consent and mutual respect. How is that to be achieved?

❏ **Those who are in a position to build bridges should build them.** There are many ways in which alienation is institutionalised in our society in ways that were never voted for. Language is unintentionally exclusive, local organisations pose problems of access to people whose first language and culture are not English, and unfamiliarity breeds unease. Many cultural frictions and conflicts would be removed if those involved simply knew more about each other. National and local government, statutory bodies and organisations at a local level can achieve a great deal in this respect.

❏ **Those who are in a position to open doors should open them.** Many of the barriers between people are kept in place by default rather than by conscious choice. **A small shift in thinking can produce radical change.** Even the title of some organisations implies that ethnic minority members are not welcome, and the composition of many leadership structures certainly suggests that. Look around your boardroom and your senior staff room: what do they say to outsiders about your diversity policy? The same applies to local organisations and to public sector bodies. How many non-white faces are there in the Citizens' Advice Bureau? In the town information office? In areas with large ethnic minority populations it is likely that there will be good representation. In other areas, the absence of ethnic community faces behind public desks may well be sending a message that only the majority community is welcome. Of course, altering this perception shouldn't result in the other extreme, tokenism.

❑ **Opportunities should be created to reduce mutual suspicion.** There are innumerable ways in which the 'two circles' described by Ali Mohammed (p. 90) can be brought closer together. Formal and informal invitations to visit between communities; exhibitions, concerts and other events designed to encourage understanding and appreciation of each other's culture and traditions; expansion of existing amenities like libraries, not only to serve the ethnic minority community but also to introduce the majority community to the cultural wealth of their neighbours in the minority communities. **The business community has a major role to play in such initiatives, through sponsorship, supplying resources and in other ways promoting mutual understanding.**

11: Hidden Talents and Business Resources
Pastor Sola Fola-Alade

What I like doing is to help people get ahead. I've discovered in myself a passion for personal coaching and helping people with career and business problems. Most of my sermons result in people going out and getting jobs!

Of all the ways that people have come to make their home in Britain, coming as a missionary is more unusual than most. A missionary who is also a highly successful graphic designer and business consultant is an even more unlikely combination. And when you discover that Pastor Sola Fola-Alade is also a qualified doctor, you begin to wonder how he has managed to achieve so much in a quite short time.

He graduated from medical school in Nigeria in 1991 and practised medicine for a year and a half before deciding that he did not want to be a doctor after all. He turned instead to the fine arts – 'I was always a very creative person' – and set up in business as a screen printer and tee-shirt designer. The company prospered and he branched out into graphic design and publishing, building up an impressive client list over a period of three or four years.

Then he became a lay preacher in a denomination of around 2,500 parishes worldwide called the Redeemed Christian Church of God, and began to be recognised as a powerful and inspirational figure in the pulpit. In 1995 the church sent him to Britain to start a community church. He began with a congregation of six people and has pastored the church ever since. The congregation is now around 400 people.

Many missionaries arrive in the UK, compelled either to spread the message of new religious movements or to call post-modernist, post-Christian Britain back to true faith. Substantial numbers come from South Korea, for example, and also from Africa, the latter often descendants of those who were converted through missionaries of an earlier generation who were sent out to Africa from Britain.

Not many of them run business consultancies as well. Pastor Fola-Alade does. 'Spearhead' is a personal and professional development organisation using seminar-based methods. Its clients include some church members and a number of other individuals and organisations, and several businesses use Spearhead as general consultants too. Most of his clients are of African or Caribbean background.

'What I like doing is to help people get ahead. I've discovered in myself a passion for personal coaching and helping people with career and business problems. Most of my sermons result in people going out and getting jobs! I realised I must have a gift in that area. I also decided that I should develop a service that wasn't based in the church but under a secular umbrella. So I started to organise seminars with speakers dealing with a range of topics such as time management, entrepreneurship, E-commerce, image consultancy, systems, recruitment and the like.' Spearhead publishes *The Achiever's Journal*, a glossy up-market magazine that packs a lot of visual energy into its pages. Its launch issue contained punchy articles on subjects as varied as changing jobs, saving and investment, career profiles and reviews. While the advertisements and occasional references discreetly acknowledge the church background of many of its readers, the *Journal* features names of contributors who are achievers, by any standards, in the general business world. It's an impressive publication, not least because its publisher is fitting a couple of other careers in alongside heading up Spearhead.

Nigerians abroad

Most British Nigerians live in London and the majority of London Nigerians live in Peckham or Camberwell. Peckham High Street in many ways looks like a street in Lagos. More affluent Nigerians live in the northern suburbs – St John's Wood, Hampstead, Golders Green, Colindale and a few in East London. The Caribbean community, with whom Pastor Fola-Alade has many links, is concentrated in areas like Brixton, other south London districts, and the East End. There's a strong sense of community, helped for example by several flourishing Afro-Caribbean newspapers such as *The Voice* and *New Nation*, for which Pastor Fola-Alade has sometimes written. *Our Society* is a magazine that addresses the needs of Nigerians in the diaspora. *Ovation* – 'It's like a Nigerian *Hello* magazine' – is a handy guide to who's currently who in the Nigerian scene.

Many of the Nigerians who come to Britain come as students, though not (as is the case with many south Asians) because education opportunities don't exist in their own country. Education in Nigeria is generally of a high standard. But Nigerians are inveterate students. 'They never stop going to college. They're always studying! That's why many of them come to Britain to continue their education with higher degrees, diplomas and professional qualifications.'

We asked Pastor Fola-Alade what it is that Nigerians bring to the UK and contribute to the national diversity of skills and talents. What are their particular skills and talents, what are they good at and have made a major contribution in?

'Some have done very well in the arts, for example theatre – though the Caribbeans have made more of an impact there. What Africans bring to the British community, and particularly those who come from the West Coast – Ghana, Sierra Leone, Liberia – is more their career skills. They are very strong career professionals. A large number of Nigerians in England are professionals, accountants, medical doctors, lawyers, architects so on. Recently a lot of them have gone into Information Technology consultancy.'

The difference between the Nigerian and South Asian communities is striking. Where South Asians tend to be accomplished business people, almost irrespective of the type of business involved, Nigerians are strong in certain professions. 'Most of those who succeed in the UK come from southern Nigeria. Southerners are not particularly strong business people, but they are very intellectual. You do have the occasional exceptions, and I'm not saying that there are no Nigerian business people or entrepreneurs in Britain. They do exist; though many of them don't actually base their business in the UK. They trade across borders, for example buying here and exporting to Nigeria or vice-versa. But the main strength of the Nigerian community is in the professions. I'd say that 85% of successful Nigerians here are professionals.' Successful South Asians tend to regard professional qualifications as a preliminary to using entrepreneurial flair, and once established in a profitable line of business will prefer their own ways of doing things to the red tape and regulations of the accepted professional route to the top. The African mentality is much more inclined to the career path and continuing education. It's a distinction Pastor Fola-Alade readily accepts. 'In all the years I have been in the UK I think I have seen two or three Nigerians own a corner shop. But you see Asian corner shops all over the place. UK Nigerians, who as I've said tend to be from southern Nigeria, are not strongly entrepreneurial. Nigerians who are strong business people are generally the Ibo people from eastern Nigeria. Many of them are in America and the Far East, where there are more opportunities. Ibos are very, very good traders, and they are to be found all over the world. Go to Finland, you'll find an Ibo; go to the North Pole, you'll find an Ibo. They're very good at business.'

Using the African Resource

We asked Pastor Fola-Alade if he thought Britain is making good use of this resource – a highly motivated, highly educated community, with much to offer both business and professions. Are we doing enough to bring these people into the mainstream community, and to make available to them the business support facilities that are available to the majority business community?

'In fairness, a lot has been done and there have been core opportunities. But I'd say that not enough has been done. We really are sitting on an immeasurable amount of resources and intellectual property so far as the ethnic minorities are concerned. Literally sitting on them – the 'glass ceiling' is an all too common problem for the ethnic minorities. For example, I trained as a doctor. I know a lot of African doctors who are very good at their jobs but don't have positions commensurate with their abilities. You don't see very many African consultants and I know of no Nigerians in senior hospital management positions. So Nigerian doctors in British hospitals either stagnate at the highest position to which the system allows them to rise – or they leave and go to America.'

Of those who trained with Pastor Fola-Alade and came to Britain like him, those who have stayed here are still at the rank of senior house officers. Those who went to America are mostly consultants with very senior posts, good remuneration, incentives and reward schemes.

'There are so many more opportunities over there,' he explains. 'But it's the same with accountancy and the law. My wife is a lawyer. She studied law in the United Kingdom, graduated four or five years ago, and hasn't been able to get a legal contract yet. There is certainly a brain drain happening, and very gifted people are leaving.'

But there is one area in which the pattern is reversing. In the IT industry Nigerians have established themselves alongside the Asians. It is an industry full of opportunity and the Nigerians are quick learners, willing to invest heavily in taking courses, private study, and the sustained learning that IT demands. In the UK information technology industry Nigerians hold top jobs and earn high incomes. It's one area of work that has been very favourable for them. The fact that Caribbeans are also doing well in this industry indicates the learning curve involved: the Caribbean has sometimes suffered considerably from being forced to accept obsolete technology from the West. Supposed to ease debt repayment, it often bound the recipient countries into dependence on the Western donors, making it all the harder for those countries to keep up with the IT revolutions sweeping the globe.[1]

Culture Conflict

Casually mentioning that among his other activities he successfully studied for an MBA, Pastor Fola-Alade reflects on a course he took for that degree which dealt with trans-national management. 'Take the Japanese. They are what's called 'far/distant'. They are very deferential, they hold people in high esteem; they won't do business with just anybody, you have to as it were meet the family first and become good friends. Africans are quite like that. Nigerians in particular are very respect-conscious. They respect older people and believe that wisdom is in proportion to your age: the older you are, the wiser you are. So, if you are doing business with an older man you obviously treat him differently to yourself. The younger man will be expected to offer the best seat to the older.'

He considers that the British are curt and precise, almost cold in their approach to business. 'Africans have large hearts. With the British you just get a handshake and that's it. But Africans warm to each other. Our families get involved. If an African man does business with a British man, he expects him to come to Africa sometime, to his village, where he will be made a chief or something. Mind you, there are some things you have to watch out for with an African – particularly with Nigerians! For example the British are very particular about time. Three o'clock means three o'clock. But for a Nigerian, three o'clock means three-thirty or even four o'clock. As a Pastor I preach against that! But we Africans are very relaxed about time. We speak of "African time"!'

Pastor Fola-Alade's findings about the British style in business extend to social contact as well. 'The British are reserved. When you do business

---

1. See, for example, Gerald Sussman and John A. Lent (eds), *Transnational Communications: Wiring the Third World* (Sage, 1991).

with them you can sense them saying, "You're going to see my business face, but that's all you're going to get." Nigerians and Africans generally are very different. You'll be sitting at home and suddenly people you have been doing business with at work will appear at your door unannounced. "I was just driving past and thought I'd drop in" – which the British would not feel comfortable with at all. Most of the people I know would say, "You should have telephoned." But Nigerians will come into your house and say, "What are you having for dinner? I'll join you." It's one big happy family!'

The emphasis on the family in the sense of the extended family united by blood-ties is somewhat different to that in, for example, the Indian and Chinese communities. 'Our concept of the extended family is not as strong as it is in the Asian community, for instance, but it's closer to the Asian model than it is to the European one. An African would employ his brothers on the basis of trust, and also he feels he has a responsibility towards his family members to train them and care for them. They in their turn have obligations through service: they work in the shop, do some business errands and things like that; that's especially true of Ibos, the eastern Nigerians. They bring their brothers into the business; for example they're renowned international businessmen and traders (though having said that, you can also find among them acclaimed academics, politicians, professionals and other achievers). They will bring in somebody from their home village, show him the ropes and set him up in business – because he is from the village, the family. But it's true too of the less entrepreneurial, more business-orientated Nigerians too. My father-in-law is one of the leading industrialists in Nigeria. He began from scratch at the age of sixteen. Now he has achieved success and most of his managers and directors are his children. Nigerians tend to employ people not just on the basis of competence, but much more on grounds of relationship.'

And if the relative in question was known to be a bad worker, or incompetent in business?

'A Nigerian would employ that person, if he was a family member. He'd find *something* for him to do. It's almost like a taboo, for your relative to be in need of employment and for you to give a job to somebody else. Not quite a taboo, but it gives great offence.'

Accessing Business Support
Pastor Fola-Alade consults for a number of businesses. Mindful of the problems that some ethnic minority businesses have encountered in trying to gain access to start-up funding, sources of investment and financial support we asked him how far UK African businesses have been able to benefit from them.

'The main problem is usually funding. The banks are not at all helpful. It's not a language problem, we don't need bank staff fluent in African languages. Most Nigerians you find in the UK speak quite good English. Very, very few people who come here are illiterate (by which I mean, unable to speak or write English). There might be an accent problem, or their diction and intonation might be a little hard to understand, but I doubt whether that is a problem when you're dealing with your bank. But most of the people I speak with who have large businesses have had problems obtaining loans. It may be in part due to the bad reputation Nigeria has for international business fraud, dating back to the 1980s when the economy was severely depressed and rogue fraudulent schemes began to proliferate.'

There can indeed be few British businesses unaware of the problem. The classic Nigerian scam (usually delivered by e-mail or by post on an impressive letterhead) offers its gullible victim the chance to share in the profits of a swindle on the Nigerian government. Usually the story is that the illegal gains can only be got out of the Nigerian bank where they are currently deposited, if an overseas collaborator puts up a few million pounds equity or provides details of a UK bank account. The successful scam ends with the UK collaborator contemplating his suddenly empty bank account, unable – as the willing partner in an attempted fraud on a foreign government – to call in the police. It's an elegant swindle, as many in Britain can testify.

The Nigerian government has occasionally gone so far as to take full-page advertisements in British newspapers, warning British citizens that if anybody loses money as the result of responding to illegal approaches from Nigerian nationals, the government will in no case intervene or compensate. For the law-abiding Nigerian businessman in Britain, the frauds have made life very difficult. 'There's an almost institutionalised suspicion. People think of you not just as a businessman but as a Nigerian businessman. A front goes up. The other day I was trying to buy a travel card from a Tube station. I gave the gentleman my Visa card, which of course carries my name. The man looked at the card and he looked at me.

"Are you Dr Alade?"

"Yes, I am."

"You don't look like a doctor."

I asked him, "What do doctors look like?"

He replied, "You just don't look like a doctor. I don't think this card belongs to you."

I don't blame the system, because the bad apples have given the whole country a bad image. It's a cross we have to bear.'

Apart from the prevailing suspicion of Nigerian businessmen and the inevitable difficulties in business relationships, Pastor Fola-Alade believes there are two factors that prevent Nigerians from taking up business support, grants and the like. One is the bureaucracy of systems that run on red tape and paper work, which creates a frustration that makes many applicants give up at an early stage. The second is lack of awareness of what is available. 'You would be amazed how many people know nothing at all about government schemes and support for business. The first time I heard that things like Business Link existed, and that their advice and help was free, I thought, "It can't be true. Nothing goes for nothing." So maybe there is an issue of education to be dealt with. A large number of people think, "It won't be for people like us, we would never get it. It's not worth making an application because we'd never get a reply."'

Unlike some of the UK ethnic minorities, Nigerians do not have well-established financial networks within their community and from which they would borrow in preference to conventional funding. 'They would go to banks and government agencies if they thought they would get help, but I think the general perception is that nothing much ever comes of applying, so it's a waste of time and effort.'

British Nigerians?

Pastor Fola-Alade is sceptical about political agendas for ethnic integration. 'Tony Blair made a conference speech just before taking office, about the poor representation of minorities in public and professional life. There's a degree of political rhetoric there, I feel, because in four or five years I don't think very much has changed. He made a similar speech at the Afro-Caribbean Evangelical Alliance conference in Brighton, and I feel he was chiefly there to encourage political support for his party. The sentiments are admirable, and it would be nice to see the dream come to fruition. But I don't see it happening in the near future.'

So what would it take to bring about change?

'A good start would be much more tolerance and willingness to give the ethnic minorities a better chance. If people were judged fairly, more by the skills and the competences that they bring to the table than by the colour of their skin, that would help a great deal. So would the disappearance of the old boy network, so that professionals like my wife and those in many other fields are given a fair chance at interviews and even before that, at the application level. If their applications were not disregarded because they didn't go to Oxford or Cambridge, or their names don't sound right, that would be a start. Because there is a lot of intellectual property among our communities that is just draining away.'

Suppose every UK African were to leave the country tomorrow, we asked, and emigrate to Africa. What would Britain lose?

'Britain would lose a significant proportion of her hard-working, intelligent, career-minded and business professionals. She would lose a great human resource. In many professions, the Africans are a key element and in some they are the best brains there. In the NHS, for example, they are a mainstay of the system; along with the Asians they basically keep the NHS going. In the IT industry they are emerging as a core element. And that's significant, because in many areas where Africans are prominent, their presence and contribution are visible and well-established. In IT the contribution is much more recent and certainly a great deal less visible. And that should be a warning, because the on-going brain drain and the bottling up of so much ability will do a lot more damage to Britain if it is unnoticed.'

❖

Postscript

Our last interview highlights a number of issues.

❑ **There is a brain drain happening.** We have already discussed the skills loss earlier in this book (Section 1 Chapter 4), but this interview is a reminder that not all the skills lost to the UK are from the communities one might expect: the skills and mobility of the South Asian community are widely known in the majority business market, those of the African and Caribbean communities less so.

❑ **Britain is not serving entrepreneurs from the ethnic minority communities adequately.** Pastor Fola-Alade's experiences are an indication that help needs to be given at levels deeper than the merely cosmetic: for example, a philosophy of banking needs to be changed, even more than a policy of how one constructs the banking interface with everyday customers.

❑ **The services of business advisory agencies are still not widely enough publicised.** Again, this is not just a matter of distributing information. It is a matter of being aware of barriers to accepting help, what sectors of the community are being passed over, and the need to contextualise information: it is possible to translate a British document into a foreign language and still have a document that only makes sense to people whose first language is English and who belong to the majority population.

❑ **Initiatives within the ethnic minority communities often come from agencies other than public sector and government sectors.** Pastor Fola-Alade is a pastor of a church; many business, welfare and educational programmes are initiated by leaders of faith communities, and by similar people. **The business community, in supporting such initiatives, might usefully reflect on why acceptance is often higher in such cases, and see if any lessons can be learned from them.**

Interlude
Observing the Conventions:
A Practical Exercise

To be aware of many of the cultural and social differences between ethnic communities takes practice. You're adopting a new way of looking at things that probably never seemed significant before: how you sit, whether or not you shake hands, whether you should assume that a 'Yes' really does mean a 'Yes' – these are usually matters of habit or of instinct. Dealing with people from other ethnic communities means changing the mindset we're used to. It means looking twice at things that we would normally not bother to look at once.

This practical exercise is intended to help in developing this change of perspective, and to allow you to identify in a practical situation some of the ethnic characteristics we talk about in this book.[1]

The Scenario

Do this exercise when you are attending a dinner – not a formal dinner-jacket affair, nor a family get-together, but a dinner at which you will be meeting people you haven't previously met and which will be hosted by a couple or an individual. It should be a dinner held in a private home. If you don't have such an event in your diary, you can still get some good results by applying the exercise to the last such dinner you attended.

If the guests are from your own ethnic community, the exercise will give you an insight into how you appear to other ethnic communities and the significance of apparently minor details of etiquette and social customs. If the guests are from one or more other ethnic communities you will get even better results, because you will be applying much of what this book covers in a real-life situation. In either case, you will be developing your people skills for future meetings with people from the ethnic communities.

It can be helpful if you do the exercise with somebody else who is at the dinner, and compare notes. The exercise is based round a list of questions:

---

1. The exercise is based, with permission, on one devised by Prof. Prabhu Guptara of Advance: Management Training Ltd, Surrey, UK.

if the opportunity arises it can be useful to discuss the questions with other guests. If you do this, note not only what they say, but also their reaction to the questions. The fact that somebody finds a question surprising or trivial can in itself be a comment on what's being discussed.

The Questions

Here are the questions that form the heart of the exercise. If you can discreetly write your comments at the time, it will be useful for later review, but be aware that a guest busily taking notes about other guests can change the nature of a social occasion very quickly!

Where you are asked to compare, make comparisons with your own ethnic community if you are dining in the home of members of a different ethnic community. If you are dining within your ethnic community, compare with other countries, or with ethnic communities in the UK of which you may have some knowledge – and don't forget that television and film give us all a wide experience of how other cultures live. You could even do the exercise watching a television or film portrayal of a dinner party in another ethnic community (but be aware that some films are very unlike the reality they represent!).

The room

- As you go into the room, notice its size and shape. Is the room larger or smaller than such rooms would be in other ethnic communities, in a similar town or venue?

- What colours are used, and in what combinations? Are these in any way different to what you have seen in other ethnic communities?

What do you think those differences signify?

The décor

- Is the décor different in any way to the décor you would expect in other ethnic communities, in similar venues?

- If so, is it because of different materials? Style? Objects in the room?

What explanation can you think of for these differences?

The table

Notice how the table is set:

❑ Are there name-cards?

❑ How are crockery and cutlery arranged?

❑ The glasses and drinks?

❑ The butter, salt and pepper?

❑ (Are these things present in your particular dinner anyway?)

❑ The space between seats around the table, and between objects on the table?

❑ The way diners react when food is served?

The people

❑ What do you notice about how people dress?

❑ About how they enter the room, walk, stand?

❑ Can you detect any differences from other communities in what sort of people they talk to, or in the way they talk to people, or how long they talk to someone?

Body language

❑ How far away from you do people feel comfortable standing? Try to get close and see what happens. Move slightly further back and see what happens.

❑ Can you see differences from other communities in what they do with their eyes while talking? What about the forehead? Face? Gestures? Body as a whole?

Topics of conversation

❑ With what sorts of subjects do people seem to feel most comfortable and most uncomfortable?

❑ What are the 'I see' topics? Do they progress abruptly or smoothly to 'I think'/'I feel' topics?

❑ Does the host/hostess, or other people in particular, steer the conversation?

Humour

Listen carefully to the humour and jokes around the table.

□ Do you think British people place the same emphasis on humour that people in other ethnic communities do?

□ If not, in what ways is humour different?

Language

□ How loudly do people speak? Is this different to other ethnic communities with which you are familiar?

□ How fast do people speak?

□ What is the rate of flow of ideas?

□ Do people work systematically through topics – or just jump about?

□ If you are dining with people from a different ethnic community, try to imitate them in these respects. See what happens.

□ What do your dinner companions do when they can't understand something?

□ What aspects of the language strike you – for example, the number of questions, the kind of questions, the number and kind of statements, the length of sentences, the importance of precision in language or thought …

□ Do people ask questions and state opinions directly, or indirectly? Straight out, or only after a small or large amount of 'preparation'?

Silence

□ Do you think silence is regarded in this ethnic community in the same way as it is in others, or in other countries you may have visited?

Section 3
Reference Section : Face to face

In what follows we use the term 'people groups' because many come from more than one country – either because of the natural expansion of a people group beyond its original borders, or because of forced dispersion ('diaspora') through war, political oppression or other forces. Punjabi Sikhs, for example, might have the Punjab or East Africa as their country of origin and Chinese people might originate in Malaysia or Hong Kong.

The characteristics of a people group are established by culture and religion. As most people groups contain followers of more than one religion, and most religions are global, this chapter is divided into two sections. First we list people groups, and provide demographic, historical and cultural information about each group including the religions its members follow. Then we provide information about each religion, its beliefs and practices, and further information on cultural and other characteristics of that religion.

We have selected information that will be of most use to business people. Religious festivals and holidays, of course, will be significant when drawing up staff timetables in a multi-cultural business. We tell you which festivals are the most important ones for each religion and also what flexibility exists in observing them. We have not gone into detail about theology, but employers do need to be aware, for example, that Muslims are required to pray at intervals throughout the day, including working hours. We point out areas of sensitivity (Muslim women prefer to avoid any physical contact with male colleagues – and that includes handshakes), explain religious customs that may seem strange to an outsider, and highlight any other information we think business people will find useful.

The 1991 Census was the first to report ethnicity and has been used whenever no other source is quoted. Where more recent figures have been used we mention the source (where this is given as '1999', for example, we have used the Guardian Unlimited website 'A-Z of religions in the UK')[1].

---

1. http://www.guardianunlimited.co.uk/religion

We have made use of a wide range of other sources. Unlike some European countries, there have been no major reductions of UK ethnic minorities since 1991 (for example the German community in several countries decreased sharply when many Germans returned to the newly united Germany). There have been some increases (there are now 18,000 Armenians living in London, for example), but the overall situation has remained stable. The largest increase in the ethnic minority population comes from the births in ethnic communities already resident in Britain.

Because ethnic identifiers are only recent additions to censuses, it has not always been possible to obtain up to date figures for some UK ethnic communities; we have simply noted 'not known' in such cases. The problem is particularly significant where long-established groups exist and where only one partner in a dwelling belongs to the group in question. Some groups, like the Koreans, have large short-term student populations in the UK, and others, like the Australians, have very large numbers of holiday visitors to the UK who are not allowed to work while living in Britain.

The 'Pointers' sections are drawn from personal experience and a range of other sources. Such lists are prone to stereotyping. It's quite possible to meet a quietly-spoken Arab, an Australian whose speech is full of polite admiration for Britain, or a Japanese businessman who scribbles train times on a business card he has just been given. Remember, too, that many ethnic minorities in the UK have been Westernised to a greater or lesser degree, and some would be exposed to Western influences in their home countries. If in doubt play safe – if left-handed, change to your right for multicultural meals; if a man wondering whether to shake hands with a lady, wait for her to offer her hand first. The broad principles outlined here, plus common sense and tact, should get you through most situations. For intensive dealings with a particular people group, explore the specialised books mentioned in the Bibliography, p. 251.

The interviews in Section 2 contain useful information about culture, religion and etiquette in the communities to which the interviewees belong. For much more detailed descriptions and comparisons of cross-cultural issues, some valuable books are listed in the Bibliography.

People Groups

African

Mother country	African nations, eg Nigeria, Somalia
Religions	Muslim, Christian, others
Languages	Somali, Yoruba, Ibo, Hausa, others
Numbers	The 1999 *Annual Abstract of Statistics* reports 351,000 UK Black Africans

Cultural pointers

☐ Africa is a large continent; customs vary. Many are influenced by the local religions.

☐ Most Africans coming to the UK are already familiar with Western ways. If you are a guest of UK African businesses or homes, watch your hosts and do as they do.

☐ Nigerians are punctual when doing business with Westerners, use only the right hand for eating, and consider the foot to be unclean.

☐ Ghanaian children avoid eye contact with adults – it's considered aggressive to look you in the eye.

☐ If a Kenyan gives you a present, don't take it with your left hand: this disparages the gift and its giver.

☐ Moroccans often kiss each other on the cheek as a greeting – the more kisses, the closer the acquaintance.

☐ Zambians avoid physical contact between sexes when greeting each other, and also avoid extended eye contact between sexes – it could be seen as flirting.

☐ Zimbabweans regard it as very rude to point at someone.

☐ Bribery is a common business practice in several African countries. There may be ulterior motives behind that generous gift …

❏ Africans are very hospitable and expect others to be the same. Family visits to business acquaintances, unannounced and out of office hours, are not unusual.

American

Mother country	America
Religions	Christianity, with many religions practised by small religious groups and ethnic communities
Languages	American English, and the languages of ethnic communities
Numbers	Not known, but large.

Cultural pointers

❏ American business is highly entrepreneurial. Success is usually defined in material terms, and progress within companies is by achievement and results.

❏ American business people value motivation, aspiration and getting results as quickly as possible – see most business bookshops' shelves.

❏ The dominant style is informality. However the American office usually generates a lot of paper. Robert Townsend's classic *Up The Organization* (Michael Joseph, 1971) is an insider's subversive view.

❏ Humour, often boisterous, sometimes aggressive, is often used to 'oil the wheels' of a discussion.

❏ Eye contact is important whether in business or socially.

❏ Time is valued highly and meetings etc are designed to make best use of it. A short, focused trip or meeting should not be seen as rude.

❏ Signing a contract closes the deal.

❏ Most Americans treat their national flag with great respect, an attitude encouraged in schools.

❏ As in Britain, women sometimes object to having doors opened for them, etc, on the grounds that it is sexist and demeaning.

Arab

Mother country	Arabs include any Arabic-speaking peoples living in an area that extends from Mauritania in West Africa to SW Iran, including the entire North African Maghrib (Morocco, Algeria, Tunisia), Egypt and the Sudan, the Arabian Peninsula, and Syria and Iraq.
Religions	Islam is the dominant Arab religion. Other, minority, religions include Bah'ai and Zoroastrianism (Parsism), the religion of the Iranian Parsis.
Languages	Arabic
Numbers	Unknown. At least 1,500,000 Muslims live in the UK.

Cultural pointers

❑ Business is conducted at a very personal level. Arabs wish to be praised for working well; in discussion they sit much closer to you than Westerners find comfortable; in Arab countries, a businessman may hold your hand. Pulling yours away is a major *faux pas*. Eye contact is very important. (None of the foregoing, however, applies to your meetings with Arab women.) Be interested in your Arab colleagues as people and enquire about their families' well-being.

❑ Avoid controversial topics or subjects that might be regarded as depressing (such as corruption, bribes and polygamy).

❑ Westerners want to make the deal and then develop the business relationship: Arabs prefer to build a relationship of trust and then move on to selling. Be prepared to drink a lot of coffee and spend many hours in small talk before concluding a deal (this is true of most Middle Eastern countries).

❑ Arabs regard a contract as agreement in principle – subject to a business relationship developing and the Western partner being satisfactorily tested. Be aware that Arabs tend to regard a verbal commitment as worth more than a written one. 'My word is my bond' still carries much importance.

❑ Arabs enjoy negotiating and a good bargain. Don't deprive them of this pleasure.

❑ Keeping to agreed time schedules is considered less important than building relationships and bringing matters to a formal conclusion. Similarly, timekeeping on social occasions is not considered vital.

❑ In business discussion (which can get quite noisy and exuberant) strive to be seen as genuine and transparent (often speaking loudly conveys this well). Avoid anything that might be interpreted as an insult – either verbal or non-verbal (for example, just picking at a meal prepared in your honour).

❑ The Qur'an (Koran) is treated with the greatest reverence. Never put it on the floor (or anywhere lower than your feet), or anywhere that might seem demeaning. Avoid treating written Arabic casually, it may contain the name of Allah or quotations from the Qur'an – so don't clean your shoes with old newspapers.

❑ Arabs do not believe in gender equality in the Western sense: they see men and women as having different roles. In Arab countries women wear veils in public and are not often seen by Westerners who are visiting their husbands.

❑ The feet and the left hand are considered inferior. The right hand is used for eating, touching, giving gifts. Never pass anything to an Arab with your left hand, and don't let the soles of your shoes be seen (so don't sit cross-legged).

Australian

Mother country   Australia.

Religions   Australia is a secular State. The main religious groups are Christian (c. 75%) and non-religious (c. 20%).

Languages   English, though Australia has 111 living Aboriginal languages, and the 20% immigrant population retains strong cultural and linguistic diversity.

Numbers   Not known. About 417,000 live in the EU, and thousands visit the UK annually.

Cultural pointers

❑ The Australian language was formed by blending the various dialects and languages of the convict ships, was developed in the immediacy of creating a new nation, and was further enriched by aboriginal elements. Unlike British English, how you speak is not an indicator of class or education.

❑ Avoid using Australian soap operas as anything but a crude guide to Australian life (Australians do have a lot of barbecues, however).

❑ Although culturally Australia is close to Britain, the old commercial and business links disappeared when the UK joined the EEC. Australia is now aligned more with Japan (many can speak the language) and other South-East Asian countries.

❑ Australians often use derogatory terms towards the British, usually harmlessly. Casual Australian vocabulary includes several words considered swearing in Britain.

Canadian

Mother country	Canada, though the population has a high immigrant content (in 1995, 16% of the population was born abroad).
Religions	Predominantly Christian
Languages	Canada is officially bilingual (English/French)
Numbers	Not known

Cultural pointers

❑ Canadians can be as irritated when described as Americans as can New Zealanders when described as Australians. The accents are not all that similar, but beware of mistakes.

❑ A handshake plus eye contact is the standard greeting, though women sometimes prefer not to shake hands.

❑ In Quebec the French influence is very strong: greetings can be more demonstrative (a peck on the cheek between women, a mild hug between men).

❑ Courtesy is valued. Men often stand up when a woman arrives. In Quebec, eating in the street is frowned on.

Caribbean/West Indian

Mother country	Jamaica, Barbados, Trinidad, and other islands
Religions	Christian, Rastafarian; Hinduism and Islam are influential in Guyana and Trinidad.
Languages	English, Spanish, Dutch, Creole, Patois
Numbers	The *1999 Annual Abstract of Statistics* reports 531,000 UK Caribbeans

Cultural pointers

❑ There is almost no indigenous population in the Caribbean – the Caribs and Arawaks virtually disappeared soon after colonisation through conflict and disease. Caribbean culture today is almost entirely a product of European settlers, notably the sugar-plantation based economy.

❑ The different islands have separate cultural and historical identities, which give each island its own form of Creole/Patois.

❑ Rastafarians prefer natural/organic food and will not eat pork.

❑ Rastafarian women do not normally see a job as their first priority over home and motherhood.

❑ Certain colours are important to the Rastafarian population: black, symbolising the people; red, those who have died; green, the land; and yellow, the gold that was taken by others. Care should be taken in corporate design and publicity if many clients/customers/staff are Rastafarians.

Chinese

Mother country	Hong Kong, China, Malaysia, Singapore
Religions	Taoist, Buddhist, Christian
Languages	Cantonese, Mandarin
Numbers	The *1999 Annual Abstract of Statistics* reports 162,000 UK Chinese.

Cultural pointers

❑ Present your business card with two hands; use two hands to take theirs.

❑ Time (especially other people's) is valued, so is punctuality.

❑ Don't be over-familiar. Chinese people tend to hide their real feelings.

❑ The Chinese value people for their connections as much as for their personality. They consider returning favours important.

❑ They are competitive in business.

❑ Maintaining 'face' is important to Chinese people. If your view is prevailing in a meeting, provide a way out – make it easy for the others to save face.

❑ When visiting Chinese homes, it's usual to remove your shoes. Be sure to compliment your hosts on their cooking, home and command of English. The family is a strong unit, elders are respected, and mutual help is given throughout the family hierarchy.

❑ Table manners are distinctive. The Chinese eat noisily (it shows appreciation of the food), but blowing your nose when at table is considered disgusting.

❑ Avoid discussion about topics like Tiananmen Square, *Wild Swans*, and Tibet. Don't assume that intelligent and humane Chinese people will endorse every Western anti-Communist statement. The Chinese respect the government as authority.

❑ They appreciate a basic knowledge of the geography of China (or their country of origin), an interest in their cultural background, and praise for Chinese culture (sport, arts etc).

Devolved Regions:

Northern Ireland

Numbers: The population of Northern Ireland is c. 1,694,000 (2001 estimate, 1999 *Annual Abstract of Statistics*)

Languages: English, Irish. In Belfast more people speak Chinese than speak Irish.

Cultural pointers

❑ During the Troubles, Northern Ireland was often believed by outsiders to be a war-zone in which daily life was lived against the background of guns and bombs, a kind of local Sarajevo or Beirut. In fact large areas of the region have been almost untouched by conflict. When talking to the Northern Irish about their home region it's helpful to remember how much of an outsider's impression is formed by media coverage and television action film reportage, even today.

❑ People outside the region also receive most of their impressions of personalities through the media. The Reverend Ian Paisley, for example, is appreciated by many Protestants and Catholics as an effective local politician and community representative, quite separately from his well-known public persona.

❑ Everyday conversation can contain political messages and it's easy to accidentally politicise a casual encounter. 'Londonderry' can be a Loyalist signal, 'Derry' a deliberate Republican omission. Be careful with words like 'mainland Britain', 'province', 'Ulster' and 'Irish' (or 'British', for that matter). Culture can also be political: for example many committed Loyalists disparage Irish folk music, literature and even the mountains of the Irish Republic.

❑ Northern Ireland shares with Ireland a rather old-fashioned way of life, though to a lesser extent. Religious services can have a distinctly Victorian flavour.

❑ Like the Jews, the Irish are the best at telling jokes about their own culture. Irish jokes told by others carry an underlying judgement about people on the basis of their ethnicity. If business colleagues tell Irish jokes, play safe and don't join in. There is a tradition of such jokes throughout Europe (the Poles are favourite targets). They are usually directed at disadvantaged communities.

❑ In Belfast there is a thriving, successful Chinese business community.

❑ Northern Irish workers can be extremely hard working, and major mainland companies often hire them by choice. Much-publicised failures of government-sponsored start-ups are usually due to other causes.

❑ Surprisingly few people from mainland Britain visit Northern Ireland. Doing so has major benefits in business. Northern Irish people often feel that the rest of Britain regards them as unimportant and their troubles as safely out of the way. In fact the region is endlessly interesting with some stunning scenery and fascinating towns and villages. If you are planning business projects in Northern Ireland, consider holidaying there as well as making brief trips by shuttle.

Scotland

Numbers:	The population of Scotland is approximately 5,106,000 (2001 projection, 1999 *Annual Abstract of Statistics*).
Languages:	English, Scots, Gaelic

Cultural pointers

❑ Like the Irish, the Scots are the target of much ethnic humour and stereotyping. Jokes about the Scots' alleged meanness are unlikely to further business partnership.

❑ The term 'Scotch' should never be used of people: use 'Scots' or 'Scottish' and keep 'Scotch' for whisky.

❑ North Sea Oil, a growing electronics industry and political change have all fuelled a growing independence movement in Scotland. Most Scots resent London-centric business views of Scotland as a satellite province (still a common assumption even now).

❑ If you are not familiar with the Scots and Scotland, take a hard look at the map. English people often see Edinburgh and Glasgow as the farthest outposts of British culture and commerce, and points north as a giant playground or a place to keep the oilfields. In fact there are 250 miles of Scotland north of Edinburgh and a diversity of business.

❑ Scottish culture is very rich and its museums and other arts venues are world-famous: the Edinburgh International Festival is on a par with Salzburg, Milan and other world arts festivals; it is one of the world's largest cultural events. There is a National Gallery, a National Portrait Gallery, and the Royal Scottish Museum.

Wales

Numbers:	The population of Wales is approximately 2,947,000 (2001 estimate, *1999 Annual Abstract of Statistics*).
Languages	English, Welsh

Cultural pointers

❑ Wales has fewer natural resources than Scotland and is closer to London. But there is a strong popular feeling of independence and a small but active Nationalist movement.

❑ The decline of traditional industries (such as mining) has had severe effects on local economies and attempts to revive areas like the southern valleys have not always succeeded. The tourist industry is becoming increasingly important.

❑ Perhaps because of the success of tourism, Welsh culture has been weakened in recent years: certainly the tourist areas have been almost entirely Anglicised and Welsh is spoken only in parts of the country.

❑ The language is preserved by a vigorous programme of university teaching and cultural events such as the Eisteddfods.

Eastern Europeans

Numbers:	There are small UK communities from most of the Eastern European countries in Britain. Many come as students, some as economic migrants. They include people from Poland, Czech Republic, Slovakia, Hungary, Slovenia, Romania, Bulgaria, Serbia, Croatia, Bosnia, Macedonia and Albania.

Cultural pointers

❑ Forty years of communism tended to create two types of Eastern European worker: those who were inefficient and unmotivated (because state ownership meant you were essentially your own boss, so why bother?) and those who were entrepreneurial achievers (because they saw ways of beating an impersonal system). The legacy of this survives, often among those who have migrated to the UK.

❑ A third type of Eastern European is those of the pre-communist generation: often punctilious in business dealings, cultured and cosmopolitan in outlook and sharing many characteristics of the French and Germans.

❑ Western businesses involved in relief and development work are often not trusted immediately: promises have been broken too often. Eastern Europeans will sometimes make what seem to be binding agreements with several Western businesses and organisations and wait to see which of them comes up with the goods.

❑ Many Eastern Europeans arriving in the UK are overwhelmed by the British standard of living and prosperity and assume that businesses here have unlimited funds to contribute.

❑ Niceties like copyright, patents, and other intellectual and commercial property conventions are often taken very lightly.

❑ Bulgarians nod when they mean 'No' and shake their heads when they mean 'Yes'.

❑ Hungarians are immensely proud of their long cultural heritage. Relations with Romania are extremely difficult, especially over the rights of the Romanian Hungarian minority; many Hungarians disparage Romanian culture. Romanians, on the other hand, claim direct descent from the Roman armies and their place-names reflect this. Be aware that some places have names in several languages (For example Romanian Cluj-Napoca is the same as Hungarian Kolozsvar) and, as in Northern Ireland, using a particular version can be a political statement.

❑ Gypsies and Jews are often treated badly in Eastern Europe; be prepared for some explicit racism in business conversations.

❑ Mealtimes are often highly ritualised. Poles and Hungarians, for example, give the guest of honour the best place and treat him or her with elaborate courtesy. In Romania and some other countries, people commonly drink toasts at meals, a custom they often carry on when they move to the UK.

❑ If somebody offers you a drink by putting a bottle in front of you, you will usually be expected to drink the whole bottle. Merely sipping spirits is often frowned on: the glass should be drained in a single gulp. It's up to you to decide whether good manners are worth the drowsiness that might follow! UK East Europeans will usually accept the excuse that you are driving later.

French

Mother Country: France. There are large numbers of immigrant communities, sometimes illegally entered, and substantial numbers from North Africa. A growing number of British people now live full-time or part-time in France.

Numbers: Varies: numbers of French resident in the UK are augmented by the numbers who commute through the Channel Tunnel or who hold short-term posts.

Religion: Main religions are Christian, Muslim.

Languages: French. No significant regional languages.

Cultural pointers

❑ The media stereotype the French as much as they do the British. Most stereotypes contain a grain of truth. For example stock Gallic sitcom types (usually flamboyant and theatrical), ultra-sophisticated wine buffs, Maurice Chevalier with his heart on his sleeve.

❑ Meetings are set up and conducted with great formality.

❑ In discussion French people are logical, analytical and focused. Meetings can go on for a very long time. It will often be late in the meeting before the French will say what they want and how they expect to obtain it.

❑ French business people don't expect to make major decisions in meetings, but enjoy a good discussion and debate. Note that French is a precise, logical language: it's said that one cannot be vague in French.

❑ Like Arabs, they want to do business after first establishing good relationships. Once they trust you as a person, they can start doing business with you.

❏ The French enjoy the good things in life. Their cuisine is legendary, their wines renowned. They are world leaders in fashion. They enjoy holidays, whether it be the glamour of the Riviera or weekend camping (which they have made a fine art).

❏ Like the Swedes, the French once owned a great empire. Even today, they are very nationalistic. They have a long tradition of diplomacy and a presence in many conflict areas. They have adopted an international mediating role, for example in Africa and in Eastern Europe where French statesmen have visited Romania and Yugoslavia. All this influences how the French see themselves abroad.

Germans

Mother Country: Germany

Religion: Main religions are Christian, Muslim

Language: German

Numbers: Not known

Cultural pointers

❏ Signing a contract makes it binding on all parties.

❏ Germans tend to be literal-minded. They often misinterpret flamboyant or aggressive language from e.g. Americans and Australians. Humour is considered inappropriate in business discussions.

❏ Punctuality is valued highly, as is correct behaviour and good manners (always knock before entering an office).

❏ The Germans have a very developed sense of public order. Dropping litter in a German train will make you unpopular with the whole carriage. A child running around inside a tram will be rebuked by the adults present. In Britain, Germans find the major cities very dirty and public behaviour irresponsible.

❏ Young Germans understandably resent being associated with Hitler's Nazi Germany and its crimes against humanity.

❏ Be aware that though most Germans in Britain come from one of the world's most materially prosperous countries, an increasing number are economic migrants or other visitors from the old East Germany.

Greeks

Mother country	Greece, Greek Islands, Cyprus
Religions	Greek Orthodox
Languages	Greek
Numbers	1991 Census reports 14,610 (0.3% of UK population)

Cultural pointers

❑ Greeks are outgoing people and greetings are enthusiastic.

❑ Eye contact is important; not just socially but also when speaking in meetings.

❑ Nodding upwards or raising the eyebrows means 'No'. 'Yes' is indicated by shaking the head side-to-side or tilting it to one side.

❑ The Greeks do not queue.

Irish

Mother country	Ireland, but the Irish diaspora is large and many Irish come from other countries, eg USA.
Religions	Christian (predominantly Roman Catholic)
Languages	English, Irish
Numbers	Not known.

Cultural pointers

❑ Do not refer to the currency as the 'punt' – call it the Irish pound.

❑ On humour, see Devolved Regions: Northern Ireland.

❑ Irish life is slow-paced by comparison with Britain and a much more relaxed view is taken of business (the lack of signposts in many parts of Ireland is symptomatic of this approach).

Japanese

Mother country	Japan
Religions	Shinto, Buddhist, folk religion
Languages	Japanese
Numbers	Not known

Cultural pointers

❑ Traditional Japanese people avoid shaking hands and prefer to bow when greeting each other. In crowds they avoid eye contact. The Japanese value the exchange of gifts when meeting business partners.

❑ Ritual is a subtext in most business dealings, nowhere more than the formal exchange of business cards (you must receive your colleague's with both hands, look at it with admiration, place it prominently in front of you, admire it again several times during the meeting, and *never* put it in your back pocket).

❑ The Japanese consider blowing your nose in public to be as revolting as the British consider picking your nose in public to be.

❑ In business, avoiding confrontation or losing face is more important than always telling the truth. Never confront or rebuke them in public.

❑ The Japanese allow adequate time for business discussion; but each discussion has its logical stages and these must be carefully spelled out and correctly followed. Also, the Japanese work long hours; they are not clock-watchers.

❑ Visiting business contacts from Japan expect to have all their time mapped out for them. Thoughtfully allowing them time to enjoy exploring Britain on their own will be interpreted as being cold and distant towards them.

❑ Like the British, the Japanese like to feel their way towards solutions, unlike for example the French who are very logical and precise.

❑ Contracts are not considered binding but as opening moves in a developing relationship. The Japanese don't like to say 'No', so they say 'Yes'. This does not mean that they agree with you. It means that they have heard what you said.

❑ Business decisions will always be referred to higher management for approval. This can mean UK deals being held up waiting for Tokyo to agree.

❑ If you make a joke, it will be dutifully acknowledged and probably taken literally.

Jews

- Jews are a religious and an ethnic people group. See Religions: Judaism (p. 241) for information

- Orthodox Jews avoid shaking hands with the opposite sex, even when exchanging business cards. However, Israelis in general shake hands enthusiastically.

- If an Israeli (including Arab Israeli) man does not offer his hand in greeting, women should not do so – there may be religious reasons for this. A nod is an acceptable greeting.

- Israelis, like Arabs, tend to stand close to each other when talking.

- Be aware of their eating needs – 'kosher' means food prepared according to Jewish law. (The word is used in the majority community to mean 'genuine or approved'. Avoid.)

Koreans, South

Religions	Large Christian and Buddhist groups
Languages	Offical language is Korean
Numbers	Growing in the UK: eg 8,600 students in UK in 1999, over 125,000 applications received in 2000

Cultural pointers

- Many Korean customs are similar to Japanese; for example, business cards are treated with similar respect. Koreans regard themselves as better and more dedicated workers than the Japanese.

- Koreans attach great importance to saving face. They also accept jokes and humour in business dealings.

- It is relatively easy to get Koreans to sign a contract, but they do not always regard it as binding.

- Koreans prefer to avoid physical contact whenever possible, except that two members of the same sex holding hands are merely displaying friendship.

- It is considered rude to make somebody walk behind your back; it's acceptable to walk through a group of people, who are then expected to stand aside to let you through.

❏ Traditionally Koreans remove their shoes before entering somebody's home (in the UK this custom is often not observed).

❏ The elderly receive great respect. They are served first at meals, and it's usual to stand up when they enter.

❏ Avoid blowing your nose in public and don't put the tissue or handkerchief back in your pocket.

❏ Where you sit in meetings or at meals is important: wait to be shown your seat.

❏ At meals, do not fill your own glass; allow other guests to pour for you, and do the same for them. Pass food to others with your right hand. Cover your mouth with your hand when you laugh and when you use a toothpick. Start to eat only after your host has started.

New Zealanders

Mother country   New Zealand

Religions   Major religion is Christianity. 1.5% other religions

Languages   English, Maori increasingly spoken.

Numbers   Not known

Cultural pointers

❏ Don't make the common mistake of regarding Australians and New Zealanders as the same people group, or of getting the two confused. New Zealanders dislike being called Australians.

❏ New Zealand society is less culturally mixed than Australia's, and its English and Scottish roots are still very apparent.

❏ There is a large independence movement in Australia, but New Zealanders tend to value their links with Britain more.

❏ In business they are often creative and do well. Many migrate to Australia looking for work, and usually prosper.

❏ Much social interaction is governed by reserve and British/Continental practice. Handshakes, positive eye contact, moderation in speech and behaviour are all important. Put your hand over your mouth if you yawn; don't chew gum or use toothpicks in public.

❑ Relations with the Maori population are on the whole more successful than are Australia's with the Aborigines.

❑ Where Australia's commercial hinterland is Japan, other South-East Asian countries and the Far East, New Zealanders are more local to the Pacific.

Scandinavians

Various numbers of Scandinavians reside in Britain. Their religions are the main European religions.

Cultural pointers

❑ For Scandinavians, signing a contract closes the deal.

❑ Scandinavians prefer you to state time in the 24-hour clock format.

❑ Scandinavians resemble Germans in many ways; Scandinavians are somewhat more friendly and family-orientated.

❑ They are innovative and creative in looking for new products and solutions.

South Asians (People of the Indian Sub-continent)
Indians, Pakistanis, Bangladeshi, Nepalese, Bhutanese, Sri Lankans and Maldive Islanders

The South Asian community is highly entrepreneurial, especially in the retailing sector: South Asians own approximately two-thirds of all UK retail outlets. But they are active in other business sectors too: many work in the computer and IT industries and other advanced technology markets, and they are a major element in the Health Service and the medical sector generally. They have sometimes experienced considerable social disadvantage in the UK (Asians are more likely to be unemployed than are the majority community, for example), yet they include some of the richest men and women in Britain, regularly appearing in 'rich lists': on the other hand, as is the case with many minority communities, their representation in public life is not proportionate to their numbers.

The UK South Asian population is around 1.85 million, and its disposable income is between £7.5 and £10 billion.[2] The main South Asian people groups in the UK are:

INDIANS

Numbers:	Britain has the largest concentration of Indians of any single country in the world (apart from India). Leicester is the second largest Indian city outside India, after Durban. The *1999 Annual Abstract of Statistics* reports 929,000 UK Indians.
Mother Country:	The Indian States. Some significant UK communities are Bengalis from NE India around Calcutta), Punjabis (from the Punjab in North India/Pakistan, and also from East Africa), and Gujaratis (from Gujarat in NW India and from East Africa).
Religions:	The three major religions of India are Islam, Sikhism and Hinduism: Sikhs come chiefly from the Punjab. There are also Buddhist, Jain, Parsi and Christian communities.
Languages:	The official language of India is Hindi. Other languages include Sylheti (mainly spoken by Bangladeshis), Punjabi (Eastern Dialect) and Gujarati.

Cultural pointers

❑ Indian culture has a long history; its literature pre-dates Anglo-Saxon literature, and Indians were pioneers in the film industry.

❑ Few UK minority ethnic communities maintain such close economic two-way links with their mother country; Non-Resident Indians (NRIs) are significant in the Indian economy. Much UK Indian business depends on the scattered world-wide Indian 'diaspora'.

❑ The Indian community is still strongly based on the family and the extended family, and so is Indian business, which tends to look to the extended family in preference to high street banks. The family focus

---

2. Updated estimates from South Asian Development Partnership based on the 1992 SADP Report *The £5 billion Corridor*.

can lead to problems when the founder retires or dies and family succession places inadequate people at the head of the business.

❑ Personal and family honour are highly valued and embezzlement; reneging on debts etc is regarded as a family disgrace and is rare.

PAKISTANIS

Numbers:	The *1999 Annual Abstract of Statistics* reports 580,000 UK Pakistanis. They live mainly in the 'South Asian corridor'.
Mother Country:	Pakistan, East Africa.
Religions:	Muslim, Hindu, Sikh, Christian.
Languages:	The official language of Pakistan is Urdu. Punjabi is also spoken.

BANGLADESHIS

Numbers:	The *1999 Annual Abstract of Statistics* reports 208,000 UK Bangladeshis.
Mother Country:	Bangladesh
Religions:	Muslim, Hindu, Buddhist, Christian
Languages:	Bengali, Sylheti

Thai/Malaysians

Numbers are difficult to obtain, as many in this group come to Britain from countries that are not their country of origin.

❑ There are three main Malaysian people groups – Chinese, Indian and Malay. Customs vary between them. Chinese and Indian Malaysians usually follow the customs of their mother country; refer to the appropriate sections in this chapter for more information.

❑ For Malays, clearing your throat and blowing your nose at mealtimes are considered so rude that it is usual to do so in the bathroom.

❑ Use only the right hand for eating, and for handing food to others (when the left hand is sometimes used to support the right).

❑ Malays are polite and deferent in business.

❑ Pointing your feet at another person is considered highly insulting (an important consideration when setting up conference and meeting rooms – or hotel bedrooms for that matter). Also, avoid placing anything of importance on the floor or below your feet.

❑ Thais are not business people by disposition and most business is in the hands of Thai Chinese. There are very strong links with America.

Spanish

Mother country   Spain, Latin America

Religions   Christian (mainly Roman Catholic), Muslims, Jews.

Languages   Spanish, with regional versions (Spanish is the third-most used language in the world)

Cultural pointers

❑ The Spanish pay remarkably little attention to social class.

❑ The quality of the person wanting to do business with them is of more interest to them than the deal being offered.

❑ In a survey published in March 1990 by the *Financial Times*, 11,000 students from all over Europe were polled. 53% of Spaniards thought business was immoral (and 92% wanted a career in business). 63% were prepared to work all hours to achieve success.

❑ Spaniards respect aggressive business dealings.

❑ Honour is of the greatest importance, and Spaniards' dignity is important to them.

Religions

Why include religion in a book about business? There are three main reasons.

❑ We provide basic information that employers and all doing business with religious groups need to know. For example, are your employees likely to require time off for religious observances? Are there sensitivities affecting workplace and amenity provision?

❏ In many ethnic communities the whole of life revolves around religion, and that includes running, or working for, a business.

❏ Attitudes to business ethics and business practice are often dictated by the values and beliefs of the religion. Zoroastrians, for example, are known for their integrity and trustworthiness in business because those values are required by their religion.

We have included the main religions of UK ethnic minorities, allocating space in proportion to the number of British followers of each religion.

Baha'i

Numbers and distribution

There are about 6,000 followers of the Baha'i religion in the UK [1999].

Main beliefs and principles

Baha'i's originated in Shi'a Islam and in the Babi sect founded in the mid-nineteenth century by Mirza Hoseyn Ali Nuri (called 'Baha Ullah' – 'Glory of God'. His 'forerunner' was Mirza Ali Muhammad, called the Bab (Gateway), a Persian who taught the coming of a new prophet. His followers took the name of Baha'i. Baha'i teaches the unity of humanity and of all religions, which are stages in God's plan to instruct humanity; the founders of the great religions were manifestations of God. Baha'is are dedicated to abolishing class, racial prejudice and religious intolerance. From the beginning Baha'i has suffered severe persecution. Baha'i has no initiation ceremony, sacraments or clergy. Members must fast regularly, obtain parental consent for marriage, and abstain from narcotics, alcohol, and mind-affecting substances.

Scriptures

The writings of the Bab, Baha Ulla and Abd ol-Baha (Baha Ullah's oldest son) are considered sacred.

Place of worship

Members congregate in temples, but there are no rituals: worship consists of the recitation of the scriptures of all religions.

Social aspects

Strict dietary laws (see above) are maintained. Members have a high regard for social ethics and universal harmony, which is reflected in relationships.

Business aspects

Members are obligated to attend each Nineteen Day Feast. The feasts do not integrate into the normal calendar, so special arrangements will be needed. Normal consideration for dietary and ethical sensitivities apply.

The calendar

The Bab declared a calendar of 19 months of 19 days plus 4 extra days (5 in leap years). Every month begins with the Nineteen Day Feast – a local festival of prayers, scripture reading, cultivating community spirit and personal relationships. All members must attend. Other events:

Naw-Ruz (March 21)	New Year's Day
Ridvan (April 21-22)	Commemorating Baha Ullah's decaration of his mission.
Declaration of the Bab (May 23)	Celebrating Mirza Ali Muhammad's declaration of his mission as forerunner of Baha Ullah
Ascension of Baha Ullah (May 29)	
Martyrdom of the Bab (July 9)	
Birthday of the Bab (October 20)	Celebrates Mirza Ali Muhammad's birth in 1819
Birthday of Baha Ullah (November 12)	

Buddhism

Numbers and distribution

Buddhism has many followers who may not be attached formally to the Buddhist religion. UK Buddhist numbers are between 30,000 and 130,000. There are 134 Buddhist groups and 55 Buddhist centres [1999].

Mahayana Buddhism is found in China, Vietnam, Korea and Tibet; Japanese Zen Buddhism derives from it. Theravada Buddhism is found in Sri Lanka and South-East Asia.

Main beliefs and principles

Buddhism teaches a 'middle way' and an eight-fold path to enlightenment – right views, aspirations, speech, conduct, livelihood, effort, mindfulness, and meditation. Buddhism was founded by Siddhartha Guatama, the Buddha ('Enlightened One'), between 500 and 350 BC, who taught Four Noble Truths of which the fourth advocated the eight-fold path as a way to enlightenment and nirvana (release from one's transitory human existence). Theravada Buddhism goes back to the most ancient traditions and teaches rules and community regulations to lead to arhatship, the highest spiritual attainment. Mahayana Buddhism draws on later traditions and practises compassion to others. The esoteric and highly ritualised Tantric Buddhism arose in India in the 7th Century AD.

Scriptures

Theravada Buddhist read the *Tipitaka* (Three Baskets), with sections on discipline, discourses and scholasticism. Mahayana Buddhists also use texts that appeared between the 2nd century BC and the 2nd century AD.

Place of worship

Buddhists worship in temples and Buddhist monks enter monasteries. There are 55 Buddhist centres in the UK.

Social aspects

Tolerance is a characteristic of most Buddhist teaching. However, certain topics that are often joked about are of great concern to Buddhists: the protection of all life, however apparently insignificant, is one. Conversations about rat poison and exterminating wasps could cause genuine distress.

Business aspects

No real implications for business.

The calendar

Parinirvana (15 February)	This marks the final passing of the Buddha.
Wesak (29 May)	A celebration of the birthday, enlightenment and death of the Buddha

Dhammacakka/Asala (28 July)	Commemorates the first sermon of the Buddha, at Benares in India
Bodhi Day (8 December)	Celebrates the Buddha's attainment of nirvana.

Christianity

Numbers and distribution

Missionary outreach from the Christian West and more recently from countries like Korea and Nigeria means that most UK people groups include a Christian element. Christianity has tended to grow under persecution and previously atheist countries like Albania and China are seeing major growth. Britain's status as a nominally Christian nation makes it hard to establish the numbers in Britain from Census returns. The *UK Christian Handbook* estimates the total church membership of Britain at just under 6,000,000. There are a number of divisions (Protestant, Roman Catholic, Orthodox etc) and denominations within those divisions (Anglican, Methodist, Pentecostal etc). Christianity is the constitutionally established religion of Britain. It is growing especially in the black minority communities.

Main beliefs and principles

Christianity has its roots in the Jewish faith. It was founded by Jesus Christ, who commanded his disciples to tell the world about his life, death and resurrection. The Christian calendar dates from his birth. Christians believe in one God, the Creator. The human race is spiritually fallen and cannot meet God's standards of perfect love and perfect purity and is therefore under God's righteous judgement. God, in the person of Jesus Christ, has rescued humanity from this state by coming into this world and dying by crucifixion – thus taking on himself God's wrath. He rose from the dead – thus validating his power to save. Christians believe that these events enable them to live with God forever (definitions of 'heaven' and 'hell' vary). The Communion (Mass/Eucharist) is a sacramental memorial of Christ's death and resurrection. Christians believe that having received salvation for free, they need do nothing to earn it, though Christians will want to please God, live holy lives and bring others to worship him. Evangelism and personal witness are priorities. Different systems of priesthood are used in different church traditions.

Scriptures

Christians acknowledge the authority of the Old and New Testaments, which together form the Bible, a collection of 66 books written over several centuries before and after Christ's birth. Roman Catholics and some others also recognise the 'Apocryphal' Scriptures. Widely used Prayer Books, Missals, Creeds etc do not have the status of Scripture.

Place of worship

'Church' for Christians means the people, not the building. A variety of premises is used, from cathedrals and churches to rooms in people's homes. Nothing is needed to make a location suitable for worship.

Social aspects

Christians believe that Jesus is the only way to God, but most Christians respect other people's right to their own beliefs. Modern Britain is not always so generous in the other direction. Care with general conversation (sexual topics, profanity etc) should be taken when with devout Christians and many topics taken lightly in today's culture (blasphemy, extra-marital sex, the occult and matters such as Hallowe'en) are sensitive areas for Christians. Many modern jokes and a great deal of media entertainment are offensive to Christians, as they are to several other religions.

Business aspects

Ethical issues tend to influence business practice to a significant degree. A major problem for many Christians is Sunday Trading, which as for some other religions prevents attendance at Sunday worship: this is a matter of civil liberty as well as personal consideration. Some Christians do not drink alcohol, or smoke, and many will not engage in business activities on Sunday. A business conference occupying an entire weekend is problematic for many Christians, though a Sunday morning break to allow church attendance will often resolve matters.

The calendar

The main Christian holidays are also national public holidays and do not interfere with business commitments. Most Christians will be willing to occasionally forego observing them in case of special needs such as maintaining essential public services.

Lent (March)	Forty days of preparation for Easter, usually involving some form of self-denial. All the Easter festivals from Lent to Pentecost depend on the date of Easter, which changes each year.
Good Friday (preceding Easter Sunday: April)	The memorial of Jesus' crucifixion.
Easter Sunday (April)	The celebration of the resurrection of Jesus Christ, and the major festival in the Christian calendar. A state bank holiday follows.
Ascension Day (May)	The celebration of Jesus' ascension to heaven, forty days after Easter.
Pentecost/Whitsun (June)	The celebration of the sending of the Holy Spirit and the founding of the church, ten days after the Ascension.
Christmas (25 December)	Celebrates the birth of Jesus Christ (though the actual date is not known). Preceded by Advent, a preparation for Christmas, and followed by a Boxing Day, a state bank holiday.

Confucianism

Numbers and distribution

Difficult to estimate, as Confucianism is a philosophy rather than a religion. It is found almost exclusively in the Chinese community.

Main beliefs and principles

Confucianism is an ancient moral philosophy followed for the past 2,000 years in China. Its founder Confucius lived after the six books of Confucian instruction were written (see below). He taught ancestor worship and himself became the object of worship. His sayings became the basis of Confucianism.

Five virtues are taught: *Jen*, or benevolence and courtesy; *Li*, or respect; *Yi*, or duty; *Chih*, or wisdom and knowledge; and *Hsin*, or integrity and trustworthiness.

Confucius was inspired by the concept of Heaven, but that of God is barely articulated. Consequently Confucians often also follow a religion.

Taoism, China's other philosophical religion, was founded by Lao-Tzu, whose *Tao Te Ching* is a very influential book. Taoism teaches a of inaction and a turning away from a goal-directed life.

Scriptures

The *Confucian Analects* collects sayings of Confucius and is the foundation of Confucian belief. Six other books are central: The Book of Changes (the well-known aid to divination, *I Ching*); The Book of History; The Book of Poetry; The Book of Rites; The Book of Music; The Spring and Autumn Annals

Business aspects

Concepts drawn from these belief systems can influence the way a Chinese business operates. Great emphasis on personal trustworthiness and respect for authority are Confucian hallmarks. Aggressive American-style goals-focused strategy will not make a big impact on a Taoist.

Hinduism

Numbers and distribution

Hinduism is the majority religion of India. Between 400,000 and 550,000 Hindus live in Britain [1999], an increase of 40% since 1975. They live in London (especially Wembley and Harrow), Birmingham, Coventry and Leicester. The biggest Hindu temple in Europe is in Neasden, London.

Main beliefs and principles

Hinduism is a civilisation (the word comes from the Persian word for 'Indian') and a religion. It has no founder or creeds. Over 3,000 years Hinduism has grown, drawing on many traditions and religions. The ultimate High God is Brahman. There are also numerous lesser gods including Vishnu (the Preserver), Krishna (the most popular of the gods and featuring in many religious epics) and Shiva (the Destroyer). Folk Hinduism is essentially polytheist. Educated Hindus often see the lesser gods as different aspects of the High God, Brahman. One can be a Hindu and also follow another religion.

For the Hindu, everything is integrated. God is in your books and in everything you do. Conversation is often punctuated by phrases such as 'By the grace of God' and 'Thank God'. Everything is God-driven. God is One, but called by many names. Hindus believe that there are many paths to the one God, and are tolerant of other faiths, though in modern India militant Hindus have campaigned violently against Muslims and Christians.

The Law of Karma decrees that human beings are accountable for what they do and will reap the consequences of their wrongdoings. Reincarnation is a cycle that continues until one is liberated from the effects of karma. This doctrine is connected to the Hindu caste system, a complex ordering of society that until recently rigidly separated Hindu social groups and especially determined which marriages were allowable. Hindus are guided by seven 'sacred instructions', the last three being: Always speak the Truth; Always do your Duty; Always read the Scriptures. The concept of *dharma*, or duty, is central to Hindu beliefs and practice.

The cow is considered sacred, and so is the River Ganges in India, washing in which is considered to be spiritually cleansing.

Scriptures

The *Vedas* are ancient writings compiled by the Great Veda Vyas. Among them are the *Upanishads*, which contain an early statement of the doctrine of reincarnation. The chief holy book is the *Bhagavad-Gita*, contained in the epic *Mahabharata*. The *Rig Veda*, a hymnal, is the world's oldest religious literature that is still in use; it was completed by c900 BC.

Place of worship

The Hindu temple is called a 'Mandir'. Hindus also make a shrine in their homes and light a candle there each day. They pray to the sun at dawn. Watering the sacred plant, Tulsi, is a form of worship. Temple worship is not compulsory. Hindus worship individually and as families, not usually in congregations.

Social aspects

Hindus usually dress modestly; married women often wear the *bindi* on their forehead to show they are married. Hindus have a Personal, a Complementary, and a Family or Sub-Caste name. There is no exact equivalent to British surnames; the last name can cover more than one family. Nor are there exact equivalents to Mr, Mrs etc. When addressing Hindus, 'Shri' (Mr), 'Shrimati' (Mrs) and 'Kumari' (Miss) can be used. The middle name is sometimes used to show respect; and 'Devi', 'Kumari' or 'Wati' can replace the last name for women. A wife will often refer to her husband as 'Mr ...'.

They are hospitable people but are sometimes reluctant to accept invitations from strangers or member of other ethnic communities, being unsure how to behave. However, they do not expect invitations in return when they have entertained visitors. Guests in Hindu homes are expected to eat everything offered. It is usual for the meal to be served as long as two hours after arrival. Hindus do not eat beef and many are vegetarian (some do not eat eggs), so care is needed when offering food.

Traditional signs of respect include touching a respected person's feet.

Hindus have a high view of marriage and divorce is considered a disgrace to the family. Arranged marriages have a success rate that compares well with the high failure-rate of modern British marriages; do not assume that all young Hindus are opposed to it.

Business aspects

Handshakes are rare in Hindu circles, and then only between men. Touching one's hands together and raising them to the forehead – the *namaste* – is the preferred way of greeting women.

The central importance of the extended family has business implications. Many Hindu companies are owned by the family rather than by individual family members. Be aware that unexpected (because elderly or distant) family members may be very influential in the business. The workforce is often considered to be an extension of the extended family, and is looked after comprehensively; an unwillingness to allow Trade Union membership may be because the family considers that workers are treated better as they are.

Because worship is home-centred and Hinduism has many variants, it is unlikely that special arrangements will be needed to allow religious observance.

The calendar

Dates of Hindu religious festivals vary according to the lunar calendar. Different regions have local festivals as well as the main festivals, which are:

Shivatri (February or March)	Celebrates the birthday of Lord Shiva, a principal deity.
Holi (March or April)	Ancient spring harvest festival, marked by bonfires. Hindus throw coloured water and brightly coloured powder at each other.

Ramnavani (Late spring)	A festival celebrating the birthday of Lord Rama.
Raksha Bandhan (August)	A celebration of brotherhood and sisterhood, though not exclusively blood relations.
Janmashtami (August or September)	A major festival celebrating the birthday of Lord Krishna. Particularly significant to the Hare Krishna group.
Navratri and *Dashera* (October)	Two celebrations of the Mother Goddess and the triumph of good over evil. *Navrati* means 'nine nights' (of folk dancing and worship), culminating in *Dashera*, 'the tenth day' – considered by Hindus as a very good time to start a new business.
Divali, (October or November, shortly after *Dashera*)	'The festival of lights', a major festival regarded by many Hindus as the end of the year. It somewhat resembles Christmas: visiting friends, giving presents, wearing new clothes and decorating the home with candles and oil lamps. The festival is a time for emphasising knowledge over ignorance, right over wrong, light over darkness. It is associated with the Indian epic drama *Ramayana* and its stories of Rama and Sita. It is followed next day by:
Annukuta	The start of the Hindu New Year, when sweets and food are offered at the temple.

Islam (Muslims)

Numbers and distribution

There are around 1,500,000 Muslims in Britain (more than double the 1975 number); around 990,000 are active members [1999]. There are significant numbers of Muslims (in decreasing order of membership) in the Pakistani, Indian, Bangladeshi, Arab, African and English communities. Muslims can be found in the Asian 'corridor' – large populations in the West Midlands, West Yorkshire, Bradford and Lancashire, and also in Greater London and in Central Scotland. There are two main Muslim groups: Sunni Muslims (90% of world Islam) follow the example of the first four 'rightly guided' caliphs, and recognise four sources of Islamic law of which one is the Qur'an. Shia Muslims recognise the authority of *imams*, who are interpreters of the Qur'an.

Main beliefs and principles

Muslims believe that their religion was revealed to the Prophet Muhammad in 622 AD. It is usual to add the words 'Peace Be Upon Him' (often abbreviated to 'PBUH') to his name.

'*Islam*' means 'submission'. Muslims believe that one must live in submission to the will of the one God (Allah). Islam – by which Muslims mean not so much a religious label as a way of life and a pattern of legal, moral and social behaviour, revealed by God to his prophets – is the one true religion that has always existed. Muslims believe in the one-ness of God, the equality of mankind, man's innate innocence (no original sin), and that religion and politics are intertwined. The 'five pillars' of Islam include Muhammad's status as prophet of God, prayers (*salat*) said five times each day, and a tax, *zakat*, which is distributed to the poor.

Muslims are required to make a pilgrimage (*hadj*) to Mecca (in Saudi Arabia) during their lifetime, if they have the health and financial resources to do so. The title *Hadji* or *Hajji* indicates somebody who has made the pilgrimage.

Islam believes that all mankind is equal and recognises followers of some other religions, notably Christians and Jews, as 'People of the Book'. It has no doctrine of incarnation, though Jesus Christ is respected as a prophet.

There are many fundamentalist movements world-wide that wish to inaugurate the Islamic *sharia* law in their countries, and some militant Islamic movements that are aggressively committed to world conversion. In the UK, separatist fundamentalist Muslim groups have attracted disproportionate press coverage. Our interview with Mohammad Ali (p. 88) illustrates a different Muslim view of multi-culturalism.

Scriptures

The *Qur'an* (Koran), which Muslims believe to be the actual word of God, is the primary authority on spiritual and material matters. The *Hadith* is a collection of the words and deeds of Muhammad.

Place of worship

Muslims worship in the mosque, which usually has a prominent place from which Muslins are called to prayer five times daily.

Social aspects

Muslims must eat *halal* food; meat prepared in other ways is *haram* (unlawful). They do not drink alcohol. Social occasions or business entertaining will require obvious planning, but offering a devout Muslim food containing even gelatine or other meat products, or a sherry trifle, for example, will cause embarrassment.

Practising Muslims are sensitive to how women dress. The garment should cover and should not reveal the shape of the body. A practising Muslim woman will avoid unnecessary physical contact with men outside the family – this includes handshakes. Muslim girls at non-Muslim schools will wish to wear the headscarf as well as any uniform; conflicts can arise. Great care is needed when discussing fashion, films or similar topics with Muslims especially if women are present.

Be aware that issues such as the *fatwa* against Salman Rushdie revolve around extremely detailed theological issues to do with the nature of Qur'anic revelation. It's not a simple issue of censorship, and requires considerable homework if one is to understand why Muslims were so angry about Rushdie's *The Satanic Verses*. It is not a subject for casual conversation with Muslims.

Gambling is forbidden. This includes the National Lottery, although many Muslims do take part. Similarly, though alcohol is forbidden in Islam, many Muslims own off-licence stores and pubs. It is dangerous to assume that what one Muslim does is typical of others, even in the same group: if you are part of a mixed group of Muslims and somebody begins to talk about the Lottery, don't rush to join in the conversation: the rest of the group may disapprove strongly, especially if they are practising Muslims.

Implications for business

Good practice when employing Muslims means allowing them time to pray (the time-slot is quite wide, so it is usually possible to arrange prayer times around normal work breaks). Consideration should be given during the Ramadan fast, so that Muslims do not have to watch non-Muslims eating as usual – this may mean arranging separate recreational accommodation. Devout Muslims are offended by sexually suggestive material such as pin-up calendars; staff may need to be encouraged to be sensitive to their Muslim colleagues.

Company practice should be flexible so that employees are not prevented from religious observance. In 1998 *The Muslim News* reported the case of a female employee of McDonald's who was told to remove her head covering or lose her job. The reason given was Health and Safety requirements. Where compromise is possible, it should be adopted. For example, time off should be negotiated for observing major festivals such as *Eid ul-Fitr* (see below). In the wider area of business discussions it's important to recognise that Islamic law forbids *riba* (interest). This affects many areas of business, as we saw in relation to Islamic banking (p. 43).

The calendar

Dates of festivals are calculated according to the lunar calendar and the date of Mohammad's flight to Medina. In the Christian calendar this happened in 622 AD. Muslims call that year AH 1. So in the Christian calendar's year 2000, the Muslim New Year of AH 1421 began on 5 April.

Ashura (10 Muharram, the first month in the Calendar)	Particularly important to Shi'a Muslims. *Ashura* is the anniversary of the death of Imam Hussein, who was martyred on the plain of Kerbala. Hussein, grandson of the Prophet Mohammad, was opposed to moral corruption in the city of Baghdad. The anniversary of his death is the most solemn and sorrowful day in the Shi'a Muslim calendar.
Ramadan (or *Ramzan*)	Perhaps the best-known Muslim observance. A month's fast to commemorate the first revelation of the Q'ran to Mohammad.
Lailat al-Qadr	The 27th night of Ramadan, and a very sacred time; Muslims are required to spend it in prayer and worship.
Eid ul-Fitr	The day of the end of Ramadan is a festive celebration called which is a time of special prayers, giving of presents, visiting friends and wearing new clothes. A Muslim will usually take one or two days off work to celebrate *Eid ul-Fitr*.
Eid ul-Adha	A festival at the end of *Haj*. It lasts four days and includes animal sacrifice, recalling Abraham's sacrifice of a ram.
Milad al-Nabin	Celebrates the birthday of Mohammad.

Jainism

Numbers and distribution

There are approximately 25,000 Jains in Britain. Almost all Jains live in India and the total world membership is around 3,000,000.

Main beliefs and principles

Jains do not believe in creation; the universe is eternal. History is cyclical, and each cycle brings twenty-four *Tirthankaras* ('fordmakers') who are to help others across the river of transmigration. The last fordmaker, Mahavira, was a contemporary of the Buddha. There are similarities in his life to that of Gandhi, who admired Jainism.

Jainism teaches that full salvation is only possible by starving oneself to death at the end of one's life (as Mahavira did). *Karma* is the result of action, and clouds the soul; it is acquired by materialism, anger and greed, worldliness and religious error. It can be shed by the renunciation of all activity; the vows of a Jain monk are five vows of renunciation. The worst of all karma-inducing activity is the taking of life, and Jains will go to great length to avoid harming even insects. The reward of a life freed from karma and ended correctly is *nirvana*, or eternal bliss.

Scriptures

The Svetambara canon is the written version 45 orally preserved texts.

Place of worship

Jains worship in temples, in which images of the fordmakers are found. Many Jains pray to Hindu Gods and put images of them in their temples.

Implications for business

Jains are vegetarian. Their prohibition against taking life means that their choice of work is limited. Jains tend to work in commerce and money-lending and some have prospered as merchants and bankers.

Judaism

Numbers and distribution

Judaism is a faith and also an ethnicity. There are 330,000 Jews in Britain – the second largest Jewish community in Europe [1999]. There are three main Jewish groups. The Orthodox observe strict dress and dietary rules; they observe the Sabbath on Saturday and are traditionalists in teaching and practice. Reform Jews have adapted to contemporary circumstances, and Progressive Jews follow a synthesis of Judaism and liberal political and social thought. Most British Jews are from the European Ashkenazic tradition, which included Liberal and Progressive Judaism, with a smaller Sephardic community whose origins are in Spain and Portugal.

The majority of UK Jews live in Greater London. There are significant communities in Manchester, Leeds and Glasgow.

Main beliefs and principles

Jews believe that as an ethnic group and a religious faith they are the descendants of Abraham and receive the benefits of the covenant God made with him c2000 BC. Judaism is a religion of ethical monotheism; Jews believe that as the Chosen People they are a witness to God throughout the centuries to the peoples of the world. Judaism does not proselytise strongly.

Scriptures

Judaism's main spiritual guide is the Torah, the Five Books of Moses (the same five books that begin the Christian Bible), which contains early Jewish history and Mosaic law.

Place of worship

Jews worship in synagogues. The UK Central Synagogue is in London.

Social aspects

Jews have a legendary sense of humour and a distinct Jewish view of life. It is best to let them tell the Jewish jokes – it avoids offence and they are much better at it anyway. Weekends are dominated by the Sabbath, which begins at sunset on Friday and continues on to Saturday. Home and family are the religious and social core of Jewish life. Jews observe strict dietary laws deriving from the status of food as 'clean' or 'unclean' (they do not eat pork, for example).

Business aspects

Jews are not allowed to work during the weekly Sabbath and the main religious festivals, which (because Jews count days from one evening to the next) begin on the evening before the calendar date of the festival. A practising Jew does not do his daily work on any of the festivals listed in the table below, and non-Jewish businesses with Jewish employees need to bear this in mind when planning. There are also a number of minor festivals that do not prevent Jews from working. These include *Chanukah* (December, eight days commemorating the re-dedication of the Second Temple in Jerusalem in c.168 BC); *Purim* (February or March, one day, commemorating the deliverance of the Jews from the Persian empire in the time of Esther); and *Tisha Be'av* (July or August, a one-day fast commemorating the destruction of the First and Second Temples).

The calendar

The calendar is reckoned by lunar and solar periods, so festivals move their date from year to year.

The Sabbath	Begins at sundown each Friday evening with the recitation of the prayer *Kiddush* at the family meal.
The year begins with the 'High Holy Days', beginning (in September or October, at the start of the Jewish month Tishri), with:	
Rosh Ha-Shanah	The Jewish new year. A sober and penitent festival, it is intended to set the spiritual priorities of the year and to urge self-examination and repentance. It inaugurates the ten days of atonement.
Yom Kippur (Day of Atonement)	The culmination of the ten days of atonement. It is the most important Jewish fast. It lasts for twenty-four hours and includes five separate synagogue services, the first being *Kol Nidre*, the setting aside of vows.
Sukkot (Festival of Tabernacles, September or October)	This lasts for eight days. The first of the three Jewish harvest festivals, it commemorates the Jews' forty years of tent-dwelling in the wilderness as Moses led them from Egypt to the Promised land. Devout Jews each year construct *Sukkah*, or dwellings made of leafy branches, and eat in them during the festival.
Simhat Torah (Rejoicing in the Law)	Follows immediately after the eighth day of *Sukkot*, it celebrates the Jewish Law and the Scriptures. (*pto ...*)

Hanukkah (Feast of Dedication)	The last of the autumn holidays, it commemorates the Maccabean victory over the Syrian army in 165 BC, in which Judas Maccabeus re-secured the Temple for Jewish worship.
Pesach (Passover. March or April)	An eight-day period commemorating the Exodus of the Jews from Egypt. On the first two nights families eat the *seder* meal, a symbolic re-enactment accompanied by readings that explain the significance of the various parts of the meal
Shavuot (The Feast of Weeks – Pentecost)	The last spring festival of the Jewish calendar, seven weeks after *Pesach* begins: it commemorates the giving of the Torah to Moses on Mount Sinai. In the past the seven weeks have sometimes been observed, like the Christian Lent, as a period of austerity and self-denial.

Orthodox Churches

Numbers and distribution

There are Greek Orthodox and Russian Orthodox communities in Britain, governed by the Archbishops of Thyateira and of Berlin respectively. UK membership of the Greek Orthodox Church is 350,000 [1999]. Russian Orthodox churches are in London, Woking, Felixstowe, Liverpool and Yorkshire. There are Greek Orthodox communities throughout the UK.

Main beliefs and principles

The Orthodox Church is a Christian tradition going back to before the Reformation. The Eastern Orthodox church was established in 1054 when the Great Schism separated the Greek and Latin churches over the issue of leadership, the Greek, Russian, Syrian, Armenian, Serbian and Coptic churches are all Orthodox churches within the Eastern tradition

The core beliefs are those of Christianity, and are drawn from Holy Scriptures and Holy Tradition. The seven 'Ecumenical Councils and Creeds' are important authorities.

Scriptures

The Bible.

Place of worship

Churches and chapels.

Social aspects, business aspects

See Christianity

Main holy days and festivals

See also Christianity. Note fixed dates for Easter Day (Pascha), April 11; Ascension Day, May 21; and Pentecost, May 23.

Epiphany (January 6)	The first manifestation of Jesus to the Gentiles
January 7	Russian Orthodox Christmas
Advent (November 30)	The beginning of the preparation for Christmas
Christmas Day (December 25	January 7 in the Eastern Calendar.

Rastafarianism

Numbers and distribution

Rastafarian numbers in the UK are unknown. Almost all Rastafarians belong to the Afro-Caribbean community. Many UK Rastafarians are not associated with the worldwide governing bodies, so practice can vary within Britain.

Main beliefs and principles

Rastafarianism began in 1953 when its beliefs were first formally stated. Members believe that the black peoples are the reincarnation of the Children of Israel, that Africa is their true home and heaven on earth, and that former emperor of Ethiopia, Haile Selassie I, was the Messiah and the champion of the black races and can still be known spiritually, as 'Jah'. (Haile Selasse, before being crowned, was Ras ('Prince') Tafari). In its earliest form, Rastafarianism taught that ill-treatment by the white community over the centuries was divine punishment for sin, and looked to an eventual repatriation to Africa where white people would be their servants. Today Africa is still at the heart of their teaching but repatriation is less taught. Rastafarians reject Afro-Caribbean, European and Christian cultural models and seek to develop a lifestyle that expresses their beliefs, especially their ideal of world harmony. Singing and drumming are important in Rastafarianism.

Scriptures

Parts of the Christian Bible are accepted as Scriptures.

Place of worship

None. Rastafarians meet in each others' houses for discussion and debate.

Social aspects

Rastafarians wear dreadlocks (matted locks of hair) and do not comb their beards. Many are vegetarian and eat only organic food, and the smoking of marijuana is a religious sacrament. Pork is prohibited, and many will not drink alcohol. Marriage ceremonies are not used, and cohabitation is treated as marriage, though there is a major emphasis on faithfulness within that relationship. There are no special ceremonies at death, which Rastafarians believe to be an illusion.

Business aspects

Dress, appearance, dietary rules and the religious use of narcotics (marijuana) all require sensitive understanding. Rastafarians do not work on 23 July, Haile Selassie's birthday.

Main holy day and festivals

The calendar is based on the Ethiopian calendar, which begins on 11 September and has 13 months, the last of which has six days.

Birthday of Emperor Haile Selassie (July 23)	One of the holiest days in the Rastafarian calendar
Birthday of Marcus Garvey (17 August)	Marcus Garvey founded the 'Back to Africa' movement that was influential in the early 1950s. Almost as important a celebration as Haile Selassie's birthday.
September 11	The Ethiopian New Year
Coronation of Haile Selassie (2 November)	One of the holiest days in the Rastafarian calendar.

Sikhism

Numbers and distribution

There are around 500,000 Sikhs in Britain [1999] with concentrations in Birmingham, Bradford, Cardiff, Coventry, Glasgow, Leeds, Leicester, Greater London especially Southall, and Wolverhampton. Membership has tripled since 1975.

Sikhism was founded in the Indian Punjab in the fifteenth century by Guru Nanak, the first of the Ten Gurus of whom Sikhs are disciples. Sikh society is organised along business or professional lines (unlike the caste system in Hinduism). The main groups are *Bhattras* (traders), *Ramgharias* (craftsmen) and *Jats* (agriculturalists).

Bhattras were early arrivals in Britain: Sikh door-to-door salesmen are probably Bhattras, and they are also often established as market traders. Many Ramgharias moved to East Africa in the 1890s, especially Kenya and Uganda, to work on building roads and railways. At Independence many came to Britain. In 1972 Ramgharias were among the Asians expelled from Uganda by Idi Amin. They have a strong cultural and religious identity, usually marry within their own community, and can be found in all kinds of work: law, medicine and education, and also shop-keeping and in factories. Jats are the majority Sikh group in the Punjab, where they are agriculturalists, often owning large estates. Known for hard work, determination and military leadership (they often become soldiers), Jats are divided into clans based in particular village regions. Surnames are not used in the Punjab, so Jats arriving in Britain adopted the name of their clan – hence the small number of surnames among them. Jats are proud of their Sikh cultural heritage.

Main beliefs and principles

Sikhs believe there is only one God, to be followed in prayer and obedience; thereby the soul will pass through various transmigrations eventually becoming one with God. There is no official priesthood. Sikh religious observances can be carried out by men or women. Reading of the Scriptures is a major part of all Sikh festivals and worship.

Scriptures

The chief writings of the Gurus are contained in the *Guru Granth Sahib*, which is read in its entirety (*Akhand path*) over 48 hours.

Place of worship

Sikhs worship in a Gurdwara, always identified by the Sikh flag. An, building can be used as a Gurdwara, but it must contain a copy of the *Guru Granth Sahib*.

Social aspects

The formal way of address Sikhs is *Sirdar* (Mr) or *Sardani* (Mrs); if you de not know their name, use *bhai-ji* or *bahin-ji*. Sikh women do not have casual conversations with men outside their family; social overtures are best kept same-sex. (Younger UK Sikhs may not follow this convention) Most Sikhs do not eat beef or its derivatives. Punctuality is not a priority for Sikhs. As in most Asian cultures, the family unit is very strong: if you invite a man to a social gathering, it will be assumed the whole family i invited.

Implications for business

Sikhs are unlikely to require major adjustment to staff hours, holidays etc to accommodate their faith. Outside the Punjab they have adopted the practice of observing festivals on the nearest non-working day. They also have no equivalent of the Christian Sunday. However, the lack of visible religious observance should not be taken to mean that Sikhs are not very religious. They pray every day: by the time a Sikh arrives for work he or she will have already spent several hours in *nitnam* (a daily prayer, reading and meditation programme). They have the same sensitivities as any religious group.

Late arrival at meetings is a cultural matter and does not necessarily mean inefficiency. When the meeting begins, a Sikh may spend some time in small talk before approaching the main issues.

There may be issues of health and safety and of uniform: the Sikh turban for example has been an issue in road safety (crash helmets) Devout Sikhs join the *Khalsa*, the full initiation into Sikhism, and will not cut their hair and will wear a special hair comb, bangle, shorts and dagger.

The calendar

Sikh religious festivals follow the lunar year and so are not on fixed dates except *Baisakhi*, commemorating the founding of Sikhism in 1699 (13 April).

Baisakhi (April 13)	The start of the Sikh New Year. It is also the anniversary of the 1919 Amritsar massacre, a very sensitive topic for modern Sikhs.
August	The celebration of *Guru Granth Sahib*'s installation by Guru Gobind Singh in Nanded, three days before his death in 1708.
Diwali (October or November)	A different celebration to Hindu *Divali*, it celebrates the escape from captivity of the Sixth Guru, Guru Hargobind. Like the Hindu festival it is a festival of lights. The *gurdwara* (place of worship) is illuminated, and homes and gardens: a Sikh district at Diwali can be quite dramatic, with hundreds of electric lights or candles throughout the streets.
Hola Mohalla (February or March)	*Hola Mohalla* has a military theme and concerns the art of self-defence.

The *Gupurbs* commemorate events in the lives of the Gurus: the martyrdoms of Guru Arjan, the fifth Guru (May or June), of Guru Nanak, the first Guru (November), of Guru Tegh Bahadur, the ninth Guru (November); and the birthday of Guru Gobind Singh, the tenth Guru (December). The *Sikh Almanac* lists the dates of the festivals for the current year. Where they fall on a weekday, public festivals are observed at the weekend. The focus of the festivals is on the life and writings of the Ten Gurus.

Zoroastrianism

Numbers and distribution

Zoroastrianism is the most important pre-Islamic religion of Iran. There are a few Zoroastrians in Iran today but most emigrated to India after the Muslim conquest; they are today known as the Parsi sect (Zorastrianism is also called Parsiism or Parsism). In 1992 the Parsi population of India was estimated at 0.01%. There are only a handful of UK Parsis.

Main beliefs and principles

Zoroaster (In Persian, 'Zarathustra) taught that the Wise Lord, Ahura Mazda, and the Evil Spirit, Angra Mainyu, are locked in struggle but good will finally triumph. In that battle human beings are called to fight by living pure and good lives. Parsis seek the 'Good Life' in thoughts, words and deeds. The good you do will be rewarded and the bad done to you, punished. Parsis believe in life after death, a coming saviour of the world, resurrection and the salvation of all mankind.

Scriptures

The *Avesta* contains texts written over a long period. They include the most ancient text in Zoroastrianism, the *Gathas* – songs believed to be by Zoroaster himself. These are part of the *Yasna* or liturgy. The *Vendidad* contains rituals for purification and disciplining offenders. *Yashta* is a book of hymns and prayers.

Place of worship

The Fire Temple is an important part of worship: fire is a symbol of the Wise Lord, Ahura Mazda. The dead are taken to isolated Towers of Silence. These customs are necessarily modified in the UK.

Social implications

When initiated into their faith, Parsis receive a sacred thread and a shirt, both religiously symbolic, which they will wear as part of their normal dress. They do not try to convert others, believing that one should follow the religion of one's birth. Priests wear robes and turbans.

Implications for business

Parsis pray five times daily and observe rituals of birth, puberty, marriage, the birth of children and death. Festival observance is important. They are known for their high ethical business standards and their philanthropy, and are exceptionally hard working.

The calendar

Ghambars	Times of seasonal celebration at such times as New Year, when feasts and religious services are held
Farvardega	Memorials of the dead. Flowers are taken to the towers of silence and sandalwood is brought to the temples.
Jashans	Various anniversaries, the most important of which is Zoroaster's.

Section 4
Reference Section : Resources

(Abbreviations: *T:* Telephone; *F:* Fax; *E:* E-mail; *W:* Web site address)

For Further Reading: a Select Booklist

INTER-CULTURAL BUSINESS AND THE MULTI-CULTURAL SOCIETY

Askenos, Peter and Angus Stewart, *Social Inclusion: Possibilities and Tensions* (Macmillan Press, 2000)

Axtell, Roger E., *Gestures: The Do's and Taboos of Body Language Around the World* (John Wiley, 2nd illustrated edn 1998).

Bentley, Trevor and Sue Clayton, *Profiting From Diversity* (Gower, 1998).

Cohen, Phil (ed.), *New Ethnicities, Old Racisms?* (Zed Books, 1999).

Green, A. E. and D. W. Owen, *Where are the Jobless? Changing Employment and Non-Employment in Cities and Regions* (Policy Press, 1998).

Guy, Vincent, and John Mattock, *The New International Manager: An Action Guide for Cross-Cultural Business* (Kogan Page, rev. edn 1993).

Hampden-Turner, Charles and Fons Trompenaars, *Mastering the Infinite Game: How East Asian Values are Transforming Business Practices* (Capstone, 1997).

Hampden-Turner, Charles and Fons Trompenaars, *Riding the Waves of Culture* (Nicholas Brealey, 1997).

Hampden-Turner, Charles and Fons Trompenaars, *Building Cross-cultural Competence* (Wiley, 2000).

International Institute for Management Development, *IMD World Competitiveness Yearbook 2001* (Lausanne: IMD, 2001).

Lewis, Richard D., *When Cultures Collide: Managing Successfully Across Cultures* (Nicholas Brealey, 1996).

Sassen, S., *The Global City: New York, Lonodn, Tokyo* (Princeton University Press, 1991).

Saxenian, AnnaLee, *Silicon Valley's New Immigrant Entrepreneurs* (Public Policy Institute of America, 1999).

Sonnenschein, William, *The Diversity Toolkit* (Contemporary Books, 2000).

INTERNET DOCUMENTARY SOURCES

A search under the name of an organisation using e.g. www.google.com will usually yield good results. The following are samples of what is available.

Commission for Racial Equality – a large collection of freely downloadable texts on a range of topics relevant to this book is maintained on the CRE website, www.cre.gov.uk

European Commission, Directorate-General for Employment and Social Affairs – a large collection of documents of various kinds is maintained on the website. Not all are relevant to this book but a good search engine is provided: www.europa.eu.int

Particular people groups and religions

AMERICANS

Moody, Fred, *I Sing the Body Electronic: A Year with Microsoft on the Multimedia Frontier* (Penguin, 1996).

Townsend, Robert, *Up the Organisation* (Michael Joseph, 1970). A short and pithy insight into the action-orientated American business mind.

Updike, John, *In the Beauty of the Lilies* (Hamish Hamilton, 1996). A major novel presenting a canvas covering most of the twentieth century and exploring the contemporary American psyche.

BRITISH

There are countless reviews of twentieth-century **Britain**, mostly profusely illustrated, advertised by book clubs and easily found in second-hand and remainder book shops. We like Brian Moynahan, *The British Century: A Photographic History of the Last Hundred Years* (Weidenfeld and Nicholson, 1997).

An authoritative historical study of the **English**, *The Pelican History of England* (Penguin, various dates), is published in several highly readable paperbacks.

There are not many people-focused and accessible books about the **Welsh**: Meic Stephens (ed.), *The Oxford Companion to the Literature of Wales* (OUP, 1986) has useful information.

The literature of **Northern Ireland** is large. Brendan O'Leary and John McGarry, *The Politics of Antagonism: Understanding Northern Ireland* (Continuum International Publishing Group – Athlone Press: 2nd edn 1996) attempts an overview. E. Estyn Evans, *Mourne Country: Landscape and Life in South Down* (Dundalgan Press, 4th edn 1989) is a people-focused portrait of one community.

There are many books about the **Scots** and every aspect of their culture, from bagpipes to tartans. David Daiches (ed.), *The New Companion to Scottish Culture* (Polygon, 1993), is a good starting point.

BRITISH EMPIRE AND COLONIES

Morris, James, *Pax Britannica* (Trilogy comprising *Heaven's Command, Pax Britannica* and *Farewell the Trumpets*: Faber & Faber, completed 1978).

CHINESE

Bonavia, David, *The Chinese* (Penguin, rev. edn 1989). Bonavia, who was an internationally respected foreign correspondent, provides 'a realistic picture of life today in the People's Republic of China' – hence the omission of Chinese communities in other countries and ethnic minorities within China.

EASTERN EUROPE

Broun, Janice, with Grazina Sikorska, *Conscience and Captivity: Religion in Eastern Europe* (Ethics & Public Policy Centre/University Press of America, 1988). Covers much more than religious background, and gives useful background to current events.

HINDUISM

Chinmoy, Sri, *Commentaries on the Vedas, the Upanishads and the Bhagavad Gita: The Three Branches of India's Life-Tree* (Aum Publications, 1997). A 'poetic commentary' on Hinduism's three ancient and fundamental scriptures.

Flood, Gavin, *An Introduction to Hinduism* (Cambridge University Press, 1966). More detailed than Kingsland, below. Combines historical account with analysis of beliefs, traditions and ritual.

Kingsland, Venika M., *The Simple Guide to Hinduism* (Global Books, 1997).

ISLAM

Bowker, John, *What Muslims Believe* (new edn 1998). Based on interviews conducted for the BBC World Service.

Ruthven, Malise, *Islam in the World* (Pelican, rev. edn 1991), includes historical survey and an analysis of the main Muslim sects.

Sarwar, Ghulam, *Islam: Beliefs and Teachings* (Muslim Educational Trust, 3rd edn 1984). A general introduction, by Muslims, in English.

JAPANESE

Yoshimura, Noboru, and Philip Anderson, *Inside the Kaisha: Demystifying Japanese Business Behavior* (McGraw-Hill, 1997). A Japanese and a British author contribute their different perspectives.

JEWS

Rosenberg, Stuart E., *To Understand the Jews* (Hodder & Stoughton, 1966). An older, but engaging and authoritative, book.

SIKHS

Cole, W. Owen and Piara Singh Sambh, *The Sikhs* (Sussex Academic Press, 1995). Introductory.

Pettigrew, Joyce J. M. *The Sikhs of the Punjab* (Zed Books, 1995).

SOUTH ASIANS

Gidoomal, Ram, with David Porter, *The UK Maharajahs: Inside the South Asian Success Story* (Nicholas Brealey, 1997). Discusses the diversity, strengths, and vulnerability of the UK South Asian business economy.

Reference works

Annual Abstract of Statistics, compiled by the Office for National Statistics (The Stationery Office, annually). Statistical data and analysis from a wide range of official and authoritative sources.

Diversity Directory, The: Your Guide to Equality and Diversity Consultancies, Diversity UK, 3 Abbey Square, Turvey, Bedford MK43 8DJ. Tel: 01234 881 380, 17th edn Spring 2000. Whole-page entries on diversity consultancies, a useful gazetteer of national agencies concerned with EO issues, and feature articles. 142 pp, pbk. *E*: mary@diversityuk.co.uk *W*: www.spectrum-universal.co.uk, www.the-diversity-directory.co.uk

Social Trends, compiled by the Office for National Statistics (HMSO, annually). Wide range of social data, some useful information on ethnic minorities.

Social Focus on Ethnic Minorities, compiled by the Office for National Statistics (The Stationery Office). One of a series examining individual social groups or issues in greater depth.

Whitaker's Almanack: Information for a Changing World (The Stationery Office, annually). 'One of the most comprehensive references sources for the modern world' (publisher's quote), this is said to contain the most-consulted index of any British reference book.

Religious Bodies

Baha'i
Baha'i Information Office
27 Rutland Gate,
London SW7 1PD.
T: 0207 584 2566

Buddhism
British Buddhist Association
11 Biddulph Road,
London W9.
T: 0207 286 5575

Buddhist Society
58 Eccleston Square
London SW1V 1PH.
T: 0207 834 5858

Tibet Foundation
2 Bloomsbury Way
London WC1A 2SH.
T: 0207 404 2889

Hinduism
National Council for Hindu
    Temples (UK)
Bhaktivedanta Manor,
Dharam Marg, Hilfield Lane,
Aldenham,
Watford,
Herts WD2 8EZ.
T: 01923 856269/857244

Arya Pratinidhi Sabha (UK) and
    Arya Samaj London
69a Argyle Road,
London W13 0LY.
T: 0208 991 1732

International Society for Krishna
    Consciousness
Bhaktivedanta Manor (as above).
T: 01923 857244

Islam
Muslim World League
46 Goodge Street,
London W1P 1FJ.
T: 0207 636 7568

Islamic Cultural Centre
146 Park Road,
London NW8 7RG.
T: 0207 724 3363

Union of Muslim Organisations
    of the UK and Eire
109 Campden Hill Road,
London W8 7TL.
T: 0207 229 0538/221 6608

Muslim Council of Britain
PO Box 52,
Wembley,
Middlesex HA9 7AL.
T: 0208 903 9024

Jainism
Jain Centre
Oxford Street,
Leicester LE1 5XU.
T: 0116 254 3091

Judaism
Chief Rabbinate
Adler House, 735 High Road,
London N12 0US.
T: 0208 343 6301

Board of Deputies of British Jews
Commonwealth House,
1/19 New Oxford Street,
London WC1A 1NF.
T: 0207 543 5400

Reform Synagogues of Great
    Britain
Sternberg Centre for Judaism,
80 East End Road,
London N3 2SY.
T: 0208 349 5640

Union of Liberal and Progressive
    Synagogues
The Montagu Centre,
21 Maple Street,
London W1P 6DS.
T: 0207 580 1663

Union of Orthodox Hebrew Congregations
140 Stamford Hill
London N16 6QT.
T: 0208 802 6226

United Synagogue Head Office
As for Chief Rabbinate, but
T: 0208 343 8989

Sikhism
Sikh Missionary Society UK
10 Featherstone Road, Southall,
Middlesex UB2 5AA.
T: 0208 574 1902

World Sikh Foundation
33 Wargrave Road,
South Harrow,
Middlesex HA2 8LL.
T: 0208 864 9228

Zoroastrianism
World Zoroastrian Organisation
135 Tennison Road,
London SE25 5NF

Commissions, Public Sector Organisations, Business Consultancies, and other Agencies

Asian Business Association
London Chamber of Commerce &
Industry, 33 Queen Street,
London EC4R 1AP.
T: 0207 248 4444
F: 0207 489 0391

Centre for Ethnic Minority Studies and Equal Opportunities
Royal Holloway University of
London, Egham,
Surrey TW20 0EX.
T: 01784 443815

Centre for Inter-Cultural Development
27 Langland Gardens,
London NW3 6QE.
T: 0207 431 1712
F: 0207 431 6080
E: john.twitchin@btinternet.com
W: www.diversityworks.co.uk;

and:

122 Park Road,
Loughborough LE11 2HH.
T/F: 01509 234628
E: john.twitchin@btinternet.com
W: www.diversityworks.co.uk

Centre for International Briefing
Farnham Castle, Farnham,
Surrey GU9 0AG.
T: 01252 721194
F: 01252 711283

Centre for Research in Ethnic Relations, University of Warwick,
Coventry CV4 7AL.
T: 01203 524956

Chinese Information Centre Co-op Ltd
5th floor, Wuhan House,
16 Nicholas Street, Manchester
M1 4EJ, *T:* 0161 237 3821
W: www.china-britain.org

Churches Commission for Racial Justice, Inter-Church House,
35-41 Lower Marsh,
London SE1 7SA.
T: 0207 523 2121

Commission for Racial Equality
Elliot House,
10-12 Allington Street,
London SW1H 5EH.
T: 0207 828 7022
F: 0207 630 6664
W: www.cre.gov.uk

Diversity UK
3 Abbey Square, Turvey,
Bedford MK43 8DJ.
T, F: 01234 881 380
W: www.the-diversity-directory
.co.uk

Equal Opportunities Commission
Overseas House,
Quay Street, Manchester M3 3MN.
T: 0161 833 9244

**Equality Commission for Northern
Ireland,** Andras House,
60 Great Victoria Street,
Belfast BT2 7BB.
T: 028 90 500600
F: 028 90 331544 *E:*
info.race@equalityni.org
(*In October 1999 the Commission took
over the functions of several NI Equality
commissions. It now enforces Northern
Ireland's equality legislation on disability,
race relations, religion and politics, sex
discrimination and equal pay.*)

Equality Foundation Ltd
St Lawrence House,
29-31 Broad Street,
Bristol BS99 7HR.
T: 0117 929 7780
F: 0117 929 2573 *E:*
elfgeneral@aol.com

**European Monitoring Centre on
Racism and Xenophobia, UK
Secretariat,** Elliot House,
10-12 Allington Street,
London SW1H 5EH.
T: 020 7932 5272 *F:* 020 7932
5220 *E:* secretariat@cre.gov.uk

**Inclusive Management Solutions
Ltd**
St Lawrence House,
29-31 Broad Street,
Bristol BS99 7HR.
T: 0117 929 7780
F: 0117 929 2573
E: elfgeneral@aol.com

Indo-British Partnership
DTI, Bay 444, Kingsgate House,
66-74 Victoria Street,
London SW1E 6SW.
T: 207 215 4825
F: 0207 215 8626

**Local Authority Race Relations
Information Exchange**
Layden House,
76-86 Turnmill Street,
London EC1M 5QU.
T: 0207 296 6781

London Skills Forecasting Unit
2nd floor, Peek House, 20
Eastcheap, London EC3M 1EB.
T: 020 7648 6450
F: 020 7626 1601
E: info@skills-unit.com
W: www.skills-unit.com

**National Association of Minority
Contractors and Businesses**
c/o Inner City Employment Ltd,
5 Acre Lane,
London SW2 5SD.
T: 0207 926 3341

**National Association of Racial
Equality Councils**
8-16 Coronet Street,
London N1 6HD.
T: 0207 739 6658

**National Mentoring Consortium
University of East London**
Romford Road,
London E15 4LZ.
T: 0208 590 7000 EXT 4343

**National Organisation of Asian
Businesses,** 100 Alcester Street,
Birmingham B12 0QB.
T: 0121 666 6157

**Pakistan Cultural and Welfare
Association**
30 Richard Stagg Close,
St Albans AL1 5AT.
01727 846 485

Race Equality Unit
The Home Office,
Queen Anne's Gate,
London SW1H 9AT.
T: 0207 273 3992

Race Relations Employment Advisory Service, Dept for Education and Employment,
14th floor, Cumberland House,
200 Broad Street,
Birmingham B15 1TA.
T: 0121 244 8141, 8142, 8143
E: hq.rreas@dfee.gov.uk

Runnymede Trust, The
133 Aldersgate Street,
London EC1A 4JA.
T: 0207 600 9666

South Asian Development Partnership
PO Box 43, Sutton,
Surrey SM2 5WL.
T: 0208 770 9717
F: 0208 770 9747

Southern Asia Advisory Group
(SAAG), Kingsgate House,
66-74 Victoria Street, London
SW1E 6SW. *T:* 0207 215 4825
F: 0207 215 8626

Tamil Information Centre
720 Romford Road,
London E12 6B
T. 0208 514 6390

UK Race and Europe Network,
Secretariat
Runnymede Trust,
133 Aldersgate Street,
London EC1A 4JA.
T: 0207 600 9666
F: 0207 600 8529
E: Runnymede@trt.demon.co.uk

United Kingdom Institute of Inclusive Design
150a Church Lane,
London SW17 9PU.
T: 0208 682 0518
F: 0208 6823027
E: consultable@compuserve.com

Embassies and High Commissions
(* = High Commission)

Africa:

Algeria:
54 Holland Park
London W11 3RS.
T: 0207 221 7800

Angola:
98 Park Lane
London W1Y 3TA.
T: 0207 495 1752

Botswana:
*6 Stratford Place
London W1N 9AE.
T: 0207 499 0031

Burkina Faso:
Honorary Consulate
5 Cinnamon Row
Plantation Wharf
London SW11 3TW.

Cameroon:
84 Holland Park
London W11 3SB.
T: 0207 727 0771/3

Central African Republic:
30 Rue des Perchamps
F-75016, Paris,
France.
T: Paris 4224 4256

Chad:
Boulevard Lambermont 52
B-1030 Brussels,
Belgium.
T: Brussels 215 1975

Congo:
26 Chesham Place,
London SW1X 8HH.
T: 0207 235 6137

Congo-Brazzaville:
Honorary Consulate,
4 Wendle Court,
131-137 Wandsworth Road
London SW8 2LH.
T: 0207 622 0419

Cote D'Ivoire:
2 Upper Belgrave Street
London SW1X 8BJ.
T: 0207 235 6991

Eritrea:
Honorary Consulate
96 White Lion Street
London N1 9PF.
T: 0207 713 0096

Ethiopia:
17 Prince's Gate
London SW7 1PZ.
T: 0207 589 7212/3/4/5

Gabon:
27 Elvaston Place
London SW7 5NL.
T: 0207 823 9986

Gambia, The:
57 Kensington Court
London W8 5DG.
T: 0207 937 6316/7/8

Ghana:
* 13 Belgrave Square
London SW1 8PN.
T: 0207 235 4142

Kenya:
* 45 Portland Place
London W1N 4AS.
T: 0207 636 2371/5

Madagascar:
Honorary Consulate
16 Lanark Mansions,
Pennard Road, London W12 8DT.
T: 0208 746 0133

Malawi:
* 33 Grosvenor Street
London W1X 0DE.
T: 0207 491 4172/7

Mauritius:
* 32-33 Elvaston Place
London W7.
T: 0207 581 0294

Morocco:
49 Queen's Gate Gardens
London SW7 5NE.
T: 0207 581 5001/4

Nigeria:
* 9 Northumberland Avenue
London WC2N 5BX.
T: 0207 839 1244

South Africa:
* South Africa House, Trafalgar
Square, London WC2N 5DP.
T: 0207 451 7299

Sri Lanka:
* 13 Hyde Park Gardens
London W2 2LU.
T: 0207 262 1841/7

Sudan:
3 Cleveland Row
London SW1A 1DD.
T: 0207 839 8080

Tanzania:
High Commission
43 Hertford Gardens
London W1Y 8DB.
0207 499 8951/4

Uganda:
* Uganda House
58-59 Trafalgar Square
London WC2N 5DX.
T: 020 7839 5783

Zambia:
* 2 Palace Gate
London W8 5NG.
T: 0207 589 6655

Zimbabwe:
* Zimbabwe House
429 Strand
London WC2R 0QE.
T: 0207 836 7755

America (South)

Argentina:
65Brook Street
London W1Y 1YE.
T: 0207 318 1300

Bolivia:
106 Eaton Square
London SW1W 9AA.
T: 0207 235 4248

Brazil:
32 Green Street
London W1Y 4AT.
T: 0207 499 0877

Chile:
12 Devonshire Street
London W1N 1FS.
T: 0207 580 6392

Colombia:
Flat 3a, Hans Crescent
London SW1X 0LN.
T: 0207 589 9177

Ecuador:
3 Hans Crescent
London SW1X 0LN.
T: 0207 584 1367

French Guiana:
French Overseas Dept.
c/o French Embassy
58 Knightsbridge
London SW1.
T: 0207 235 8080

Guyana:
* 3 Palace Court, London W2 4LP.
T: 0207 229 7684

Paraguay:
Braemar Lodge
Cornwall Gardens
London SW7 4AQ.
T: 0207 937 1253

Peru:
52 Sloane Street
London SW1X 9SP.
T: 0207 235 1917

Uruguay:
2nd Floor, 140 Brompton Road
London SW3 1HY.
T: 0207 589 8735

Venezuela:
1 Cromwell Road
London SW7.
T: 0207 584 4206

America (Central)
& Mexico:

Belize:
* 19a Cavendish Square
London W1M 0JR.
T: 0207 499 9728

Costa Rica:
Flat 1
14 Lancaster Gate
London W2 3LH.
T: 0207 708 8844

El Salvador:
159 Great Portland Street
London WC1.
T: 0207 436 8282

Guatemala:
13 Fawcett Street
London SW10 9HN.
T: 0207 351 3042

Honduras:
115 Gloucester Place
London W1H 3PJ.
T: 0207 486 4880

Mexico:
42 Hertford Street
London W1Y 7TF.
T: 0207 499 8586

Nicaragua:
8 Gloucester Road
London SW7 4RB.
T: 0207 584 4365

Panama:
119 Crawford Street
London W1H 1AF.
T: 0207 487 5633

America (North)

United States of America:
24 Grosvenor Square
London W1A 1AE.
T: 0207 499 9000

South-East Asia:

Indonesia:
38 Grosvenor Square
London W1X 9AD.
T: 0207 499 7661

Philippines:
9a Palace Green
London W8 4QE.
T: 0207 937 1600

Canada:

Canadian High Commission:
1 Grosvenor Square
London W1X 0AB..
T: 0207 258 6600

Caribbean:

Antigua & Barbuda:
* 15 Thayer Street
London W1M 5LD.
T: 0207 486 7073

Bahamas:
* 10 Chesterfield Street
London W1X 8AH.
T: 0207 408 4488

Barbados:
* Great Russell Street
London WC1B 3NH.
T: 0207 631 4975

Cayman Islands:
Cayman Islands Government
Office
100 Brompton Road
London SW1.
T: 0207 581 9418

Cuba:
167 High Holborn
London WC1.
T: 0207 240 2488

Dominica:
* 1 Collingham Gardens
London SW5 0HW.
T: 0207 370 5194

Eastern Caribbean States:

High Commission for the Eastern Caribbean States (incl. St. Kitts & Nevis, St. Lucia, St. Vincent & the Grenadines)
10 Kensington Court
London W8 5DL.
T: 0207 937 9522

French Caribbean Territories:
French Overseas Dept.
c/o French Embassy,
58 Knightsbridge
London SW1.
T: 0207 235 8080

Grenada:
* Collingham Gardens
London SW5 0HW.
T: 0207 373 7808

Jamaica:
* 1 Prince Consort Road
London SW7 2BQ.
T: 0207 823 9911

Trinidad & Tobago:
* 42 Belgrave Square
London SW1X 8NT.
T: 0207 245 9351

Europe:

Austria:
18 Belgrave Mews West
London SW1X 8HU.
T: 0207 235 3731

Belgium:
103-105 Eaton Square
London SW1W 9AB.
T: 0207 470 3700

Bosnia-Hercogovina:
4th Floor,
Morley House
320 Regent Street
London W1R 5AB.

Bulgaria:
186-188 Queen's Gate
London SW7 5HL.
T: 0207 584 9400

Croatia:
21 Conway Street
London W1P 5HL.
T: 0207 387 2022

Cyprus:
* 93 Park Street
London W1Y 4ET.
T: 0207 499 8272

Czech Republic:
26-30 Kensington Palace
 Gardens
London W8 4QY.
T: 0207 243 1115

Denmark:
55 Sloane Street
London SW1X 9SR.
T: 0207 333 0200

Finland:
38 Chesham Place
London SW1X 8HW.
T: 0207 838 6200

France:
58 Knightsbridge
London SW1X 7JT.
T: 0207 201 1000

Germany:
23 Belgrave Square
London SW1X 8PZ.
T: 0207 824 1300

Greece:
1a Holland Park
London W11 3TP.
T: 0207 229 3850

Hungary:
35 Eaton Place
London SW1X 8BY.
0207 235 5218

Iceland:
1 Eaton Terrace
London SW1 8EY.
T: 0207 590 1100

Ireland, Republic of:
17 Grosvenor Place
London SW1X 7HR.
T: 0207 235 2171

Italy:
14 Three Kings Yard
Davies Street
London W1Y 2EH.
T: 0207 312 2200

Latvia:
45 Nottingham Place
London W1M 3FE.
T: 0207 312 0040

Liechtenstein:
Represented by Swiss Embassy

Lithuania:
84 Gloucester Place
London W1H 3HN.
T: 0207 486 6401

Luxembourg:
27 Wilton Crescent
London SW1X 8SD.
T: 0207 235 6961

Macedonia:
10 Harcourt House
19a Cavendish Square
London W1M 9AD.
T: 0207 499 5152

Malta:
* Malta House
36-38 Piccadilly
London W1V 0PQ.
T: 0207 292 4800

The Netherlands:
38 Hyde Park Gate
London SW7 5DP.
T: 0207 590 3200

Norway:
25 Belgrave Square
London SW1X 8QD.
T: 0207 591 5500

Poland:
47 Portland Place
London W1N 3AG.
T: 0207 580 4324/9

Portugal:
11 Belgrave Square
London SW1X 8PP.
T: 0207 235 5331

Romania:
Arundel House,
4 Palace Green
London W8 4QD.
T: 0207 937 9666

Spain:
39 Chesham Place
London SW1X 8SB.
T: 0207 235 5555

Sweden:
11 Montagu Place
London W1H 2AL.
T: 0207 917 6400

Switzerland:
16-18 Montagu Place
London W1H 2BQ.
T: 0207 616 6000

Yugoslavia:
No current diplomatic
representation in the UK

Far East:

China:
49-51 Portland Place
London W1N 4JL.
T: 0207 636 9375/5726

Hong Kong:
Hong Kong Economic and
   Trade Office, 6 Grafton Street
London W1X 3LB.
T: 0207 499 9821

Japan:
101-104 Piccadilly
London W1V 9FN.
T: 0207 465 6500

Korea, (South) Republic of
60 Buckingham Gate
London SW1E 6AJ.
T: 0207 227 5500

Malaysia:
45 Belgrave Square
London SW1X 8QT.
T: 0207 235 8033

Singapore:
* 9 Wilton Crescent
London SW1X 8RW.
T: 0207 235 8315

Taiwan:
Taipei Representative Office
50 Grosvenor Gardens
London SW1W 0EB.

Thailand:
29-30 Queen's Gate
London SW7 5JB.
T: 0207 589 2944

Vietnam:
12-14 Victoria Road
London W8 5RD.
0207 937 1912

Indian Sub-Continent (South Asia):

Bangladesh:
* 28 Queen's Gate
London SW7 5JA.
T: 0207 584 0081

India:
* India House,
Aldwych
London WC2B 4NA.
T: 0207 836 8484

Maldives:
22 Nottingham Place
London W1M 3FB.
T: 0207 224 2135

Nepal:
12a Kensington Palace Gardens
London W8 4QU.
T: 0207 229 1594/6231/5352

Pakistan:
* 35-36 Lowndes Square
London SW1X 9JN.
T: 0207 664 9200

Middle East:

Bahrain:
98 Gloucester Road
London SW7 4AU.
T: 0207 370 5132

Brunei:
* 19-20 Belgrave Square
London SW1 8PG.
T: 0207 581 0521

Egypt:
12 Curzon Street
London W1Y 7FJ.
T: 0207 499 2401/3304

Iran:
16 Prince's Gate,
London SW7 1PT.
T: 0207 225 3000

Iraq:
Represented by Jordanian Embassy

Israel:
2 Palace Green,
Kensington
London W8 4QB.
T: 0207 957 9500

Jordan:
6 Upper Phillimore Gardens
London W8 7HB.
T: 0207 937 3685

Kuwait:
2 Albert Gate,
London SW1X 7JU.
T: 0207 590 3400

Lebanon:
21 Kensington Palace Gardens
London W8 4QM.
T: 0207 229 7265/6

Libya:
Represented by Saudi Arabian
Embassy

Oman:
167 Queen's Gate
London SW7 5HE.
T: 0207 225 0001

Saudi Arabia:
30 Charles Street
London W1X 7PM.
T: 0207 917 3000

Turkey:
43 Belgrave Square
London SW1XD 8PA.
T: 0207 393 0202

United Arab Emirates:
30 Princes Gate
London SW7 1PT.
T: 0207 581 1281

Yemen:
57 Cromwell Road
London SW7 2ED.
T: 0207 584 6607

Pacific:

Australia:
* Australia House, Strand
London WC2B 4LA.
T: 0207 379 4334Fiji:
34 Hyde Park Gate
London SW7 5DN.
T: 0207 584 3661

New Zealand:
* New Zealand House
Haymarket
London SW1Y 4TQ.
T: 0207 930 8422

Russia and Neighbours:

Afghanistan:
31 Prince's Gate
London SW7 1QQ.
T: 0207 589 8891

Georgia:
3 Hornton Place
London W8 4LZ.
T: 0207 937 8233

Russian Federation:
13 Kensington Palace Gardens
London W8 4QX.
T: 0207 229 2666/3268/6412

Internet Resources

Search engines

❏ Google (http://www.google.com) is an incredibly fast, intelligent engine.

❏ Copernic 2000 (http://www.copernic.com) is a sophisticated search engine that has useful facilities for serious web-searching. Worth paying to register, as the registered version has substantial extras.

❏ Ask Jeeves
(http://www.askjeeves.com or http://www.askjeeves.co.uk). Slick presentation and permits natural-language queries, but less effective than Google.

Relevant government Web sites

□   Central Office of Information (COI), http://www.coi.gov.uk/coi

□   Department for Culture, Media and Sport (DCMS),
    http://www.culture.gov.uk

□   Department for Education and Employment (DfEE),
    http://www.dfee.gov.uk

□   Department of Trade and Industry (DTI), http://www.dti.gov.uk

□   Foreign and Commonwealth Office, http://www.fco.gov.uk

□   Home Office, http://www.homeoffice.gov.uk

□   National Assembly for Wales, http://www.wales.gov.uk

□   Northern Ireland Office, http://www.nio.gov.uk

□   Office for National Statistics (ONS), http://www.statistics.gov.uk

□   Scotland Office, http://www.scottishsecretary.gov.uk

□   10 Downing Street, http://www.number-10.gov.uk

Other useful Web sites

□   UK Black Links Recruitment & Business Directory,
    W: www.ukblacklinks.com.

□   Centre for Research in Ethnic Relations (CRER),
    http://www.warwick.ac.uk/fac/soc/CRER_RC.
    CRER at Warwick University publishes a range of resource and much of it is
    available on the Internet.

□   Cities project,
    ttp://www.gla.ac.uk/Acad/Urban/Cities/Projects/21-1049.htm
    This project led by academic from Leicester and Birmingham looks in
    particular at 'break-out' – the entry of ethnic minority business into the
    mainstream business community.

□   Judicial Studies Board, http://www.jsboard.co.uk/header.htm
    This web site contains the *Judges' Bench Book on Ethnic Minorities*, designed
    to ensure proper treatment of ethnic minorities in English courts. Available
    in its entirety for download.

□   National Ethnic Minority Data Archive project (NEMDA),
    http://warwick.ac.uk/~errac/nemda.htm.
    Established by CRER (above) in association with the Commission for Racial

Equality, NEMDA presents data drawn from a wide range of data sources. A useful summary of key data is at:
http://www.warwick.ac.uk/~errac/keyinf.htm
(the home page of Dr David Owen, who runs NEMDA, is at http://warwick.ac.uk/~errac, and provides further information).

❑ International Institute for Management Development, http://www.imd.ch
This site has up-to-date rankings on world competitiveness of 49 countries, summarised from the IMD Yearbook listed in the Reading list, p. 251.

❑ Youth Anti-Racist Alliance, www.blacknet.co.uk/youthara

Media

Newspapers and Periodicals
(d=daily; w=weekly; f=fortnightly; m=monthly; q=quarterly)

Arabic

Ad-Diplomasi News Report (w)
PO Box 138, London SW3 6BH.
T: 020 7286 1372
F: 020 7266 1479

Al-Alaam (w)
Banner House,
55-57 Banner Street,
London EC1Y 8PX.
T: 020 7608 3454
F: 020 7608 3581

Al-Ahram International (w)
Al-Ahram House,
203-209 North Gower Street,
London NW1 2NJ.
T: 020 7388 1155
F: 020 7388 3130

Al Arab (d)
159 Acre Lane,
London SW2 5UA.
T: 020 7274 9381
F: 020 7326 1783

Al Hayat (d)
Kensington Centre,
66 Hammersmith Road,
London W14 8YT.

T: 020 7602 9988
F: 020 7602 4963
W: www.alhyat.com

Al Muhajir (f)
132 Mill Lane,
London NW6 1NE.
T: 020 7813 5553
F: 020 7813 6234

Asharq Al Awsat (d)
Other publications: *Almajalla,
Sayidaty, Hia, Aljamila, Alrajoul*
Arab Press House,
182-184 High Holborn,
London WC1V 7AP.
T: 020 7831 8181
F: 020 7831 2310

Bengali

Ananda Bazar Patrika
(d and Sunday w magazine,
Bengali/English)
48 Beverley Gardens,
Wembley,
Middlesex HA9 9QZ.
T: 020 8904 2533
F: 020 8908 2625
E: shrabani@abplondon.demon
.co.uk

Daily Deshbarta (d)
170 Brick Lane,
London E1 6RU.
T: 0207 377 1584
F: 0207 247 0141

Janomot (w)
Unit 2,
20B Spelman Street,
London E1 5LQ.
T: 020 7377 6032
F: 020 7247 0141
E: janomot@easynet.co.uk

Notun Din (w)
Room 5,
Brady Centre,
*192-196 Hanbury Street,
London E1 5HU.
T: 020 7247 6280/0578
F: 020 7247 2280
E: nohin@din.demon.co.uk

Probashi Samachar (q)
20 Orchard Avenue,
London N14 4ND.
T: 020 8886 4231

Surma (w)
40 Wessex Street,
London E2 0LB.
T: 020 8980 5544
F: 020 8981 8829
E: surmanews@I12.com

Weekly Potrika
Suite 210, Wickham House,
10 Cleveland Way,
London E1 4TR
T: 020 7423 9270.
F: 020 7423 9122

Chinese

Chinese Business Impact (publishes
translations of existing publications)
Chinese Information Centre,
4th Floor, 16 Nicholas Street,
Manchester M1 4EJ.

T: 0161 228 0420
F: 0161 228 3739

Shang Ye Xian Feng (bi-m)
194 Old Brompton Road,
London SW5 0AW.
T: 020 7835 2183
F: 020 7370 6245

Sing Tao Daily (European edition)
46 Dean Street,
London W1V 5AP
T: 020 7287 1525.
F: 020 7734 0828

English language

The African (m)
25 Hester Road,
Upper Edmonton,
London N18 2RF.
T: 020 8350 0684
F: 020 8351 0516

The American In Britain
Yewlands House, Milbrook,
Nutley, East Sussex TN22 3PH.
T: 01825 713676
F: 01825 713687

The Asian
Sunrise House, Sunrise Road,
Southall, Middlesex UB2 4AU.
T: 020 8574 9292
F: 020 8574 9393
E: editor@asianweekly.co.uk

The Asian Age (d)
Media Asia (Europe) Ltd,
Dolphin Media House,
Spring Villa Park,
Spring Villa Road,
Edgware HA8 7EB.
T: 020 8951 4878
F: 020 8951 4839
E: arvind@asianage.com

Asian Entertainment Guide (w)
18 Molyneux Street,
London W1H 5HU.
T: 020 7723 6797
F: 020 7724 2971

Asian Express (f)
211 Piccadilly,
London W1V 9LD.
T: 020 7439 8985
F: 020 7537 2141

Asian Trader, Garavi Gujarat,
Pharmacy Business
Garavi Gujarat House,
12 Silex Street,
London SE1 0DW.
T: 020 7928 1234
F: 020 7261 0055

The Asian News (English)
192B Stoney Lane, Balsall Heath,
Birmingham B12 8AN.
F: 0121 449 1725

Asian Telegraph (Telegraph On Line)
21A Park Road,
London NW1 6XN.
T: 020 7723 5042
F: 020 7607 6705
W: www.telegraph.com

Asian Times
3rd Floor, Tower House,
141-149 Fonthill Road,
London N4 3HF.
T: 020 7281 1191
F: 020 7263 9656

Asian Times (w national
publications), Unit 2.01
Whitechapel Technology Centre,
65 Whitechapel Road,
Whitechapel, E1 1DU.
T/F: 0207 650 2000
E: easterneye@hotmail.com

Asian Voice
Asian Convenience Retailer
8-16 Coronet Street, (off Old
Street), London N1 6HD.
T: 020 7729 5453
F: 020 7739 0358
E: gujarat@
gujarat-samachar.com

Asian Voice Scotland (w)
51 Forth Street, Glasgow, G41 2SP.
T: 0141 420 6811
F: 0141 420 6833

Awaaz Asian Voice (d)
PO Box 15, Batley,
West Yorkshire, WF17 7YY.
T: 01924 510 512
F: 01924 510 513

Black Perspective (q)
PO Box 246, London SE13 7DL.
T/F: 020 8692 6986
E: editor@blackperspective.free-
online.co.uk

Caribbean Times (w)
Unit 2.01, Whitechapel
Technology Centre,
65 Whitechapel Road,
Whitechapel, London E1 1DU.
T/F: 0207 650 2000
E: caribbeantimes@hotmail.com

Cineblitz (m)
Cine-Asia Publications,
Dolphin Media House,
Spring Villa Park,
SpringVilla Road,
Edgware, Middlesex HA8 7EB.
T: 020 8381 1166
F: 020 8381 1177

Cipher (bi-monthly)
184 Bridgewater Road, Alperton,
Middlesex HA0 1AR.
T: 020 8903 6530
F: 020 8795 0502

Eastern Eye (w)
Unit 2.01
Whitechapel Technology Centre,
65 Whitechapel Road,
Whitechapel,
London E1 1DU.
T/F: 0207 650 2000
E: easterneye@hotmail.com

The Filipino (bi-monthly)
PO Box 20376, Golders Green,
London NW11 8FE.
T: 020 8731 7195
F: 020 8458 1055
E: editor@filipino.co.uk

The Gleaner (w)
Unit 220-223, Elephant & Castle
Shopping Centre,
London SE1 6TE.
T: 020 7277 1714
F: 020 7277 1734
*E:*editorial@
   gleaner171.demon.co.uk

Impact International (m)
Suite B, PO Box 2493,
233 Seven Sisters Road,
London N4 2BL.
T: 020 7263 1417
F: 020 7272 8934
E: impact@globalnet.co.uk

India Abroad Newspaper
Flat 1, 2 Kendrick Place,
London SW7 3HF.
T: 020 7581 5244

India – Home And Abroad (q)
Park Publications, 1 Park Close,
London NW2 6RQ.
T/F: 020 8452 4182

India Link International (m)
42 Farm Avenue,
North Harrow,
Middlesex HA2 7LR.
T: 020 8866 8421
F: 020 8723 5250

India Monitor (m)
1B Claverton Street,
London SW1V 3AY.
London Correspondent:
Rakesh K Mathur (0956 568 394)
F: 020 7630 8688

India Times
Global House, 90 Ascot Gardens,
Southall, Middlesex UB1 2SB.
T: 020 8575 0151
F: 020 8575 5661

India Weekly
105 St John's Street,
London EC1M 4AS.
T: 020 7251 3290
F: 020 7251 3289
E: newsdesk@indiaweekly.co.uk

Indian Express
117 Fortress Road,
London NW5 2HR.
T/F: 020 7428 9798

Irish Post (w)
Smurfit Media UK,
Cambridge House, Cambridge
Grove, Hammersmith,
London, W6 OLE.
T: 020 8741 0649
F: 020 8741 3382

Irish World (w)
934 North Circular Road,
London NW2 7RJ.
T: 020 8453 7800
F: 020 8208 1103
W: www.theirishworld.com
E: theeditor@irishworld.com

Jewish Chronicle (w)
25 Furnival Street
London EC4A 1JT.
T: 020 7415 1616
F: 020 7405 9040
W: www.jchron.co.uk

Jewish Quarterly
Jewish Literary Trust Limited, PO
Box 2078 London W1A 1JR.
T: 020 7629 5004
F: 020 7629 5110
E: jewish.quarterly@ort.org

Jewish Recorder
Jewish Cultural Society,
18 Oak Hill Drive,
Edgbaston, Birmingham,
West Midlands B15 3UG.
T: 0121 766 6663
F: 0121 766 8135

Jewish Telegraph
4 May Terrace, Gittnock, Glasgow,
Lanarkshire G46 6DL.
T: 0141 621 4422
F: 0141 621 4333

Jewish Tribune (w)
95-97 Stamford Hill,
London N16 5RE.
T: 020 8800 6688
F: 020 8800 5000

The Leader
2 Baynes Close, Enfield,
Middlesex EN1 4BN.
T: 020 8366 5082
F: 020 8367 6941

London Irish Press
Unit 8, Concord Business Centre,
Concord Road, London W3 0TR.
T: 020 8752 1202
F: 020 8896 3654

London Jewish News (w)
50 Colindeep Lane, Colindale,
London, NW9 6HB.
T/F: 020 8358 6520

*London/Midland/Northern
Asian/Black African Caribbean* (q)
Wild Rose Publishing, 10A
Ellingfort Road, Hackney,
London E8 3PA. *T:* 020 8985 4070
F: 020 8525 1171

Mauritian International (q)
Nautilus Publishing Co,
PO Box 4100,
London SW20 0XN.
T/F: 020 8947 1912

Mauritius News (m)
583 Wandsworth Road, London
SW8 3JD.
T: 020 7498 3066
F: 020 7627 8939
W: www.mauritius-news.co.uk
E: editor@mauritius-news.co.uk

Middle East Expatriate
Crescent Court, 102 Victor Road,
Teddington,
Middlesex TW11 8SS.
T: 020 8943 3630
F: 020 8943 3701

One Asia (Internet Magazine)
64 New Cavendish Street,
London W1 M7LD.
T: 020 7612 9318
F: 020 7323 0756

The Muslim News (m)
PO Box 380,
Harrow, Middlesex HA2 6LL.
T: 020 7608 2822
F: 020 7608 1232
W: www.muslimnews.co.uk
E: editor@muslimnews.co.uk

The Nation (English/Urdu)
Links Media, 96C Ilford Lane,
Ilford, ESSEX IG1 2LD.
T: 020 8478 3200
F: 020 8478 6200
W: www.thenation.com
E: msarwar@
thenation.demon.co.uk

New Horizon (m), Icis House,
144-146 King's Cross Road,
London WC1X 9DH.
T: 020 7833 8275
F: 020 7278 4797

New Impact Journal (bi-monthly)
Anser House, Courtyard Offices,
Marlow,
Buckinghamshire SL7 1AX.
T: 01628 481 581
F: 01628 475 570

New World (w)
234 Holloway Road,
London N7 8DA.
T: 020 7700 2673
F: 020 7607 6706

The News
Jang Publications Ltd,
1 Sanctuary Street,
London SE1 1ED.
T: 020 7403 5833/4122
F: 020 7378 1653
W: www.jang.co.uk
E: thenewssell@yahoo.com

Nigerian News (fortnightly)
23 Aberdeen Court,
London W9 1AF.
T: 020 7266 4564
F: 020 7266 4057

North West Asian News (m)
Observer Buildings,
Drake Street,
Rochdale OL16 1PH.
T: 0170 635 7086
F: 0170 634 1595

Pahayagan (Filipino bi-monthly)
49 Connaught Street,
London W2 2BB.
T: 020 7402 6917

Pride Magazine (m)
Hamilton House,
Battersea Bridge Road,
London SW11 3AX.
T: 020 7228 3110
F: 020 7228 3130
W: www.pridemagazine.com
E: aminat@pridemagazine.com

Q News International
3rd Floor, Dexion House,
2-4 Empire Way,
Wembley, Middlesex HA9 0XA.
T: 020 8903 0819
F: 020 8903 0820

Rira Magazine
(Irish youth magazine)
39-41 North Road,
Islington, London N7 SDP.
T: 020 7609 9010
F: 020 7609 6716

Salaam! (m)
Intermedia Exchange Ltd,
Unit 6,
5 Rockware Avenue,
Greenford,
Middlesex UB6 0AA.
T: 020 8357 0056
F: 020 8930 2066

Scotland's Oracle
575 Pollockshaws Road,
Glasgow G41 2QQ.
T: 0141 423 9166
F: 0141 423 9166

2nd Generation (bi-m)
Unit 401A,
Bon Marché Centre,
444 Brixton Road,
London SW9 8EJ.
T: 020 7924 9966
F: 020 7924 9988

Shanti Communications
(news agency)
1 Stuart Road,
Thornton Heath,
Surrey CR7 8RA.
T: 0831 196 693
F: 020 8665 0384

The Sikh Courier International (q)
33 Wargrave Road,
South Harrow,
Middlesex HA2 8LL.

T/F: 020 8257 0359

The Sikh Messenger (q)
43 Dorset Road,
Merton Park,
London SW19 3EZ.
T/F: 020 8540 4148

Spice Magazine (m)
Tees Court,
Moseley Street,
Birmingham B12 0RT.
T: 0121 245 2424
F: 0121 245 2434
W: www.spicemagazine.com

Teamwork (bi-m),
WISC,
5 Westminster Bridge Rd,
London SE1 7XW.
T: 020 7928 7861/2
F: 020 7928 0343
E: wiscorg@aol.com

Touch Magazine (m)
1st Floor, 51 Hoxton Square,
London N1 6PB.
T: 020 7739 5727
F: 020 7739 0138
E: touchzine@aol.com

Untold Magazine (bi-monthly)
Stratford Workshops,
Unit 328 Burford Road,
London E15 2SP.
T: 020 8519 1920

The Voice (w)
370 Coldharbour Lane,
Brixton, London SW9 8PL.
T: 020 7737 7377
F: 020 7274 8994

The Weekly Awam
37-39 Woodfield Road,
Balsall Heath,
Birmingham B12 8TD.
T: 0121 446 4738
F: 0121 446 4388

The Weekly East
The Weekly Pakistan
65 North Acton Road,
Park Royal, London NW10 6PJ.
T: 020 8838 6300
F: 020 8838 2112

Greek

Parikiaki (w)
534A Holloway Road
London N7 6JP.
T: 0207 272 6777
F: 0207 281 0127
Advertising F: 0207 263 2003

Ta Nea (w)
8-10 Stamford Hill
London N16 6XS.
T: 0208 806 0169/8659
F: 0208 806 0160

Gujarati

Asian Trader (f)
(English/Gujarati/Urdu)
Garavi Gujarat (w)
(English/Gujarati)
1-2 Silex Street, off Webber Street,
Southwark, London SE1 0DW.
T: 0207 928 1234
F: 0207 261 0055
E: amg@gujarat.co.uk

The Daily Millat
2 Baynes Close, Enfield
Middlesex EN1 4BN.
T: 0208 366 5082
F: 0208 367 6941

Gujarat Samachar
(w) Gujarati/English)
8-16 Coronet Street,
off Old Street, London N1 6HD.
T: 0207 729 5453
F: 0207 739 0358
E: gujarat@
gujarat-samachar.com

Hindi

Amar Deep Hindi (w)
36 Trent Avenue
London W5 4TL.
T: 0208 840 3534
F: 0208 579 3180

Navin Weekly
Masbro Centre, 87 Masbro Road
London W14 0LR.
T: 0207 385 8966

Italian

La Voce Degli Italiani (w)
20 Brixton Road
London SW9 6BU.
T: 0207 735 5164
F: 0207 793 0385

Punjabi

Awaze quam international (w)
Gate 2, Unit 5B, Booth Street,
Smethwick,
Birmingham B66 2PF.
T: 0121 555 5921
F: 0121 555 6899

Perdesan Monthly
478 Lady Margaret Road
Southall, Middlesex UB1 2NW.
T: 0208 575 8694
F: 0208 575 8659

Pardesi Punjab
6 Emerald Square,
Southall, Middlesex UB2 5JS.
T: 0961 196 034
F: 020 8737 4513

The Punjabi Guardian (f)
129 Soho Road, Handsworth
Birmingham B21 9ST.
T: 0121 554 3995
F: 0121 507 1065

Punjab Mail International (m)
66 Dames Road,
Forest Gate, London E7 0DR.
F: 0208 522 0901

Punjab Times International (w)
24 Cotton Brook Road
Sir Francis Ley Industrial Park
Derby DE23 8YJ.
T: 01332 372 851
F: 01332 372 833
E: punjabtimes@aol.com

Weekly Des Pardes
8 The Crescent, Southall
Middlesex UB1 1BE.
T: 0208 571 1127
Fax:0208 571 2604

Turkish

Hurriyet (d)
1st Floor, 35 D'Arblay Street
London W1V 3FE.
T: 0207 734 1211
F: 0207 287 3101
E: betul@hotmail.com

Toplum Postasi (w,English/Turkish)
117 Green Lanes
London N16 9DN.
T: 0207 354 4424
F: 0207 354 0313

Urdu

The Daily Jang
Jang Publications Ltd
1 Sanctuary Street
London SE1 1ED.
T: 0207 403 5833
F: 0207 378 1653

Milap Weekly
Masbro Centre, 87 Masbro Road
London W14 0LR.
T: 0207 385 8966

Ravi News Weekly
Ravi House, Unit E1
Legrams Lane
Bradford BD7 1NH.
Tel/*F:* 01274 666 900

Sada Urdu Monthly
PO Box 630, Croydon CR0 2WN.
T: 0208 684 9429
F: 0208 251 8689

Radio Stations

Asian Sound Radio
Globe House,
Southall Street
Manchester M3 1LG.
T: 0161 288 1000
F: 0161 288 9000

Choice Fm
(South London Radio)
291-299 Borough High Street
London SE1 1JG.
T: 0207 378 3969
F: 0207 378 3936

Galaxy 102.2
1 The Square,
111 Broad Street,
Birmingham B15 1AS.
T: 0121 616 1000
F: 0121 616 1011

Galaxy 105
Joseph's Well,
Hanover Walk,
Leeds LS3 1AB.
T: 0113 213 1053
F: 0113 213 1054

Kiss 100 Fm
Kiss House,
80 Holloway Road
London N7 8JG.
T: 0207 700 6100
F: 0207 700 3979

London Greek Radio
Florentia Village,
Vale Road,
London N4 1TD.
T: 0208 880 8001
F: 0208 800 8005

London Turkish Radio
185B High Road
London N22 6BA.
T: 0208 881 0606
F: 0208 881 5151

Radio Ceredigion (Welsh)
Yr Hen Ysgol Gymraeg
Ffordd Alexandra
Aberystwyth,
Dyfed SY23 1LF.
T: 01970 627 999
F: 01970 627 206.

Radio Asia
Spectrum 558,
65 North Acton Road,
Park Royal, London NW10 6RJ.
T: 020 8838 6300

Radio XL
KMS House, Bradford St,
Birmingham B12 0JD.
T: 0121 753 5353
F: 0121 753 3111

Sabras Sound Ltd
(Asian and English language)
Radio House, 63 Melton Road
Leicester LE4 6PN.
T: 0116 261 0666
F: 0116 268 7776
W: www.sabrasradio.com

Spectrum Radio
204/206 Queenstown Road,
London SW8 3NR.
T: 020 7627 4433
F: 020 7627 3409
W: www.spectrum558am.co.uk
E: spectrum@
    spectrum558am.co.uk

Spectrum Chinese Programmes
PO Box 2288,
London W1A 1YY.
T: 0207 434 2835
F: 0207 434 2836
E: dj@558.net

Sunrise Radio
Sunrise House, Merrick Road
Southall, Middlesex UB2 7AU.
T/F: 0208 893 5900

Sunrise Radio
Sunrise House, 30 Chapel Street,
Little Germany,
Bradford BD1 5DN.
T: 01274 375 043
F: 01274 728 534

TV Stations

Asian Television
PO Box 113, Oldham,
Lancashire OL1 1LS.
T: 0161 627 1207
F: 0161 665 2361
E: atml138@aol.com

Chinese News & Entertainment
Marvic House,
Bishops Road, Fulham,
London SW6 7AD.
T: 020 7610 3880
F: 020 7610 3118
W: www.cnetv.com
E: pcne@pcnetv.demon.co.uk

Helenic TV
50 Clarendon Road,
London N8 0DJ.
T: 020 8292 7037
F: 020 8292 7042
E: helenictv@btinternet.com

Middle East Broadcasting (MBC)
80 Silverthorne Road,
London SW8 3XA.
T: 020 7501 1253,
F: 020 7501 1231

E: issa@uk.mbcctv.com

Namaste Asian Television
7 Trafalgar Business Centre,
77/87 River Road, Barking,
Essex, IG11 OJU.
T: 020 8507 8292
F: 020 8507 0809

Network East
Room 714,
BBC Pebble Mill,
Pebble Mill Road,
Birmingham,
West Midlands, B5 7QQ.
T: 0121 432 8888
F: 0121 432 8241

Sony Entertainment T.V. Asia
34 Fouberts Place, Soho, London,
W1V 2BH
T: 020 7534 7575
F: 020 7534 7585

The Pakistani Channel (Interactive)
65 North Acton Road,
Park Royal, London, NW10 6PJ
T: 020 8838 6300
F: 020 8838 2122
W: www.thepakistanichannel.
   com
E: info.pak@btinternet.com

The Persian Channel
10 Pennine Parade,
Pennine Drive,
London NW2 1NT
T: 020 8731 9333
F: 020 8731 6971

Zee TV
Zee News,
64 Newman Street,
London, W1P 3HB,
T: 020 7436 0543 OR
020 7637 4502
F: 020 7436 0549
E:anita.anand@zeetv.co.uk

INDEX

Where page references are bold, the reference is to a major treatment of the topic

Ouseley Report (Bradford Race Review,
2001) 91, 103
Pakistanis *see* South Asians
Parekh, Bhikhu *see* Runnymede Report
(2000)
Patel, Kirit 117
Peter and Janet' 179-83
Pitroda, Sam 61f
Poles 9, 45, 127-38
Police 12, 75-87; Police Initial
Recruitment Test 83; Dutch best
practice 161
Popovic, Isidora 62, 162-70
Portobello Business Centre 164
Prince's Trust, The 62, 164-5, 166-70
passim
Quad (audio) 104f
Quest for Economic Development
(QED-UK, Bradford) *see* Ali,
Mohammed
Race Equality Unit 28n, 66
Race for Opportunity 80
Ram, Monder 55
Rastafarianism 245-6
Religions: reference section 227-50;
Religious bodies, addresses 255-6
Roche, Barbara 34
Rover (vehicles) 111; Longbridge
manufacturing plant 23f
Royal Dutch/Shell Group 151-61 passim
Runnymede Report (2000) 14ff, 28f
Rushdie, Salman 21, 103
Safeway 53
Saga (insurance) 67
Sagoo, Bally 48
Sanghera, Bahilar 55
Scandinavians 224
Scotland 215
Shah, Nik 68, 75-87, 156
Shankar, Ravi 186
Shell *see* Royal Dutch/Shell Group

Sikhism 247-9
Sinclair, Clive 21
Small Business Service 150
South Asian Development Partnership 4,
65-73 passim
South Asian Voluntary Organisations
Network (SAVON), Bradford 96
South Asians 10, 18, 32, 34, 42f, 62, 71,
88-103, 116-26 passim, 192f, 195,
224-6
Spanish 227
Stone, Lord 80f
Straw, Jack 63, 66, 78
Sun Tzu, *Art of War* 144
Sure Start 98
Surinam 158
Swenson, Chester A. 67
Taggart, Neil 23
Tan, Kim 56, 61, 136, 138-50
Technics (electronics) 105
Tesco 46
Thais/Malaysians 226-7
Trade Unions [Public Sector] Charter on
under-representation of ethnic
minorities (1999) 77
Trompenaars, Fons 40
Van Klinken, Jaap 151-61
Vauxhall Nova 51
Vaz, Keith 77
Vietnamese 33, 47; boat people 139
Virgin Group 62
Viswanathan, Ashok 13n
Wales 216
Walker, Peter and Ross 104f
Watford Electronics 123
West Indians 18, 141
WorldTel (telecommunications) 61f
Yugoslavs 162-70
Zimbabwe 44
Zoroastrianism 249-50